The Infrastructure of Accountability

The Infrastructure of Accountability

Data Use and the Transformation of American Education

Edited by

DOROTHEA ANAGNOSTOPOULOS

STACEY A. RUTLEDGE

REBECCA JACOBSEN

HARVARD EDUCATION PRESS

CAMBRIDGE, MASSACHUSETTS

Library of Congress Control Number 2012953211

Paperback ISBN 978-1-61250-531-2
Library Edition ISBN 978-1-61250-532-9

Published by Harvard Education Press,
an imprint of the Harvard Education Publishing Group

Harvard Education Press
8 Story Street
Cambridge, MA 02138

Cover Design: Ciano Design
Cover Photo: Kim Steele/Getty Images

The typefaces used in this book are Sabon for text and Myriad Pro for display.

Contents

Foreword   **vii**
Jeffrey R. Henig

Introduction   **1**
Mapping the Information Infrastructure of Accountability
Dorothea Anagnostopoulos, Stacey A. Rutledge, and Rebecca Jacobsen

PART I
Building the Infrastructure of Accountability   21

1   **The Paradoxes of Data-Driven School Reform**   **23**
Learning from Two Generations of Centralized Accountability
Systems in the United States
Heinrich Mintrop and Gail L. Sunderman

2   **Trust and Numbers**   **41**
Constructing and Contesting Statewide Student Information Systems
Dorothea Anagnostopoulos and Juanita Bautista-Guerra

3   **The Accidental Revolution**   **57**
Teacher Accountability, Value-Added, and the Shifting Balance
of Power in the American School System
Chris Thorn and Douglas N. Harris

4   **Money and Measures**   **75**
The Role of Foundations in Knowledge Production
Janelle Scott and Huriya Jabbar

PART II
The Infrastructure of Accountability in Districts, Schools, and Classrooms   93

5   **Governing with Data**   **95**
The Role of Independent Review Panels in Urban Districts
Kenneth K. Wong

6 **"The Numbers Speak for Themselves"**   **113**
Data Use and the Organization of Schooling in Two Florida
Elementary Schools
Stacey A. Rutledge and Brenda Gale Neal

7 **New Data, Old Patterns**   **129**
The Role of Test Scores in Student Assignment
Lora Cohen-Vogel, La'Tara Osborne-Lampkin, and Eric A. Houck

8 **What Makes a "Good" School?**   **145**
Data and Competing Discourses in a Multilingual Charter Network
Lisa M. Dorner and Angela B. Layton

9 **Technologies for Education and Technologies for Learners**   **163**
How Information Technologies Are (and Should Be) Changing Schools
Richard Halverson and R. Benjamin Shapiro

PART III
The Infrastructure of Accountability and the Public Good   181

10 **A Tale of Two Tests**   **183**
Test Scores, Accountability, and Inequality in American Education
Jennifer Jennings and Heeju Sohn

11 **Do Good Grades Matter?**   **199**
Public Accountability Data and Perceptions of School Quality
Rebecca Jacobsen and Andrew Saultz

Conclusion   **213**
The Infrastructure of Accountability:
Tensions, Implications, and Concluding Thoughts
Stacey A. Rutledge, Dorothea Anagnostopoulos, and Rebecca Jacobsen

Notes   **229**

Acknowledgments   **261**

About the Editors   **263**

About the Contributors   **265**

Index   **271**

Foreword

JEFFREY R. HENIG

The infrastructure of data-based accountability is new. The impulses behind it are not. Enabled by new technologies, today's generation of reformers has prioritized the development of large-scale data systems. It is in the manner in which these technologies intertwine with ideas and political forces of longer standing that the full implications of this collection of essays come to the fore.

The architects of the contemporary education accountability system can be likened to the Progressive reformers of a century ago. Those Progressives, who battled with the urban machines that dominated many cities at the time, were responsible for many of the features of local governance and education governance that are still prevalent today. In general-purpose municipal governance, these included civil service laws, the city manager system, and nonpartisan elections. In education, the Progressives helped to shape a governance system specifically for public schools, assigning policy making to school boards independent from municipal governments and the political machines that often controlled them. They sowed the seeds for certification and other institutional mechanisms meant to ensure that teachers were selected and retained based on merit and not based on service to the local party. All of these reforms were portrayed as a way to empower the experts, who would both know and respect objective data, and to explicitly buffer them from political interference, patronage politics, and faddish and emotion-driven popular whims.

Today's New Progressives share key beliefs with their intellectual sires. First is a belief that institutions matter. Individuals may be ill-informed or animated by self-interest, but if they are harnessed within the right set of organizational incentives, the level of collective performance can be shifted in a positive direction. Second is a belief that expertise should drive policy details and administration. "There is no Democratic or Republican way to pave a street," was a favored slogan of the time, with the implication that there was, instead, an objectively correct way best determined via technical and scientific expertise. The third shared belief is that politics is a corrupting force. Partisan politics in particular appeals to parochial group interests, substitutes the promise of material self-interest for that of an abstract public good, and raises the goal of power maintenance over that of system performance.

One important way the older and newer Progressives differ is in their definition of relevant expertise. For the old-style Progressives, expertise was partly about management principles—this, after all, was the heyday of Taylorism and the belief that time-management studies could vastly increase productivity. But this faith in scientific management was adopted by leading education administrators who interlaced it with respect for pedagogy, curriculum, scientific understanding of children's cognitive and emotional development, and a Dewey-inspired conception of the relationship between public education and democracy. Steps they took to separate education from municipal government helped to set the stage for the expansion of a professional education sector and its manifestation in large (and some would say unwieldy and unchecked) bureaucracies, what political scientist Theodore Lowi later would label "the New Machines."[1]

The New Progressives—animated in part by a reaction against what they see as the self-serving exercise of power and discretion by education bureaucracies—focus on a different kind of expertise, one linked more to accountability for educational outcomes than to a deep understanding of the processes by which learning takes place. There are two components of this new expertise. The first involves sophisticated management of human capital—hiring and firing—in the belief that this will ensure that the most effective people will be doing the work of teaching and running schools. The second revolves around the manipulation of incentives, in the form of rewards and sanctions, in the belief that this is necessary both to motivate people to do their best and to get them to concentrate their efforts on the things that are believed to matter most.[2]

While part of their motivation has been to better monitor student, school, and district progress, the goals the New Progressives have attached to the extensive data systems being currently created extend beyond simple description and diagnosis. Data systems are intertwined with accountability via an array of mechanisms for allocating rewards and punishments. And while the contributing authors provide an intriguing diversity of evaluative stances about the consequences of the emerging accountability systems—

with some believing they are fundamentally the wrong way to go and others seeing fixable imperfections in the way we are going about it now—they all agree that accountability is having big effects. This, in itself, represents an important sea change in our understanding of education systems and the potential for effective reform. The deep-seated traditional view is that American education is immune to change. It has been seen to be immune because powerful interest groups, especially teacher unions, have an incentive to retain the status quo and because our fragmented system of educational governance provides so many veto points that these interests can succeed in blocking even broadly based reform movements. Furthermore, education delivery has been regarded as, by nature, a "loosely coupled system" with so much slack between central authority and classroom practice that successive waves of top-down directives dissipate before they reach the classroom level; teachers, behind closed doors, were believed to be beyond the reach of their superiors and essentially free to reinterpret or simply ignore the directives they receive.[3] The combination of interest group veto power and loose coupling buttressed the expectation that nothing much would ever change. Reforms, when they appeared, would prove to be superficial and symbolic.

The new accountability systems—both the test-based metrics that zero in on a teacher's value-added and the more systematic qualitative assessments being incorporated into classroom observations by principals and others—have broken through the classroom door, forcing teachers to respond in ways they have not previously. Given how fundamental this change is, its ramifications are likely to be quite considerable, though we currently have only a vague sense of what those ramifications might be. Whether they are for the better or for the worse is at this point uncertain and likely to depend on contexts that vary and on decisions yet to be made.

This collection breaks new ground on several fronts. It considers the accountability infrastructure as it runs up and down through our multilayered federal system: from Washington, DC, and the state capitals down to principals' offices and teachers' classrooms. It attends to the relationship between what is largely a governmentally constructed system and the private actors—in both the for-profit and nonprofit sectors—that have emerged as critical nodes in the implementation process as well as increasingly consequential contributors to the political coalition that is determining how the new accountability infrastructure will evolve over time. Taken as a whole, the volume is methodologically diverse and inductive in spirit: some chapters more than others are informed by theory, but none is straight-jacketed by preconceived notions about how accountability efforts should unfold.

Perhaps most important, together these essays are looking at the ways the accountability systems operate on and through real people—people who sometimes misunderstand, sometimes deliberately flout, and sometimes creatively reconfigure the incentives meant to steer them and the data meant to inform them.

This volume does not rush to judgment. It is difficult to take critical aim, after all, at a target that keeps morphing. As the editors emphasize, studies of data systems in other contexts reveal potent feedback loops and indicators and apply them in ways that the originators could not have anticipated. The system of educational accountability currently in place—if it is even realistic to imply that there is a single, defined system—is related to state efforts following A Nation at Risk, to somewhat inchoate notions embedded in No Child Left Behind, and to priorities highlighted by the U.S. Department of Education in shaping the Race to the Top competition. But this is still an immature policy regime. Even architects of the current system declare that this is a work in progress. U.S. Secretary of Education Arne Duncan emphasizes that he opposes teaching to the test, narrowing curriculum to subjects currently tested, and in general he believes that the current generation of standardized tests is simply not good enough to rely on in the ways that some states, districts, and schools do. In the middle of a high-propane controversy over the release of individual teacher value-added data in New York City, Bill Gates took pains to announce in an op-ed that a sophisticated accountability system would require greater commitment and resources than all but a few districts have made thus far: "Those who believe we can do it on the cheap—by doing things like making individual teachers' performance reports public—are underestimating the level of resources needed to spur real improvement."[4]

That this is an immature policy regime means that drawing definitive lessons is challenging. What one finds in years 1–5 of an emerging policy regime may or may not indicate what it will look like once it matures, both because the animating laws and regulations may be reconfigured and because levels of knowledge, habits, learning, and a changing cast of characters can affect how policies unfold in practice. Nor is there certainty about whether changes will steer the accountability infrastructure in good directions or bad ones. Sometimes policy regimes improve with age as individuals and organizations gain better understanding of what is expected of them, learn what works and modify what does not, develop new tools, and build informal collaborations that reduce friction and tap social capital. But experience in education and elsewhere also shows that policy regimes can grow flaccid or rigid or run out of steam. Visionary leaders burn out. Early funders cut back support while they shift their attention to the next new best thing. Accountability regimes may be particularly vulnerable to either functional or dysfunctional learning over time; there is potential for an intellectual arms race with educators and students sniffing out new ways to game the system, while those in charge hone their instruments for detecting or deflecting such tactics.

To acknowledge that things are in flux does not mean we need to wait around until things crystallize. We need to be taking measure of things as they are developing, especially if there is a risk that, despite their good intentions and technical skills, the New Progressives might be steering in the wrong direction. And on this ground there are at least three themes articulated in this volume that should at least give us pause.

First, the rush to get accountability systems enshrined in legislation and bureaucratic practice is running ahead of the evidence on its behalf, and this is true despite the fact that the architects of the accountability systems are also vocal proponents of scientifically based decision making. There is a set of unanswered empirical questions about how these new systems will affect the teaching profession overall. Will a greater emphasis on merit and the potential to target higher pay to those who are performing well attract and hold a new-style teacher, as proponents presume? Or will the profession seem stressful, uncertain, and inhospitable to innovation and professional judgment, as critics warn? The only honest answer at this point is that we do not know the answer; but it behooves us, then, to be more modest and experimental in our race to accountability and more committed to research along the way.

Second, and related, we need to know more about the cost side of the accountability equation. That includes real dollars, time, and social stress. It also includes opportunity costs. Lurking in the background of this collection are hints of other broad approaches to addressing educational achievement gaps that are languishing at least in part because the focus on test-based accountability has so dominated the scene. Mistrust of "so-called experts" has led us to build systems based on algorithms attached to automatic sanctions; in the process, have we swung too far in separating accountability for education from informed judgment by professionals? Suspicion that attention to nonschool factors—concentrated poverty, social services, housing, and public health—will be used to excuse poor teaching has led to an accountability system narrowly focused on what happens within school buildings; in the process, are we missing opportunities to build more comprehensive data bases that situate accountability for learning within broader social and economic contexts? Wariness toward the corrupting potential of interest group politics has led us to harness data tightly within administratively designed incentive systems; in the process, are we missing opportunities to inject data more forcefully into the public sphere, encouraging democratic accountability by parents and citizens who become, over time, more confident and knowledgeable about how to use data to collectively define priorities and select educational strategies?

A final theme has to do with the intersection between accountability and democracy. Fears about the corrupting influence of politics have led both older and newer Progressives to try to buffer accountability systems from interest group and electoral influence. But this is a one-dimensional view of the relationship between accountability and democracy: it poses accountability as an administrative tool at the service of publicly defined goals but disregards the role that data potentially play in shaping citizens and reframing public discourse and understanding. The relationship between data and politics is a two-way street. Politics can affect the kind of data collected, who has access to it, and the extent to which that data is applied to broad collective problems or the pursuit of narrower agendas. At the same time, data systems, and the broader regimes within which they are embedded, can alter the distribution of power and influence, pushing some groups and the values they hold to the margin while giving others stronger holds on the levers of policy change.

This volume provides the conceptual tools and substantive starting points for exploring these themes and for beginning the much-needed public deliberation on their consequences. As I read the chapters, I found myself reflecting on ideas about education and democracy articulated by John Dewey—ideas overshadowed by the contemporary emphasis on education as weaponry in the war for global economic advantage. Because of education's historical role as a shaper of citizens, it is especially important in this context to think about the question of whether accountability systems can be more supportive of more deeply democratic regimes: democratic processes, habits, conditions of thought. That calls for paying much greater attention to the role the public could play in selecting accountability metrics, for ensuring broad access to data and a plurality of interpretive applications, and for reflecting deeper on whether the outcomes we are embedding in our accountability infrastructure prepare young people for the critical tasks of democracy. These tasks—which involve wrestling with complex, multifaceted decisions under conditions of uncertainty and where values may conflict and pragmatically creating foundations of common ground though negotiation and good judgment—will ask more of tomorrow's citizens than capacity, or even proficiency, in reading and math.

Jeffrey R. Henig
Professor of Political Science and Education, Teachers College and
Professor of Political Science, Columbia University

Mapping the Information Infrastructure of Accountability

DOROTHEA ANAGNOSTOPOULOS
STACEY A. RUTLEDGE
REBECCA JACOBSEN

Test-based accountability has dominated U.S. educational policy for over twenty years. Beginning in the 1990s with a handful of states and expanding nationally with the 2001 passage of the federal No Child Left Behind (NCLB) act and, more recently, the 2009 Race to the Top initiative, state and federal policy makers have sought to induce improvements in the nation's public schools by attaching increasingly consequential incentives and sanctions for students, teachers, and schools to students' scores on state assessments. This marks a dramatic shift in educational policy away from an emphasis on regulating inputs and toward measuring, monitoring, and regulating outcomes.[1] As its hold on American education has persisted, test-based accountability has sparked ongoing debate and research, much of which has focused on its effects on student achievement and schooling practices.[2]

This book expands current debate and research by examining an overlooked dimension of test-based accountability in the United States: its information infrastructure. Test-based accountability has spurred states to create large-scale information systems that gather, process, and disseminate information on the characteristics and performance of schools, teachers, and students. Data from these systems are made available to ever-widening audiences and used to inform decisions across and beyond the educational system. Newspapers report the annual results of state assessments, and state education agencies and districts post school report cards on the Internet. State and federal policy makers use standardized performance data to distribute monies, reward and punish schools, and, increasingly, evaluate and pay teachers. District and school educators base decisions to promote or retain students, assign teachers and students, and focus curriculum and instruction based on students' test scores. Parents use school demographic and performance data to determine where to live and where to send their children to school. Educational reformers draw on the data to mobilize support and monies for particular reforms. As they determine the nature, use, and distribution of educational resources and opportunities and shape what counts as "good" schools, "good" teachers, and "good" students, these decisions have profound practical, political, and moral implications.

Yet, the performance data made ubiquitous under test-based accountability are, themselves, the products of myriad decisions about what information should be collected, how it should be encoded and processed, and how it should be inscribed into files and reports. The people who make and enact these decisions do so not only in the schools, districts, and state and federal education agencies that comprise our formal educational system but also in testing companies, software firms, research universities and consortia, foundations, consulting firms, and newspapers. Collecting, processing, and disseminating information across these people and settings requires sophisticated computing technologies that can store and process the vast amounts of information required to produce performance measures and ratings. Policies that secure the fiscal and human resources to utilize these technologies and that ensure data accuracy are also necessary. The data that fuel test-based accountability are, thus, the products of complex assemblages of technology, people, and policies that stretch across and beyond the boundaries of our formal educational system. These assemblages constitute the infrastructure of accountability.

Though essential to test-based accountability, the contours and consequences of this infrastructure remain only vaguely understood. Questions of how this infrastructure is being built, the new technologies and actors it gives rise to, how it redistributes power and influence across and beyond the formal educational system, and how it shapes what and who counts in our nation's schools have not been addressed in a comprehensive way. This book takes up these questions. Its chapters examine different parts of the infrastructure of accountability. Taken together, they provide a first mapping of this infrastructure. Though this map is partial, given the relative newness of the infrastructure of accountability and its sprawling nature, the chapters provide key insights into how it is reshaping the ways in which Americans practice, organize, participate in, and even think about the nation's public schools.

Two primary goals drive this volume. First, we use an infrastructural perspective drawn primarily from social studies of science and technology to provide new conceptual tools for further research on test-based accountability, specifically, and educational policy, more broadly. While a growing number of studies have examined schools' responses to test-based accountability and how local educators use data,[3] the information infrastructure of test-based accountability has been largely overlooked. Like the water systems that run beneath our streets and into our homes and workplaces, this infrastructure remains mostly invisible to us. It is sunken into objects, such as the computer files into which school staff upload data or the value-added models that districts use to evaluate teacher effectiveness. Once installed, these objects tend to recede into the background. The work of developing and using these objects typically occurs backstage, out of public view. In the case of creating teacher value-added models, the expertise required by such work further blunts public scrutiny of it.

The information infrastructure of accountability is further difficult to see because it is relational. It holds different meanings for different people. For state and federal policy makers it is a regulatory tool. For foundations it is a funding priority. For teachers and administrators in local schools and districts it is a surveillance technology used to monitor and regulate their decisions and practices. For researchers it is a complex equation that purchases a seat at the table with policy makers, research monies from grantors, and status among colleagues. In each case, what any one actor "sees" of the infrastructure and the meaning it holds for them depends on their position on the broader educational field and on their interests, goals, and ideologies. It is only when we assemble work that looks across the infrastructure of accountability that we begin to grasp the extent to which test-based accountability is changing the educational landscape. We hope that the infrastructural perspective we develop here will be useful to such broad-ranging research.

Secondly, we intend this volume to expand the debate on test-based accountability. Though the large-scale information systems being built to support test-based accountability are relatively new, their capacity to store and rapidly process vast amounts of information on the nation's students, teachers, and schools has expanded significantly. This expansion has been a critical, if overlooked, factor in the development of test-based accountability policies. It has been fundamental, for example, to the creation and use of value-added measures to evaluate and pay teachers. These measures require sophisticated information systems capable of tracking individual student achievement longitudinally and attaching that information to individual classrooms and teachers. The growth in the capacity of these information systems has thus enabled test-based accountability to penetrate further into the core processes of schooling—teaching and learning.

Yet, the rapid development of these information systems can threaten to outstrip our ability and will to deliberate on the nature and consequences of the performance metrics they make available. To be clear, we are not against the creation of performance metrics or the dissemination of information on the nation's schools. A robust democracy requires the widespread availability of information, particularly on those institutions, like public schools, in which participation is compulsory for most citizens and that consume significant amounts of public funding. Because standardized test scores, school grades, and teacher value-added scores appear as objective facts, however, they can blunt public deliberation and make invisible the moral and political decisions that go into creating as well as utilizing them. By making visible the infrastructure of people, technologies, and policies that must be assembled to produce and disseminate as well as use the data of test-based accountability, we hope to reinvigorate questions about how these metrics are shaping what and who "counts" in education, the purposes we ascribe to our nation's schools, and how responsibility for and authority over our schools are allocated and exercised.

INFORMATION SYSTEMS AND TEST-BASED ACCOUNTABILITY

Though the amount of information on American students, teachers, and schools and the speed at which we are able to collect, process, and store it have expanded dramatically over the past twenty years, Americans have long collected information on their schools. The U.S. Department of Education was formed in 1867 largely to collect and report educational statistics about the conditions of schooling across the country.[4] Roughly three decades earlier, prominent advocates of the Common School movement, like Horace Mann, constructed some of the first educational information systems.[5] As Massachusetts' first secretary of the state board of education in 1837, Mann was charged with collecting and "diffus[ing], as widely as possible," information on the conditions of schools across the state.[6] Through school visits, surveys, and the reports school leaders submitted to the state board, Mann compiled information on, among other things, the curriculum, teacher qualifications and salaries, grading patterns, annual school appropriations, school facilities and equipment, and parental and public interest in the common school. Mann, who disseminated this information through speeches and written reports, hoped that the information would persuade the public to support institutionalizing the public school system.

These early information systems are analogous to the colonial roads and paths on which, over time, we have installed our modern state and interstate highway systems. Both state and federal education agencies still collect and disseminate some of the same information on school conditions, student demographics, and teacher qualifications collected by Mann and his contemporaries. Yet, the information systems that have emerged under test-based accountability differ significantly in their design and capacities from their forerunners and even from the information systems in place until the late 1980s and early 1990s. Until then, most state education agencies compiled aggregate information on their schools from reports, sometimes still on paper, that districts submitted during established reporting periods. Information on different program areas, such as Title I and special education, and on students, teachers, and school characteristics was seldom integrated.[7]

Test-based accountability has prompted significant changes in educational information systems. State education agencies have created information systems that both track individual students' achievement and progress across the K–12 school system into college and beyond and link this information to individual schools and teachers. As of 2011, all but a handful of states had installed statewide longitudinal student information systems with the capacity to integrate information on student outcomes across program areas and with teacher and school information.[8] These systems also include data warehouses that integrate, store, and make available vast amounts of information for analysis by researchers, reformers, the media, and other interested individuals and groups as well as by educators.

The large-scale information systems states installed under test-based accountability constitute the main arteries of the emergent information infrastructure of accountability. They collect, process, and submit information from schools and districts to state and federal education agencies that attach incentives and sanctions to it. They also make the information available for further analysis, dissemination, and use by state legislatures, researchers, and other interested parties. Districts and schools have also installed their own local information systems that are operable with but different from the state systems. While some districts and schools have created their own information systems, a commercial market for these systems has emerged over the past two decades. Whether homegrown or commercially developed, these systems facilitate local educators' access to and use of student data collected both by the state and locally. These systems now have the capacity to produce the reports mandated by state and federal accountability policies and the customized reports on individual students and classrooms that teachers and local administrators can use to monitor individual students' progress on meeting state learning standards.[9]

Linked to state information systems, these district and school-level information systems constitute key components of the information infrastructure of test-based accountability. Like state information systems, they further connect to networks of people, technologies, and policies that extend beyond the formal educational system. Private foundations have played key roles in promoting and funding the creation of state information systems. Consultants and computer firms have also either expanded or sprung up to build information software and systems that states, districts, and schools can purchase and to assist states, districts, and schools in building, operating, and using their own systems. In addition, because test-based accountability focuses on student test scores, testing companies have been an integral part of this information infrastructure. As the stakes attached to test scores have intensified, districts and schools have implemented local assessment programs to monitor their students' progress on meeting state and federal standards.

Importantly, though the federal government has supported the development of statewide information systems, this development and the proliferation of local district and school information systems has not been centrally planned. State and local information systems have relied on various combinations of local, state, federal, and private efforts and resources. The federal Department of Education has supported the development of these systems since 2005 through its Statewide Longitudinal Data Systems Grant program.[10] The program hosts annual conferences where state staff and private vendors can share best practices and innovations in the design, implementation, and operation of statewide information systems. It also provides states competitive grants of up to $20 million per grantee.[11] More recently, the federal government launched the Common Education Data Standards initiative intended to encourage the creation of a common set of data elements that will enable information sharing across state lines. Though voluntary, this initiative has the potential to link current statewide information systems into an interstate education information system. Like efforts supporting many other parts of the infrastructure of accountability, the Common Education Data Standards initiative brings together federal, state, and professional organizations and receives funding, in part, from philanthropic foundations, specifically the Bill & Melinda Gates Foundation. It also remains voluntary.[12] Whether and how this initiative creates an interstate educational information system remains to be seen.

INVESTIGATING TEST-BASED ACCOUNTABILITY
FROM AN INFRASTRUCTURAL PERSPECTIVE

Though the information infrastructure we sketch above has been integral to the development and expansion of test-based accountability, we currently lack a comprehensive view of it. Such an understanding must take into account how people use the data made available through this infrastructure. It must also consider how the information infrastructure gets built and by whom, and how that process influences the kinds of information that come to matter.[13] This goes beyond issues of technical affordances and data use. As the chapters in this volume reveal, these are not merely technical issues whose import fades once the requisite technologies get installed. They are also political, cultural, and moral matters. Determining what kind of information about the nation's students, teachers, and schools is collected and how it is processed, disseminated, and used, by whom, in what form, and for what purposes involve questions of power. They also reflect and privilege particular ways of thinking, particular values, and particular notions of worth.

This volume contributes to the development of such a comprehensive view by delineating an infrastructural perspective. Drawn primarily from theoretical and empirical work in the social studies of science and technology,[14] an infrastructural perspective conceives of the information systems of test-based accountability as dynamic socio-technical networks of people, technologies, and policies. These networks both shape and are shaped by the social worlds they traverse.[15] An infrastructural perspective calls attention to how these networks give rise to new roles and relationships and redistribute power. In particular, we argue that the information infrastructure of accountability has given rise to a type of *informatic* power that combines strategic uses of incentives with measurement and computing technologies. Finally, an infrastructural perspective highlights the processes of quantification, standardization, and classification through which information on the nation's schools, teachers, and students gets encoded and inscribed into forms that can be used across and beyond the educational system.

Information Infrastructure as Dynamic Sociotechnical Networks

Though commonplace notions of infrastructure evoke images of material structures and objects, of pipes, bridges, computers, cable lines, etc., an infrastructural perspective envisions infrastructure as complex sociotechnical networks.[16] These networks include material objects and structures, like dams, tunnels, and computer cables; they also include the people who construct, operate, and maintain these structures and the policies that allocate resources and establish the mandates that demand, support, and regulate this work. Building the roads, bridges, and ramps that comprise the nation's interstate highway system, for example, requires assembling not only machines and materials, like bulldozers, concrete, and steel, but it also requires workers who possess the skills and knowledge to properly use these machines and work with these materials. This includes engineers, surveyors, construction workers, crane operators, etc. It also includes planners and inspectors who envision and design the system and who are charged with ensuring its safety and politicians and other advocates who garner political, fiscal, and cultural support for the system.[17]

One goal of this book is to begin to map the assemblages of technologies, people, and policies that must be created to build and operate the information infrastructure of test-based accountability. An infrastructural perspective conceives of this information infrastructure as more than the computer hardware and software needed to collect, process, and disseminate information on the nation's schools. It also includes companies and individuals who construct the state assessments, school staff that upload student information into the relevant computer files, researchers who construct the mathematical models used to compute growth and value-added scores, the state agents who determine the cut-off scores for state assessments, and the journalists who report results of state assessments, among others. Further, the information infrastructure of accountability includes the policies set at the federal and state levels and increasingly promoted by foundations that mandate and regulate data reporting and govern data use.

An infrastructural perspective highlights the dynamic nature of these networks. The information infrastructure we explore in this book, like other infrastructures, is always being built.[18] Glitches must be repaired, and, as new technologies become available, tools and practices must be updated. This is particularly true given the rapid and continual advancements in computing technologies. Large-scale information infrastructure is also always being built because it traverses so much geographic distance and so many social settings. State education agencies cannot ensure that all the schools and districts in their states have the requisite technology and expertise to collect, report, and utilize the data they must collect under test-based accountability. They also cannot directly monitor all the decisions made by people in schools, districts, testing companies, or homes that go into producing, disseminating, and using these data. State education agencies must therefore rely on people in these different settings to build, operate, and maintain much of the information infrastructure of test-based accountability. This involves installing computer systems operable with state information systems, repairing breakdowns, interpreting forms and regulations, and fitting the state information systems into the existing tools, practices, and ways of thinking that comprise the social worlds of each setting.

The information infrastructure of test-based accountability is also constitutive. We typically conceive of infrastructure as merely the material structures or technologies we use to move resources, people, or information, unchanged, from one location to another. An infrastructural perspective, however, illuminates how infrastructure alters our social and material worlds.[19] The interstate highway system, for example, enabled us to live in communities far from our workplaces and to relocate our lives in search of better opportunities. It gave rise to the creation of truck stops, motels, and diners that rose up along the highways to serve the increasing number of drivers, a new identity constituted by the expansion of automobile ownership and the construction of roads that made automobile travel possible.[20] Operating and maintaining the highway system has also given rise to new types of workers and technologies, such as toll workers and the ticket machines and computerized passes that have replaced many of them. Similarly, the public-private partnerships that many cities and states have enacted to maintain highways in the face of rising costs and budget constraints have contributed to the emergence of new types of organizations and new forms of governance. The highway system has also altered the environment. It required paving over grasslands, felling trees, and cutting through mountains. It also reshaped neighborhoods and communities, destroying and impoverishing some while creating and enriching others. In the process, the highway system entrenched and often exacerbated existing racial and class divisions.[21] The interstate highway system thus profoundly shaped our social, political, and moral imaginations, changing our sense of geographic and social distance and how we relate to each other within and across it.

The construction of the information infrastructure of test-based accountability has also given rise to new actors, including consultants who work with schools to use data, computer and software companies that assist states and districts in building and operating their information systems, and testing companies that create and score state assessments. In addition, as we note above, public-private partnerships have been essential to the construction of statewide information systems. The chapters in this book examine the rise of many of these new actors and new partnerships. They also investigate how the information infrastructure of test-based accountability gives rise to new schooling practices and entrenches established ones. Some chapters also examine how the infrastructure interacts with existing racial and, to a lesser extent, class divisions to shape both the social identities we enact and ascribe to others and our moral and political imaginations. Like the effects of the interstate highway system, these effects are multiple and often contradictory. Investigating this multiplicity is critical to understanding and deliberating on the full consequences and meanings of test-based accountability.

Informatic Power

As it identifies the new actors and relationships that infrastructure gives rise to, an infrastructural perspective raises questions of power. In the case of the information infrastructure of test-based accountability, we argue that this infrastructure gives rise to what we refer to as *informatic power*. Informatic power, as we define it, is similar to Mukerji's notion of logistic power.[22] According to Mukerji, logistic power, which inheres in the creation, implementation, and operation of large-scale infrastructures, differs from conventional notions of strategic power. The latter is a practice of social domination that relies on threats and favors to control social outcomes and preserve existing social hierarchy. The authority of ruling elites is legitimated by defining them as morally and/or intellectually superior as evidenced by their ability to impose and maintain their advantage over others. Logistic power, in contrast, is the use of the material world for political effect. It entails the physical reworking of the land to shape the conditions and possibilities for collective life. While this material construction favors some groups over others, the exercise of logistical power depends on the use of practical or formal knowledge to reshape the environment rather than on the strategic calculation of advantages. Power is embedded into the material structures. It is thus impersonal. As Mukerji notes, the built environment often seems to lie outside of politics and thus can seem as inevitable as the natural order. A system of such impersonal rule blunts resistance as power is enacted without people enforcing order. The outcome of exercising logistical power is a material regime imbued with cultural ideals and reflecting relations of power that seem inevitable, natural, or true.

Drawing on Mujerki's work, we argue that test-based accountability and, more specifically, the construction and use of the large-scale information systems at its core give rise to informatic power. Informatic power combines both strategic and logistic power as it ties systems of incentives and sanctions to measurement and computing technologies. Informatic power appears impersonal as its exercise depends on the knowledge, use, production of, and control over measurement and computing technologies. The standardized tests, mathematical models, and computing technologies that comprise key elements of the information infrastructure of test-based accountability are used to produce performance measures that appear as transparent and accurate representations of the complex processes of teaching, learning, and schooling. As they define what kind of knowledge and ways of thinking matter and who counts as "good" teachers, students, and schools, these performance metrics shape how we practice, value, and think about education. Because we view them as "objective," the standards and measures of test-based accountability blunt resistance against the practices, values, and ideologies they reflect. The standards and metrics appear as outside of politics.

Under the informatic regime of test-based accountability, state and federal education agents accrue power not only through imposing incentives and sanctions on schools, teachers, and students but also through collecting, processing, and disseminating information. State and federal policy makers become what Latour calls "centers of calculation."[23] They demand that individual students, teachers, and schools report information upward to them. They then process and return that information as objective measures of the students', teachers', and schools' performance. The information infrastructure of test-based accountability thus facilitates both the ongoing processes of measurement, through the continual collection and processing of information, and the self-awareness among students, teachers, and schools of being constantly measured. In this way the information infrastructure of test-based accountability simultaneously extends and obscures the reach of state and federal policy makers into schools and classrooms as students, teachers, and local administrators align their performances with the ostensibly objective measures.

While an infrastructural perspective helps illuminate how informatic power extends the authority of state and federal policy makers over schools, it also considers how this power circulates and is enacted, contested, and resisted as information moves across and beyond the educational system. Given the emphasis on computing and measurement, test-based account-ability extends the power of testing companies, computer firms, consultants, and researchers who create the metrics and models on which state and fed-eral policy makers rely. Private foundations play a critical part in the cre-ation of the information infrastructure of test-based accountability. As they do so, these organizations contribute to the state's calculative power. They also garner influence for themselves and, as they provide multiple models and technical options that can compete with state ones, can thus become alternative centers of calculation.

At the school level, teachers, administrators, and students do not merely passively submit to the state and federal accrual and use of informatic power. A growing number of studies document the gaming strategies that schools employ to raise student test scores without engaging in significant improvement efforts.[24] Educators and other critics of test-based account-ability have also openly resisted the use of standardized test scores as the major measure of student, teacher, and school performance.[25] Further, the data that test-based accountability produces and makes available are open to interpretation. Their meaning must be constructed. Though the apparent objectivity of numbers carries cultural authority, the performance metrics of test-based accountability are not simply objective facts that can be mined and drilled. Assigning students, teachers, and schools a numerical rating and classifying them as "failing" or "effective" says little about the causes of failure or what can or should be done about it or about school success and how to maintain it. As recent studies of school data use reveal, teachers and administrators interpret and use data in light of their existing world-views, interests, and local practices, preferences, and structures.[26] An infra-structural perspective alerts us to the interplay of the cultural authority of numbers and the local narratives of schooling in which those numbers take on meaning and get taken up into practice. The space between performance metrics and practice thus provides for and relies on local meaning making. As such, it makes room for translation, adaptation, and resistance as well as accommodation.

Finally, information is essential to democratic control over and partici-pation in the nation's schools. As noted above, Common School advocates viewed the collection and dissemination of information on schools as criti-cal to fostering broad support for public schools. As a public institution, the people are owed information on the performance of the nation's schools. However, the information that test-based accountability makes available provides only partial views of schools, teachers, and students. While the American public generally supports using students' standardized test scores to hold schools and teachers accountable, any one test can only assess a narrow range of the skills and knowledge that Americans want their schools to teach and their students to learn. Many of these skills and knowledge—such as creativity, tolerance, and commitment to democratic participation—that the public views as important goals for its public education system cannot be readily measured on standardized tests.[27] Further, this narrowed set of performance metrics has been largely determined by professionals and "experts" rather than democratically. In this way, data are still powerful, but not in the way originally conceived by current theories about public use of accountability data. Rather than empowering the people, the data may constrain what people know and how they think about their schools. While seeming to empower the public by arming them with more information on the performance of their schools, an infrastructural perspective enables us to see how significant control rests in the hands of the people and groups that establish these metrics.

In sum, an infrastructural perspective calls for tracing the networks of people, technologies, and policies through which informatic power emerges to understand both how such power can get centralized through the processes of data collection, processing, dissemination, and use and how it can get redistributed, resisted, and refracted, as well.

Quantification, Standardization, and Classification

If statewide longitudinal information systems constitute the main arteries of the information infrastructure of accountability, quantification, standardization, and classification represent its substrate. They are the processes through which information from schools and districts gets transformed into the performance metrics, ratings, and rankings of test-based accountability. Quantification, standardization, and classification are not unique to test-based accountability. They have long been part of the grammar of U.S. schools.[28] Schools have sorted and classified students and knowledge according to standardized categories associated with age, grade level, and school subject. Oftentimes, these classifications have reinscribed broader social classifications based on race, ethnicity, gender, and language. Standardized tests and the "scientific" curriculum that built on such tests to track students into ostensibly suitable courses of study have proliferated since the early twentieth century.[29] The test scores, report cards, and rankings of test-based accountability reinscribe these processes. Americans support using standardized test scores to hold teachers and schools accountable in part because it aligns with the conventional practices of "real school."[30]

An infrastructural perspective extends our view of these processes by highlighting how quantification, standardization, and classification operate in and through the information systems of test-based accountability. In their studies of information systems in health care and other fields, Star and her colleagues have shown how these processes, though distinct, are interrelated.[31] Quantification facilitates the creation of standardized measures by which people and phenomena are sorted into classification systems. The primary quanta of test-based accountability—students' standardized test scores and the standardized quantitative measures of teacher and school performance derived from them—enable students, teachers, and schools to be sorted into performance categories to which incentives and sanctions can be attached. Standardization has also taken other forms under test-based accountability, most prominently in the efforts to establish state and national learning standards. Significantly, standardized tests and the sanctions attached to them have been important to embedding the learning standards into school curriculum and teaching. It is the imbrication of quantification, standardization, and classification, then, through which these processes becomes consequential.

Along with exploring this imbrication, an infrastructural perspective asks how local processes of quantification, standardization, and classification converge or diverge with those embedded in formal policy and its information infrastructure. At points of convergence, formalized classification systems and the processes of standardization and quantification on which they rest, link up with local systems to narrow ways of thinking and acting. School practices such as "teaching to the test," devoting increased time to reading and mathematics at the expense of other subjects, and "pushing out" low-scoring students are points of convergence documented by research on test-based accountability.[32] Points of divergence, in contrast, make visible the local struggles and compromises that the creation and imposition of formalized measures, standards, and classification systems gives rise to.[33] Efforts by teachers to separate teaching to the test from the "real" curriculum and to preserve instructional practices that address their students' diverse academic needs represent such points of divergence.[34] Several chapters in this volume explore the processes of convergence and divergence. As they do so, they highlight these processes' material and moral force, documenting how educators in districts and schools allocate instructional resources, opportunities, and worth in efforts to meet state and federal performance standards and to preserve local goals and commitments.

While the emphasis on points of convergence and divergence highlight the ways in which quantification, standardization, and classification move across organizational settings (i.e., among states, districts, and schools), an infrastructural perspective also highlights the practical politics of these processes. Someone has to decide on the categories that students, teachers, and schools will be sorted into, the test scores that establish the boundaries between these categories, the percentage of a teacher's performance rating that student test scores will count for, and the learning standards that students will be expected to meet. These decisions have been the sites of public scrutiny and contestation, as evidenced by the debates surrounding national learning standards and the antitesting movement. They often, however, occur out of public view and become largely invisible as they get embedded into regulatory documents, tables, charts, and mathematical models. The contestation and negotiation through which they were constructed get erased. An infrastructural perspective seeks to recover these practical politics by asking: Who determines the tests and algorithms used to quantify student learning and teacher quality, who creates them, and who is left out of such decisions? Who sets the standards and makes the categories by which we classify student, teacher, and school performance, and how, and who is excluded from this work? These questions help illuminate the way in which power and resources circulate through the processes of quantification, standardization, and classification.

An infrastructural perspective further highlights the relationships among the processes of quantification, standardization, and classification, on the one hand, and knowledge production, on the other. This is particularly relevant to investigating the information infrastructure of test-based accountability. According to the theory of action of test-based accountability, objective performance data provide educators the information they need to address students' learning needs more effectively and efficiently. Some studies have found that test-based accountability has compelled districts and schools to target resources in ways that have improved learning opportunities for lower achieving students,[35] while others have documented increases in high stakes tests in many states.[36]

Yet, the quantitative data and performance measures of test-based accountability remain simplifications. Labaree characterizes the view of education that underlies test-based accountability and that is built into its infrastructure through the processes of quantification, standardization, and classification as a grid that "crams the complexities of the educational enterprise into the confines of ledgers, frequency tables, and other summary quantitative representations."[37] While the sense of order, rationality, and utility that these representations possess is appealing, they distort the actual complexities and uncertainties of the educational enterprise and its core processes: teaching and learning. As large-scale information systems produce increasingly precise measurements of student, teacher, and school performance, they risk substituting precision for validity and distracting from important issues, such as educational equity, diversity, and social justice, that are not easily reduced to or redressed by standardized metrics. For example, though intended to compel schools to close the racial and class achievement gaps, the intertwining of achievement categories and social categories (i.e., students' race, social class, ability, and language) under NCLB effectively increased the number of ways schools could be classified as "failing." The schools most often deemed failing under NCLB and, therefore, most often facing negative sanctions have been the schools that serve the highest percentage of students classified as racial minorities, low-income, English language learners, and special needs.[38] Building the complex knowledge base needed to improve these schools is not merely technical; it requires political will and moral commitment to redressing entrenched inequalities. Reducing issues of educational equity to standardized test scores and, increasingly to teachers' value-added performance measures, can thus provide ever more precise measurements without resolving deeper questions.

Further, as Labaree cautions, the overreliance on quantification and the intensification of standardization risk imposing reforms that erode the local practical knowledge needed to keep schools running and for teaching and learning to take place.[39] The knowledge that the infrastructure of accountability makes available is technical. As information flows up from classrooms and schools to state and federal agencies and across to testing companies and other organizations that assist in processing it, it gets quantified, standardized, and classified into rationalized categories that are abstracted from the particularities of school and classroom contexts. Labaree contrasts this technical knowledge with the local practical knowledge that arises from the interaction among people, their work, and the contexts in which they live. Local practical knowledge is critical in environments, like modern classrooms, that are characterized by both high uncertainty and complexity. Rather than rules and formula, this type of knowledge depends on rules of thumb and the judgment to determine which rule of thumb applies in which case. It also relies on "multiple measures of where things stand, multiple ways to pursue a single end, and multiple mechanisms for ensuring the most critical outcomes."[40] As test-based accountability reaches further into the core processes of teaching and learning through the creation and use of teacher value-added models, Labaree warns that such efforts risk destroying the complex ecology of schools and classrooms and eradicating the local practical knowledge that sustains it. By exploring how the technical knowledge of test-based accountability gets produced, disseminated, and used, an infrastructural perspective helps to investigate the relationship between this technical knowledge and the practical knowledge of local schools and districts. In particular, it seeks to identify those points of convergence and divergence to understand the consequences of test-based accountability and its infrastructure for the production of knowledge about and for the nation's schools.

THE STRUCTURE OF THE BOOK

An infrastructural perspective locates the large-scale information systems central to test-based accountability at the juncture of technical networks, knowledge, politics, and moral order. The chapters in this book trace the different paths of this juncture as they explore different parts of the infrastructure of accountability. Taken together, they enact an "infrastructural inversion"[41] by making visible the assemblages of people, technologies, and policies that comprise the infrastructure of test-based accountability and illuminating their technical, political, and moral consequences.

We have organized the book into three parts. Part I explores efforts to build the infrastructure of accountability occurring at the level of broad policy trends and regional, state, and district initiatives. In chapter 1, Mintrop and Sunderman identify the dysfunctionalities and paradoxes test-based accountability policies have given rise to over three distinct policy generations by documenting how these policies have motivated educators to raise standardized test scores while failing to improve the quality of students' learning experiences, and to close achievement gaps. The authors explore how state and federal policy makers have deployed informatic power in ways that have narrowed school practices and how such power might be deployed flexibly to enrich these practices.

In chapter 2, Anagnostopoulos and Bautista-Guerra draw on both science and technology studies and research on trust in organizations to document the political, organizational, and technical work required to design, build, and manage the statewide student information systems (SSIS) at the core of the infrastructure of accountability. Drawing on case studies of three state education agencies, the authors explore how SSIS have altered relationships within state education agencies and among states, districts, and schools and the implications of these changes for issues of data quality and for broader questions of trust and distrust within the educational system.

Chapters 3 and 4 explore the influential roles that actors outside the educational system are playing in the construction and operation of the infrastructure of accountability at the regional, state, and district levels. These chapters highlight the constitutive nature of the infrastructure of accountability and how power circulates through it. In chapter 3, Thorn and Harris, drawing on their experiences advising states and districts on teacher value-added evaluation and compensation systems, detail how the work of designing and implementing teacher value-added accountability policies has both facilitated collaboration among established actors and spurred the creation of new partnerships between public schools and non- and for-profit data management organizations. The authors explore the implications of these new partnerships for educational management and governance.

In chapter 4, Scott and Jabbar document foundations' growing influence on data production and policy advocacy in national and district contexts to identify three key strategic funding areas foundations have invested in to influence policy making: (1) constructing data systems for accountability, (2) the funding of education media to translate data and research to the public, and (3) grants to share research and facilitate networking. The chapter reveals how foundations are fundamentally shaping the data infrastructure for establishing "what works" in educational reform and in the public imagination.

Part II follows the infrastructure of accountability into the core of the educational system—districts, schools, and classrooms. In chapter 5, Wong, writing from the lens of a political scientist and a participant-observer, describes how the Accountability Review Council (ARC) in the School District of Philadelphia used its access to district data systems and the diverse expertise of its membership to fulfill key institutional functions. Wong argues that given growing public skepticism on the role of governmental functions, an independent review panel such as ARC can ease tensions between citizens and professional insiders.

In chapter 6, Rutledge and Neal explore the nature and impact of the infrastructure of accountability in two contrasting Florida elementary schools to document how administrators and teachers in both schools relied on the data derived from standardized materials, diagnostic tests, and computer programs to inform the organization of students, teachers, and instructional time. The chapter identifies points of convergence and divergence between local classification systems and those embedded within state accountability policy and how local contexts, student demographics, and policy pressures shape each.

Cohen-Vogel, Osborne-Lampkin, and Houck explore in chapter 7 how test-based accountability has conditioned the ways school leaders assign students to disrupt or deepen conventional student assignment practices. The chapter illustrates how districts and schools use performance data and multiple classification schemes to preserve long-standing goals of racial integration and established local practices that support heterogeneous classrooms. While chapter 7 highlights points of divergence between test-based accountability's classification systems and local practices, in chapter 8, Dorner and Layton explore points of convergence. The authors report findings from a three-year ethnographic study of the Language Immersion Charter School (LICS) to reveal how accountability pressures led charter school founders to focus on the English language development (as measured by state tests) of children from immigrant families and, over time, to reclassify these children from "bilinguals" to "limited English proficient." The LICS case illustrates how the infrastructure of accountability carries a powerful performance script that defines "good" schools as those that produce "good" data and that threatens to silence scripts of good schooling that value inquiry-based learning, multiculturalism, and global citizenship.

In chapter 9, Halverson and Shapiro contrast technologies for education, those organized to support the work of policy makers and educators, with technologies for learners that are organized to support users' (i.e., students') needs. Arguing that educators are currently overrelying on technologies that provide feedback to institutional actors (technologies for education) rather than learners, they call for greater use of technologies for learners and identify important new directions for using the information infrastructure to support dramatic reforms in teaching and learning.

Part III explores the consequences of the infrastructure of accountability for our broader moral and political imaginations. Jennings and Sohn, in chapter 10, explore how the use of high-stakes standardized test scores to measure both educational effectiveness and equity can obscure persistent racial achievement gaps even while charting improvements in test scores. Comparing outcomes on high-stakes and low-stakes tests, the authors argue that a focus on the former threatens to displace broader goals of social efficiency, social mobility, and democratic equality and to impoverish educational policy and debate.

In chapter 11, Jacobsen and Saultz illustrate how the infrastructure of accountability now reaches far beyond the schoolhouse walls to include the entire citizenry. Exploring the use of public data reports produced by the New York City school district, the authors demonstrate how media narratives about accountability data shape public understanding of performance data and public opinion of the city's schools.

The final chapter explores major themes that emerge across the chapters, focusing, in particular, on tensions between equity and effectiveness, outcomes and outputs, standardization and localism, and trust and distrust. The chapter concludes by identifying implications for policy and research.

PART I

Building the Infrastructure of Accountability

CHAPTER 1

The Paradoxes of Data-Driven School Reform

Learning from Two Generations of Centralized Accountability Systems in the United States

HEINRICH MINTROP
GAIL L. SUNDERMAN

I n organizations, the use of data is interwoven with forms of organizational management, and data infrastructures are embedded in management structures. With the advent of the accountability era of the 1990s in the United States, a new form of organizational management took hold in the public school sector that uses data to concentrate goal setting and performance monitoring functions at the state and, later, federal levels. Sennett analyzes this new centralization as a confluence of two new developments in the organization of work, one technical, the other political: (1) new data warehousing technologies and infrastructures made it possible, with relatively little administrative capacity, to set targets based on a small set of quantitative performance indicators and monitor whether these targets were reached by large numbers of relatively small performance units; and (2) increasingly deregulated workplaces, spreading from private industry into the public sector, suggested to political and managerial elites to link performance indicators and data to sanctions imposed on employees for lack of performance.[1]

In education, this has given rise to accountability systems driven by performance on standardized achievement tests. Over the last twenty years or so, accountability systems have evolved in what we see as three distinct design generations up to this point. The first generation began with a handful of pioneering states that each developed its own system designs in the early to mid-1990s. A second-generation pattern took over when the No Child Left Behind Act of 2001 (NCLB) made sanctions-based accountability universal across all federal states. At this juncture, ten years after the passage of NCLB, with many states opting out of its main requirements, policy makers and school systems are relying on a new set of design components that suggest the beginning of a third generation, this one pivoting on educator evaluations.

Generations have a common ancestry. And so it is with school accountability in the United States. All three generations of accountability designs share common elements—incentives, measureable goals, performance monitoring and assessment, and consequences for low performance. All three give primacy to central administrative levers and managerial leadership to guide the system and penetrate the technical core. In so doing, they reflect trends in public management that have been discussed in the public administration literature under the auspices of "reinventing government" or "New Public Management."[2] But these structural commonalities play out quite differently in each generation, as old system elements are abandoned and new ones are added. As each generation follows the next, we need to learn from the experiences of the previous one to avoid repeating mistakes.

We proceed in this chapter in four steps. We analyze the two successive generations in the first two sections, focusing on system functionality and outcomes. As to functionality, we look at the match between managerial goals and required capacities. Dysfunctionalities arise when goal-capacity discrepancies undermine incentives. As to student learning, we look at its impact on test scores, curriculum, and instruction. In a third step, we discuss possible theoretical explanations for the patterns we identify. In a final step, we apply these explanations to implementation scenarios for third-generation designs.

Our argument is that high-stakes accountability in the first two generations worked and did not work. The systems have turned out to be powerful motivators for educators to reach the state-sponsored goals while, overall, missing their substantive educational goals of increasing the quality of students' learning experience and closing the achievement gap. At the same time, the systems produced dysfunctionalities that strained the problem-solving capacity at each level. Drawing on public administration literature, we suggest that these patterns might be explained by a set of paradoxes: *politicized goal setting, unintended technical inflexibilities, unforeseen capacities and capacity deficits, indicator corruption,* and *performativity.* These paradoxes are loosely understood as developments or outcomes that are contrary to beliefs about how accountability should work.[3] To mitigate these five paradoxes for the third-generation design, we argue for a more comprehensive institutional framework that lessens the primacy of administrative levers in favor of mobilizing teachers' concerns around good instruction.

THE FIRST GENERATION

Given that states were key players in the early designs of the 1990s, system designs differed according to state preferences.[4] Some states, such as Maryland and Kentucky, fused the demand for immediate results with a quest for aspirational educational goals that were given teeth in performance-based tasks on state assessments. Other states, notably Texas, chose a lower cognitive goal horizon. In short order it became clear that these systems functioned quite differently. A state system such as Maryland's, with very ambitious cognitive and pedagogical goals combined with low levels of state support for school improvement, could not sustain the momentum needed to post continuous growth on state assessments and had to retreat on its goals to ensure system survival. A state system such as Texas', with less ambitious goals, posted impressive growth on state tests, largely in the basic skills dimension, and produced fewer failing schools. These different trajectories are illustrated in figure 1.1.

First-generation systems showed that the functionality of the systems depended on the interplay among the difficulty of goals (i.e., realism of growth targets, cognitive rigor of state tests), available capacity reserves, intensity of external pressure, and educators' internal valuation of accountability goals. Incentive systems, by design, locate performance problems in lack of employee motivation, here presumed lack of teacher effort and low expectations.[5] The primary accountability unit was therefore the school, which, incentivized by information, clear goals, rewards and sanctions, was expected to search for new ways of improving its collective performance.[6] Middle management (i.e., districts), presumably unwieldy, rule bound, and bureaucratic, were left out of some of the early state designs. Schools would deliver immediate and continuous quantitative results toward envisioned performance targets. Organizational learning and motivational potential, heretofore untapped, would make costly investments in capacity building unnecessary.

The systems were indeed powerful. Growth targets, performance assessments, and the threat of sanctions compelled schools and districts to pay close attention to system demands.[7] But the systems' motivational power

FIGURE 1.1   Trends in percent of students meeting standard in Texas and Maryland: Grade 8 reading, 1994–2001

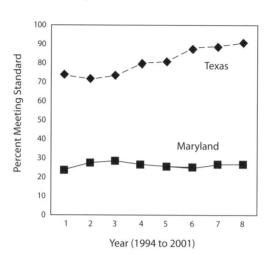

Year (1994 to 2001)

Source: Robert L. Linn, Eva L. Baker, and Damian W. Betebenner, "Accountability Systems: Implications of Requirements of the No Child Left Behind Act of 2001," *Educational Researcher* 31, no. 6 (2002): 3–16.

was double edged. The literature noted an upsurge of energy elicited by the threat of sanctions, sometimes leading to impressive turn-around.[8] The upsurge could just as well turn to demoralization, however, when test score gains were not forthcoming or could not be sustained, and when perceived unmanageable threats led to organizational rigidity.[9] Demoralization was exacerbated as sanctions were applied to whole organizations, hence to high- and low-performing teachers and principals in equal measure.[10] While teachers embraced accountability in general, teaching closely to the test, though probably widely practiced, was seen as a violation of professional norms of good educational practice.[11]

While in most pioneering states test scores on high-stakes assessments rose, it became apparent fairly early on that the number of schools facing sanctions was quite high, and a good portion of schools required external support to make it through the system. States, however, were reluctant to build up the required support and intervention capacity. Instead, they adjusted system designs to existing capacities.[12] Toward the end of this phase, districts were increasingly brought back into the picture—for example, in the 1999 California design—as key missing links for capacity building but also as prime recipients of accountability sanctions.[13]

In sum, it became apparent during this phase that performance information plus incentives eliciting educators' efforts would not be sufficiently powerful without more extensive state or district support and an intervention infrastructure. High educational aspirations clashed with the specificity of goals that needed to be translated into immediate results. On the face of it, the Texas system, designed with modest cognitive goals attached to simple metrics, seemed viable. Here, high pressure was placed on increasing the number of students reaching a specific performance threshold that was within reach of most schools.[14] The system looked promising as test scores kept rising without the need for expensive new investments in capacity building.[15] Thus, new quantitative metrics coupled with new central data warehousing capabilities and added incentives enabled state governments to powerfully influence educators' work. But problems with capacity and with steering the system toward more complex learning outcomes surfaced.

THE SECOND GENERATION

With the signing of NCLB in 2001, high-stakes accountability was made universal across all fifty states. Even though the experience of first-generation systems could have warranted more caution, the NCLB design greatly enlarged ambitions and further concentrated central control. The negative repercussions visible in first-generation experiments—namely, the difficulty for high aspirations toward complex learning to survive in a data-driven, "results now" environment and the failure of states to develop support and intervention programs commensurate to the frequency of school failure—was not imputed. Instead, with NCLB, high-stakes accountability became attached to an even purer incentive and sanctions regime stretched over an even larger distance between a goal setting center (i.e., federal level) and implementing agencies (i.e., schools and districts) than had heretofore been the case.

The quantitative performance measure became at once extremely simple (i.e., the percent of students scoring proficient on state achievement tests) and more fine-grained (i.e., separate subgroup goals for each statistically significant student subpopulation). Districts were now included as key accountability recipients. The timeline became fixed and shortened (i.e., proficiency by 2013–2014), and growth quotas toward the end goal were expected to be met. The sanctions regime was to unfold in preordained stages of increasingly severe interventions and sanctions, not adjustable to states' available support capacity. With the control of performance measures and sanctions moving to the federal level and state governments retaining control over assessments, proficiency definitions, and investments in support and intervention, the distance between goal setting and substantive implementation stretched more widely.

Thus, NCLB followed from assumptions not dissimilar to first-generation rationales, but with inflated expectations. Even more so than the first-generation systems, the NCLB sanctions regime was based on the assumption that recalcitrant local actors often block reform and that imposing reform by a distant force less entangled in local pressures, bureaucratic institutions, and politics will be more successful. It therefore needed to bank, to a considerably large extent, on the presumed power of high-stakes incentives to penetrate the system to the core and on the willingness of the states (unsanctioned by the federal government in this respect) to do the right thing: maintain ambitious educational goals and make the necessary investments to ameliorate deficits where the power of sanctions proved to be insufficient.

Measured by high-stakes state tests, the system was a success: test scores in most states tended to rise continuously.[16] As figure 1.2 indicates, these gains could not be confirmed with gains on low-stakes tests, namely the National Assessment of Educational Progress (NAEP). NAEP scores demonstrated that the achievement gap, certain modest improvements in achievement notwithstanding, lingered throughout the NCLB years.[17] NCLB failed to accelerate the rate of achievement growth or to meet its overarching goal of proficiency for all by 2014 by a long shot. Given the discrepancy between high-stakes and low-stakes test results, it is not clear what the high-stakes state tests were actually measuring. To some, a good dose of teaching to the high-stakes test explained some of the gains.[18]

Evidence accumulated that state governments under NCLB, not unlike the more ambitious state systems of the first generation, reduced the rigor of their assessments over time to keep the systems functional and intervention burden manageable.[19] Lacking capacity to intervene, states relied on districts, under tremendous pressure themselves, to support schools that persistently missed their performance targets.[20] Struggling with their own limited administrative capacity and professional competence, many districts seem to have responded as a low-capacity bureaucracy would, with relatively low-cost simplistic strategies. Test alignment, remediation, benchmarking, consultants who helped statistically identify "bubble kids," prescriptive and packaged instructional programs such as literacy and remediation programs, excessive practice and reteaching, and the like helped reinforce a low-rigor learning culture in schools.[21]

FIGURE 1.2   Discrepancy between high-stakes and low-stakes performance, 2002–2005

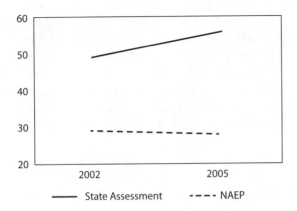

Note: Grade math proficiency trend based on state assessment v. NAEP; N=25 states.

Source: Lee Jaekyung, Tracking Achievement Gaps and Assessing the Impact of NCLB on the Gaps: An In-Depth Look into National and State Reading and Math Outcome Trends (Cambridge, MA: The Civil Rights Project at Harvard University, 2006).

The design worked as intended, and it didn't. It is probably safe to say that, during its ten-year run, NCLB became the decisive impetus for an intense dynamism of educational reform. Specifically related to the NCLB design, performance deficits of previously marginalized groups were taken more seriously due to the sting of subgroup-based sanctions.[22] Yet, the system produced dysfunctionalities that strained the problem-solving capability at each level. Evidence has accumulated that federal goal setting created much movement around the proficiency cut-off points but was unable to register growth in the below-proficiency band where many high-poverty schools operate, was insensitive to the exclusion of students, created an undue burden for schools with highly heterogeneous student populations with many subgroups, and resulted in an untenable number of failing and misidentified schools in many state systems.[23]

In particular, sanctions connected to student groups whose learning needs are not easily standardized, such as special education students or English language learners, converted many otherwise solidly performing schools into failing ones.[24] In the logic of the NCLB design, these groups, when excluded from the sanctions regime, would be pushed to the sidelines, neglected by schools under high pressure; but when included, they would make growth goals quite daunting, undermining the incentive function.

Inflexibility of growth targets and sanctions stages all but doomed the functionality of state systems that held on to rigorous standards and also faced challenging student demographics. The signaling function of the incentive system lost its punch as large numbers of schools and districts entered the corrective action and sanctions stages. In California, for example, more than half of all schools and districts had done so after seven years of NCLB.[25] High numbers of failing schools and districts linked to an increasing severity of corrective action strategies dissipated states' limited intervention capacities.

Especially in school districts serving disadvantaged populations, high-stakes pressure encouraged job design structures that were apt to reward teachers with high compliance dispositions and repulse educators with a high need for personal growth.[26] Studies suggest that rather than freeing up operational units for innovation and learning, high pressure coupled with simple metrics and the demand for scientifically proven interventions resulted in a degree of micromanagement not seen under the most rule-bound traditional bureaucracy.[27] This may have been justifiable if the systems had produced large and confirmable equity gains in the low-rigor basic skills dimension. But this has not been the case.

In view of these patterns, the basic architecture of NCLB seems to have failed in helping us reach the law's most important goals. Despite enormous district and school efforts, as documented by sizable increases in state test scores, second-generation accountability designs were dysfunctional in many states and failed to produce substantial improvements in schools' learning cultures and confirmed student outcomes. With the fading of NCLB, we need to part with the idea that a bare-bones growth quota and sanctions regime with an artificial end goal far above the stretch capacities of the system and far removed from the political realities and educational complexities of implementation in states, districts, and schools could be powerful enough to close the achievement gap and produce a high-quality learning culture in short order.

THEORETICAL EXPLANATIONS

The purpose of this chapter is not to explain why the NCLB policy regime may have failed in light of its own goal, at its most far-reaching extreme, of closing the achievement gap within a historically unprecedented thirteen years.[28] There is scholarship on the power of extraschool factors, most notably socioeconomic factors, that might provide some useful explanations that, in our eyes, have clearly gained more credibility as a result of the failed NCLB experiment.[29] Our purpose here is narrower. We need to understand how a centralized public management system with commendable social goals that holds employees accountable to outcomes with standardized data could fail a much more modest quest—that is, to put schools and districts on a continuous path of improvement in key dimensions of proper functioning. In other words, we limit our discussion to the managerial aspects of the problem. Drawing from the literature on public management, we try out a number of explanations that may help us understand the phenomena we identified earlier.

High-stakes data-driven accountability in the educational sector is the education-specific version of what is referred to in the literature as the new public management (NPM). Borrowing from private-sector principles, its founding doctrine advocated a move away from bureaucratic rule-bound service provisions to entrepreneurial management based on establishing explicit, quantitative performance indicators, incentivizing outputs, separating steering by output controls from operations, bringing accountability to smaller production units, and, in the process, cutting costs, increasing labor discipline, and stimulating organizational innovation.[30]

As NPM systems all over the world have aged, the literature on this phenomenon has matured as well. It is now widely acknowledged, even by its theoretical protagonists, that, as with other management models that came before it, initial claims for NPM models proved to be inflated, and the idea that a new organizational device could solve entrenched social problems, preferably without the outlay of new resources, looks ever more ideological than rational.[31] New paradoxes, unanticipated developments, and unintended effects have been detected.[32] Five of those seem especially applicable to high-stakes accountability systems in education: politicized goal setting, technical inflexibility, capacity deficits, indicator corruption, and performativity. Understanding these patterns can help inform the design of the next generation of policies.

Politicized Goal Setting

The linchpin of NPM designs—ambitious goal setting by the center, flattened bureaucracies in the middle, freeing work from rule-bound regulation, and learning and problem solving on the bottom—were compromised once they encountered the entrenched political and bureaucratic structures of educational systems.[33] In contrast to the presumed rationality of private-sector functioning, educational goals formulated by policy makers were still subject to politicization; and while middle layers at the regional or local levels may have lost some control, they did not vanish. Under these circumstances, the result was a tendency to repoliticize and rebureaucratize the system. In the United States, high-stakes accountability was accompanied by highly politicized goals formulated with the customary bravado of the policy-making center (e.g., being number one in math and science in the year 2000; closing the achievement gap in the year 2014) that were wholly unrealistic by any standards of rational management and, fixed in policy and caught in political posturing, could only be revised with great difficulty.

When first-generation systems were designed, districts were left out of the picture. In some pioneering states (e.g., Maryland and Kentucky), they weren't direct recipients of sanctions, and neither were the structures of local governance or administration changed. Especially after the passage of NCLB, middle managers in districts were not only made directly accountable, but they responded vigorously with increasing regulation and micromanagement of instruction, an approach that may make sense in light of customary bureaucratic practices, prevailing learning theories, and limited instructional know-how.[34] Such a dynamic would tend to incentivize quiet acceptance of external regulation on the part of workers, rather than lively problem solving, producing increased conformance and isomorphism while diminishing aspirations outside of the narrow bounds of prescriptions, benchmarks, tests, and sanctions.

Technical Inflexibility

First-generation systems started out with very ambitious goals as well, but they were softened or rolled back as high performance demands ran up against high failure rates. Second-generation systems, by contrast, became victims of their own political rhetoric. While there was considerable push back by states and local education agencies to many of the NCLB accountability requirements, the basic framework remained unchanged.[35] At the core, two-way communication between top and bottom was weakened by the adversarial stance of a demanding center that suspected "excuses" whenever performance did not rise up to expectations.[36] The result was that the top (the federal government under NCLB) could not learn from the feedback that lower levels of the system (states, districts, and schools) could provide, creating what Collingridge calls an "inflexible technology" that forestalls "normal trial-and-error learning" within the system. Data may flow up and down infrastructural lines, but they do not speak.[37]

Unforeseen Capacities and Capacity Deficits

Capacity building played an insignificant role in the theorizing about new outcome-driven public management systems, since these systems were designed with the arguable idea that lack of motivation on the part of employees is responsible for performance deficits and that powerful incentive systems can remedy this situation.[38] We know now that this "willingness" hypothesis is right and wrong at the same time. The determined focus of schools to improve scores on high-stakes tests may speak to the motivational power of incentives, and the continuous increase in high-stakes test results without concomitant verification by low-stakes tests speaks to a very specific capacity of schools and districts to streamline their operations to correspond to the measured performance indicators.

But there is a set of persistently low-performing schools, often located in impoverished community environments, that does not even have the capacity to do that due to their lack of basic teaching skills and organizational instability.[39] The literature has pointed to the lack of effective support and intervention programs for this set of schools. Episodic infusions of discretionary money or changing modes of governance (e.g., charter convergence) have not produced consistent results.[40] Capacity building for this set of schools may need to go beyond the managerial dimension (e.g., data infrastructure, outcome monitoring, work incentives, episodic resource allocation, governance changes). More comprehensive remedies would involve multiple institutions beyond the public school system that aim to strengthen the supply of qualified teachers and administrators, improve school-community relationships, and target extraschool risk conditions.[41]

Indicator Corruption

At first glance, new public management systems, as well as high-stakes accountability, stress design characteristics such as clarity, consistency, authoritativeness, and stability that would seem to bode well for effective implementation.[42] After all, the systems are presumably clear and specific in their simplicity, accurate in their measurability, authoritative in their top-down execution, and stable in their relentlessness, relative to far more loosely structured policy initiatives of the past. And indeed this upturn in rationality may explain their penetrating power.

But clarity and simplicity in design are vulnerable to indicator corruption, a phenomenon widely recognized in a variety of literatures. In the public administration literature, Campbell's dictum about large-scale evaluations of planned change is famous: "The more any quantitative social indicator is used for social decision-making, the more subject it will be to corruption pressures and the more apt it will be to distort and corrupt the social processes it is intended to monitor."[43] Holmstrom and Milgrom, drawing from principal-agent theoretical models, hypothesize that employers, when incentivizing complex work with rewards based on simple performance indicators, will encourage distortions as employees tend to concentrate efforts on only those dimensions for which they will be rewarded.[44] NPM theorists have pointed to work distortions and indicator inflation in outcome-driven management and accountability systems in many countries and various areas of public administration and government.[45] It is perhaps no surprise that these same distortions were found in educational accountability systems.

Performativity

Indicator corruption might be useful in explaining creative compliance or indicator inflation, such as teaching to the test or concentrating on "bubble kids," but it does not seem powerful enough to explain the paradoxical disconnect between output and outcome that NPM systems seem to produce.[46] The most visible sign of this disconnect in present-day U.S. education is the discrepancy between high-stakes and low-stakes test results. That is, while the systems produce the demanded output, they fail to produce the outcomes on which this output is supposed to deliver, such as substantive learning gains that can travel from school to life (or at least from one test to another) and young people's engagement in their learning (to at least make it past high school).

Ball, drawing from the work of Lyotard, has attempted to capture this pattern of deep seriousness about outputs divorced from valued outcomes as performativity.[47] In simplified terms, performativity in Lyotard's formulation describes the tendency of postmodern society to legitimate knowledge, truth, and right action in terms of "what works" as measured by increasingly more fine-grained scientific measures, objective indicators, and defined externalized performances that apply to narrow roles or organizational fields.[48] Performativity, thus, freezes out the "bigger picture" and ethical judgments that were previously interpreted by, and derived from, grand narratives, such as religion or prominent ideologies (e.g., liberalism, Marxism). When we become preoccupied with what works, we give up on what we ultimately value—our aspirations. Output trumps outcome. The performances themselves "stand for, encapsulate or represent the worth, quality or value of an individual or organization within a field of judgment."[49]

Ball uses the concept of performativity to describe what occurs when a proliferation of externally imposed measures, indicators, rewards, sanctions, programmatic prescriptions that in the present day carry the aura of authority and scientific objectivity become internalized as appraisals of self and others. In the performativity pattern, the traditional defensiveness against bureaucratic intrusion and inwardness of teachers' communication with learners in the enclosed space of classrooms turns into defenselessness and externalized auditability and "fabrication." Fabricated practices, Ball stresses, are not mere artifice but are acted out for real, sometimes with earnestness and conviction.[50] Yet, enacting them may still invoke personal struggle and a sense of lost authenticity and judgment. The performativity pattern may explain how accountability systems of both generations could succeed in producing output while neglecting to produce valued outcomes.

The Paradoxes Put Together

Of the five paradoxes of new public management regimes discussed here, two of them—capacity deficits and indicator corruption—were already well recognized in the analysis of earlier modes of public administration and management. But under NPM they appear in a different light. Capacity appears double edged. There is the capacity to fabricate audited performance, to speak with Ball, resulting in demanded output, and there is the capacity to produce valued outcomes. The imposition of NPM-like systems may have revealed astounding proportions of "fabrication capacity" in schools and districts, while the capacity to produce valued outcomes may have actually declined, most notably due to simple inattention.

Indicator corruption may have to be rethought in the era of NPM. As part of a much more comprehensive work regime and a concomitant society-wide social psychology, indicator corruption may fold into the more thorough performativity pattern. The paradox of technical inflexibility is unique to NPM. It is indeed paradoxical that a management mode explicitly designed to free schools from bureaucratic rules and regulations in order to stimulate problem solving close to clients would end up micromanaging schools with ever more tightly interwoven outcome and process controls that rigidified to the degree that the politicized top "management" of the system could not learn from its faulty goal setting.

In light of the experiences of the two preceding accountability generations and the analytical literature on modes of NPM, we need to design
third-generation systems that avoid the traps of politicized goal setting,
technical inflexibility, capacity deficits, indicator corruption, and performativity lest we continue the disconnect of output and outcome.

THIRD GENERATION

With the Common Core State Standards project, the federal Race to the
Top initiative, the School Improvement Grants program, and the ESEA flexibility waiver program, high-stakes accountability has entered a new design
phase, even though it is not clear if this loosely patched package of initiatives will survive state-level or congressional politics.[51] Even so, new accents
are set:

- The Common Core State Standards reintroduce aspirational educational goals, namely college readiness.
- The simplistic sanctions regime is abandoned, at least at the federal
  level and, with it, realistically, all inflated hope that management by
  results via quantitative growth quota disaggregated to the level of subgroups could close the achievement gap in short order.
- Investment in support and intervention is concentrated in the bottom 5
  percent of the most needy schools.
- The demand to evaluate educators based on achievement tests and measures of practice attenuates the centralization of goal setting by sharing the control over data between center and local districts and schools,
  while at the same time requirements for extended data systems will
  enable "management" to measure performance with finer grain size and
  down to ever smaller performance units.

We assume for the moment that these are indeed the contours of third-
generation designs to come, especially the combination of unsanctioned
aspirational educational system goals and sanctioned individual teacher performance. Inferring from the experience of the previous two generations, we
have a new system that can potentially go in either of two directions: greatly
expand on the educational experience of students by stimulating instructional quality and student learning gains in tandem, or greatly reduce it by
extending the reach of rebureaucratized levers of instructional micromanagement into the last vestiges of teachers' classroom work. The direction,

we infer from previous generations, depends on the way the management system becomes embedded into the larger institutional infrastructure.

There can be little doubt that a high-stakes system that drills down to the level of the individual teacher will become extraordinarily powerful in motivating work behavior. But what type of modal behavior will be motivated is not clear. One scenario imagines a highly problematic repeat of the patterns from previous generations. To begin with, there is presently an intense debate on the reliability and validity of value-added measures calculated for individual teachers.[52] For all practical purposes, the motivational power of these scores will be decided by the recipients, regardless of statistical properties, based on the scores' practical correspondence with a host of other quality criteria held by teachers. If the value-added scores repeatedly appear arbitrary, they may be discounted as valid judgments of work, but this does not mean that they are inconsequential. If the performativity pattern holds, they could be at once discounted and accepted as objective truth, in the face of which individual teachers would defenselessly make themselves "auditable" and produce the demanded output given their fabrication capacity.

Third-generation designs move key improvement levers from outcomes back to inputs by standardizing the evaluation of instruction and attaching sanctions to these evaluations for ineffective teachers. Presumably, a paramount purpose of this procedure is upgrading teaching quality. This in turn requires complex tools for judging the planning and execution of lessons that can structure deep analytical conversations between evaluating and evaluated parties. It is likely that this kind of sophistication is a stretch for the instructional leadership capacity of many local schools and districts, especially those at the lower end of the performance distribution. The default reaction to this situation of high-pressure, low-capacity, but high-"scientific" legitimacy is, as we have seen, a breaking down of task complexity and a simplified version of external (in this case district) performance monitoring per checklist. In this scenario, evaluations may become trivialized and discounted by high-performing teachers.[53] An upgrading of instructional quality becomes stalled, and the negative dynamics of previous generations become more likely. Performativity is heightened when high test pressures and trivialized teacher evaluations go hand in hand.

In a more sanguine scenario, the higher-performing segment of teaching faculties in schools and districts embrace the performance assessments. The assessments turn out to generate robust judgments of teaching quality that are consistent with classroom observations and other quality criteria that practitioners may intuitively entertain. That is, high-performing teachers feel validated in their expertise and effort. Districts eschew their tendency to attach simple monitoring devices to high-pressure situations and share responsibility for evaluations with expert educators, though the latter may be relatively few in number initially. As a result, judging instructional quality is a matter of measurement and instructional expertise. Districts oversee the process, external experts support it, and internal experts are empowered to set the norms of excellence for faculties.

Good instruction is deeply embedded in a web of interconnected and highly institutionalized relationships and links: community relations, professional connections, administrative hierarchies, and societal standards of proper comportment and required skills and knowledge.[54] Community relations exert influence on teachers' work when local elites or parents, oftentimes in direct personal contact, voice their preferences and interact with local officials and educators. As professional workers, educators draw from a fund of established knowledge and internalized norms of good education and acceptable performance. They receive professional socialization and special training in higher education institutions. Internal relationships with colleagues in schools and interactions with external experts maintain and reinforce professional standards, norms, and skills. Administrative means of influencing instruction (i.e., rules, resource allocations, rewards, and sanctions for teachers and students, most notably performance, career, and remuneration criteria) reinforce these professional standards.

Third-generation designs that avoid preceding patterns need to avoid inflexible accountability "technologies." They need to attenuate politicized goals that are currently disconnected from the real growth potential of the system. Goals need to be challenging and persistent, but high pressure and relentlessness fosters rigidities that squelch aspirations and learning. Feedback loops that help goal-setting executives learn from experiences and adjust their expectations are essential. To turn a phrase from Osborne and Gaebler: those who row the boat cannot but help to watch the ones that steer; but those who steer need to train their eyes on the crew as they decide what course to chart and how far to go.[55] To counterweigh the tendency of district administrations to respond to performance pressures with micro-controls of teaching, instructional experts—partly housed within district administrations, partly housed in the professional sphere outside of the K–12 school system—need to become key actors in teacher evaluations.

Given levels of capacity, embedding new complex standards for teaching into daily practice will require broad development of new skills and competencies among teachers and administrators and systematic recruitment of excelling instructional leaders. This is a task that surpasses the capacity of management and administrations. It brings professional organizations of all kinds—universities, associations, reform organizations, and new institutional bodies—into the center of the picture. An important step has been taken in shifting key accountability functions downward, back to local systems. It is imperative to recognize that instructional excellence probably cannot emanate from the perch of the center or the primacy of administration; it must be an internal striving of actively participating professional workers who are sensitive to articulated community needs.

CHAPTER 2

Trust and Numbers

Constructing and Contesting Statewide Student Information Systems

DOROTHEA ANAGNOSTOPOULOS
JUANITA BAUTISTA-GUERRA

Test-based accountability has made available unprecedented amounts of information on the nation's students, teachers, and schools. State education agencies, districts, newspapers, and numerous organizations, both nonprofit and for-profit, publish school report cards, state testing results, and teacher evaluation ratings through a variety of media. As Jacobsen and Saultz note in chapter 11 of this volume, this unprecedented availability of educational performance data has significant consequences for Americans' trust in their public schools. While the public reporting of educational performance data can be used to shame and embarrass schools and educators, it can also boost confidence by providing the public a way to monitor its investments in the schools.

In this chapter, we explore issues of trust as they relate to the development and operation of the statewide student information systems (SSIS) that produce these numbers. State education agencies (SEAs) are responsible for installing and managing SSIS. While SEAs can and do integrate data auditing tools into their SSIS, they must ultimately rely on staff in districts and schools to collect and report accurate information to them. Yet, under test-based accountability, collecting and reporting data to SSIS are highly fraught for districts and schools. SSIS represent the main arteries of the information infrastructure of test-based accountability (see the introduction to this volume). They track the progress of individual students across the K–12 system, through college, and beyond. When linked to personnel and other information systems that collect data on teachers, school safety, and school finance, SSIS produce the performance data that state and federal policy makers use to monitor, reward, and punish schools and teachers. SSIS also make this data publicly available, making schools and educators vulnerable to public shaming by the media and politicians.[1] In short, SSIS implicate students, teachers, and administrators in collecting the very information used to monitor, regulate, and punish them. The development and operation of SSIS are thus shot through with issues of trust and distrust.

We examine these issues through case studies of the implementation and operation of SSIS in three states. We conducted these studies in 2007–2008 with our colleague Valentina Bali. In each state we collected state legislation, budgets, and documentary data pertaining to the SSIS and conducted semi-structured interviews with administrators and staff members in SEAs who were directly involved in the development and operation of the SSIS (SSIS staff). We selected the states in our study according to the comprehensiveness of their SSIS as identified by the Data Quality Campaign (DQC). In 2007, the Emergent State was in the early stages of developing its SSIS (low DQC index), the Accelerated State had recently implemented a relatively comprehensive SSIS with plans for further expansion (medium DQC index), and the Established State had a highly comprehensive SSIS that included a data warehouse and the capacity to link to other data systems (high DQC index).[2]

Comparing the development of the SSIS across the three states illuminates the work of creating and maintaining the infrastructure of accountability. Designing and operating SSIS are not merely technical matters. They require securing and mobilizing significant fiscal, political, and organizational resources. They also depend on establishing trust among SEAs, districts, and schools. This work has significant implications for the quality of the data on which test-based accountability rests.

FRAMING IDEAS

Educational research has identified trust as a critical resource for schools. Though definitions of it vary, trust essentially entails the willingness to rely on another person or group to ensure one's best interests competently and with care. This willingness is based on the perception that the other party is benevolent, reliable, competent, honest, and open.[3]

Educational researchers have found that trust among parents, students, teachers, and principals facilitates school reform efforts and positively contributes to student achievement.[4] In schools, as in other organizations, trust facilitates the sharing of information, cooperation, and efficient problem solving. It contributes to productivity by reducing the costs and complexities of coordination and management both within and across organizations.[5] Conversely, distrust reduces productivity. As distrust increases feelings of anxiety and insecurity, people focus their resources on protecting their vulnerabilities rather than on accomplishing work objectives. Importantly, under conditions of distrust, the sharing of information suffers as people in subordinated positions tend to withhold information and distort upward communication.

Though beneficial, trust within and across organizations is variable and dynamic. Levels of trust can vary within and across individuals, groups, and organizations. High levels of trust can exist among some groups around some operations, while lower levels of trust can exist among the same groups around other operations. The degree to which people view others as trustworthy is shaped by organizational structures, policies, and culture. Changes in any of these can affect the types and levels of organizational trust. Trust is also shaped by individual dispositions and individual, group, and organizational histories. Importantly, the introduction of technologies of surveillance (i.e., tools to monitor and regulate work behavior and practice) has been found to increase distrust among both those being monitored and those doing the monitoring.[6] In short, trust in organizations is provisional. It is vulnerable to breaches caused both by internal changes and events as well as external shocks and pressures.

Though a growing number of studies documents the importance of trust in schools, few studies have examined issues of trust as they relate to the collection and reporting of data and, in particular, to the operation of large-scale information systems, such as SSIS. Identifying these issues requires understanding the work of developing and operating these systems. Sociological studies of technology, scientific innovation, and large-scale information systems have identified three processes central to this work.[7] *Problematization* refers to the processes through which SSIS staff attempt to tie the interests of other personnel in schools, districts, and SEAs to the SISS. If such attempts are successful, the latter come to view the SISS as critical to meeting their goals and securing needed resources. *Enrollment* involves SSIS staff ensuring that staff in schools, districts, and SEAs collect and report information accurately and in the correct form. The goal is to embed the SSIS into people's everyday work across the educational system in a way that meets SEAs' specifications and is amenable to SEA coordination. *Mobilization* refers to SSIS staff's ability to garner support for SSIS by enlisting other groups and individuals as spokespeople for the systems. Researchers have identified three types of strategies for attaining the goals of these processes: *coercion* by physical force, legal statute, or incentives; *communication*, including written and electronic; and *standardization* of personnel training and tools.

If SSIS staff can attain the goals of problematization, enrollment, and mobilization, they can increase the stability and efficient operations of SSIS. However, because SSIS require assembling and coordinating the work of vast amounts of technological resources and personnel across schools, districts, SEAs, and other settings (e.g., testing companies, software vendors), control over these systems is never entirely secure.[8] SSIS are not merely technical systems whose development and operation can be managed through technical fixes. Rather, they are dynamic sociotechnical systems that require ongoing political, organizational, and technical work. Indeed, while SSIS staff can utilize technologies to monitor school and district data reporting, given ever-expanding demands for data from schools, SSIS staff must rely in large part on personnel in schools and districts to submit accurate data. In short, SSIS also require trust across the educational system.

THE DEVELOPMENT AND OPERATION OF SSIS IN THREE STATES

We now examine the development and operation of the SSIS in our three case study states. After briefly describing the history of SSIS development in each state at the time of our study, we explore the work SSIS staff engaged in to install, operate, and/or expand the SSIS. Concerns about trust arose throughout this work. SSIS staff addressed these concerns through a variety of strategies. These strategies had consequences for the ability of SSIS staff to coordinate data collection and reporting across the educational system and to mobilize support for the SSIS.

Overview of the States

Table 2.1 identifies the number of elements that the SSIS in each case study state contained at the time of our study. According to the DQC, fully functioning SSIS contain ten elements, including unique student identifiers, capabilities to link student and teacher information, and longitudinal capacities across K–12 and higher education data. In 2007, SSIS comprehensiveness varied considerably across the case study states. Table 2.1 also reports whether the states had enacted legislation or statutes regarding SSIS, the degree of district centralization in each state, and the total state general fund balance as a percent of total expenditures. The latter is a measure of

TABLE 2.1   **Classification of case study states by number of SSIS elements and state-level influences, 2007**

State	Number of SSIS elements	SSIS legislation or mandate	Number of school districts per 10,000 students	Percent of budget balance*
Emergent	3–4	no	5.0	4
Accelerated	6–7	yes	7.0	14
Established	9–10	yes	0.3	17

* Total state general fund balance as a percent of total expenditures.

Source: Dorothea Anagnostopoulos and Valentina Bali, "Implementing Statewide Student Longitudinal Data Systems: Lessons Learned from the States" (unpublished final report to the IBM Center for the Business of Government, 2008).

each state's fiscal health. In a prior analysis we found that these conditions related to SSIS development. States with more comprehensive SSIS tended to have state legislation, fewer school districts, and better fiscal health than states with less developed systems.[9]

Emergent State

As Table 2.1 indicates, in 2007 the Emergent State had just begun developing its SSIS. It depended heavily on an external consultant to design and create its system. At the time of our study, the consultant had created unique student identifiers for all students in the state and had attached them to state assessment data. The system did not have longitudinal capacities.

Several factors appear to have slowed SSIS development in the Emergent State. First, there was little state legislative support. No state legislation regarding the SSIS had been enacted. SSIS staff characterized the state legislature as largely uninterested in utilizing data. Second, fiscal resources to support the creation of SSIS were somewhat constrained. As Table 2.1 reports, the Emergent State had less than a 10 percent total state general fund balance as a percent of its total expenditures. Third, school governance was decentralized. There were well over seven hundred districts within the state. This posed significant coordination costs. Finally, a highly publicized testing failure had created considerable tensions between the SEA and the districts and schools. Prior to our study, the testing company the SEA had hired to administer and score the state assessments had failed to return accurate assessment results in time for the SEA and districts to meet federal reporting deadlines. The districts, facing significant revenue losses, held the SEA responsible. Several pressured the state legislature to investigate, and the legislature held public hearings on the matter. SSIS staff reported that, as a result, the SSIS had become a "hot potato." Project managers who oversaw the SSIS development resigned. There was little interest in the SEA in taking ownership of the SSIS. Tensions between district personnel and SEA staff remained high at the time of our study. A staff member of the external consultant that developed and managed the emergent SSIS reported that she avoided being seen with SEA staff members when she interacted with district and school personnel because the former were "lightning rods" for district and school anger.

Accelerated State

The Accelerated State had implemented a fairly comprehensive SSIS the year before our study. As Table 2.1 indicates, the system contained between six and eight elements and had longitudinal capacity since its inception. Though the number of districts in the Accelerated State was relatively high, other conditions were conducive to the rapid development and implementation of the SSIS. Among the most important was state legislative support. When the SEA's application for federal funds for SSIS development was rejected, the state allocated roughly $25 million over three years for this work. With this support, the number of SSIS staff doubled from twenty to more than forty. The support also enabled SSIS staff to purchase computer technologies and, when needed, consultant services. The latter was important to the creation of a data warehouse that required technological expertise SSIS staff did not yet possess. The state legislature also used its coercive power to tie school funding to participation with the SSIS in the first year of the system's implementation. All districts and schools were thus compelled to go through the SSIS to secure state funds.

SSIS staff employed several strategies to mobilize support for the SSIS across the educational system. One of the first statements the SSIS director released to districts explained the state and federal mandates behind the data collection and specified how SSIS staff would safeguard the privacy of the information being collected. The SSIS director also sent letters to parents informing them about the data mandates and providing an opt-out opportunity. This move was intended to establish the trustworthiness of the SSIS staff and of the SSIS itself. SSIS staff intended the letters to signal that they could be trusted with information, much of which made districts and schools vulnerable to state intervention.

Established State

The Established State in our study began developing its SSIS in the early 1990s, during the first phase of test-based accountability (see Mintrop & Sunderman, chap. 1 this volume). By 2007, its system was fully comprehensive. It collected over three hundred different types of information on students across the K–16 school system and beyond and included a fully operational data warehouse. Several conditions supported the system's development. Many of the staff who designed the system in the 1990s continued working with it in the 2000s. They possessed a deep knowledge of the SSIS and of the state's educational system. They also had established relationships with people within and outside the SEA that facilitated the SSIS's development and operation. The state legislature was also very supportive of the SSIS and of data use more generally. At the time of our study, the legislature had recently allocated funds for the creation of the data warehouse. When combined with federal funds the SEA had received, the SSIS had stable funding. Finally, as Table 2.1 indicates, there were very few districts in the Established State, thus reducing the coordination costs for SSIS staff.

We turn next to the challenges that SSIS staff faced across the three states as they created, installed, and operated the SSIS and the strategies they used to address these challenges. We highlight the issues of trust that arose in relation to these challenges. We organize our discussion around the processes of problematization, enrollment, and mobilization essential to the development and stabilization of SSIS.

PROBLEMATIZATION AND THE LIMITS OF COERCION

Problematization is the process through which SSIS staff attempt to convince others that their valued interests can only be secured through participating with the SSIS. Federal data reporting mandates associated with No Child Left Behind (NCLB) legislation that attached incentives and punishments to information on student achievement compelled schools and districts across all three states to participate in their states' SSIS. State mandates in the Accelerated State and Established State that tied state school funding to data reporting placed further pressure on schools and districts to do so. Interestingly, both state legislatures issued these mandates early in the development of each state's SSIS. This was particularly important in the Established State, which began developing its system prior to NCLB. Installing a computerized data system that collected data at the individual student level marked a significant departure from the previous paper-based system in which data was collected in the aggregate. SSIS staff reported that districts mounted considerable resistance to the new system. According to SSIS staff, it was not until the state legislature tied school funding to participating with the SSIS that most districts in the state got on board. Across the three states, state and federal mandates were thus crucial to defining schools' and districts' interests in ways that made the SSIS central to securing them.

While the coercive power of state and federal legislation facilitated the processes of problematization, it also posed challenges for SSIS staff. As the SSIS became increasingly critical to schools and districts attaining funding and avoiding sanctions, the reliability and competence of the SSIS staff also came under scrutiny. A SSIS staff member in the Established State questioned the capacity of the aging technology within the SEA. Others recognized that SSIS staff bore increasing responsibility as the stakes attached to data intensified for schools and districts; system breaches or breakdowns had increasingly significant implications. The testing failure that occurred in the Emergent State was so heated because of the stakes federal mandates attached to the data. Because the SEA had difficulty redressing the problem created by the testing company, the failure cast doubt on its reliability and competence, straining SSIS staff's relationship with the state's districts and schools.

Enrollment and Trust Among SEAs, Districts, and Schools

Because they rely on the work of vast numbers of people and technology across the educational system, SSIS pose significant coordination challenges for SEAs. Solving these challenges requires, in part, ensuring that people involved with the SSIS have sufficient knowledge, skill, and technological resources to accurately collect and report a wide range and amount of information. Ensuring the quality of this information requires making the use of these resources predictable and reliable. This is the work associated with enrollment. The SSIS staff in the three states employed a range of strategies to engage in this work. This work variously rested on and established the bases for different types of trust among SEAs, districts, and schools.

SSIS staff in both the Accelerated State and Established State maintained several forms of communication with school and district personnel that enabled them to assist the latter in collecting and reporting SSIS data. They produced and distributed numerous guidebooks and alerted school and district personnel about system changes through postings on the SEAs' Web sites. They maintained help desks, provided trainings and workshops across their states, and worked over the phone with district and school personnel. In addition, SSIS staff in the Accelerated State created several listservs through which they communicated with superintendents, district personnel, SEA program area staff, and school personnel. SSIS staff in the Established State held an annual data conference where they interacted directly with district and school personnel to address the latter's questions and assist them in meeting new demands and understanding system changes.

Importantly, in the Emergent State it was the staff of the external consultant the SEA hired to design and operate the SSIS, rather than SSIS staff, who maintained ongoing communication with district and school personnel. The consultant staff wrote the guidebooks, maintained the help desk, and conducted workshops. This was a result of both the SEA's decision to place the primary responsibility for the SSIS on the external consultant and the testing breach. Given the tension surrounding the testing failure, the consultant staff reported that they consciously separated themselves from the SEA during their interactions with district and school personnel. One consultant staff member described how he positioned himself as a go-between when working with the districts, noting, "We play the role of not being part of the Department of Education (DOE) . . . [We tell districts and schools] we do not understand DOE policy . . . but we're more than willing to listen to your question and take it back to somebody at the DOE." The consultant staff thus functioned as a type of third party conduit providing information to the districts from the SEA and vice versa. They did not, however, use this position to help repair trust between the districts and the SEA. Instead, they appear to have utilized their position to secure their continued employment with the SEA. They remained the individuals with the deepest knowledge of the SSIS and with the communication channels with the districts and schools critical to the operation of the SSIS.

The ongoing communication with district and school personnel served several purposes. It provided the personnel with just-in-time support to address unique district or school needs. SSIS staff in the Established State also described using ongoing communication with district personnel to resolve inaccuracies in the data districts sent to them. SSIS staff stated that when they identified these inaccuracies they tried to work things out with the district personnel through phone conversations and e-mail communications. Importantly, if they felt that the district personnel were not addressing the problem, the SSIS staff said that they "kicked [the problem] up" to program area staff, including those in the school finance division, who had the authority to penalize the district or school. "Kicking it up" thus served as a credible threat, a necessary condition for the repair of trust within organizations.[10] It also reveals how issues of data quality cannot be addressed merely through technical fixes. Though the Established State's SSIS included a data auditing component, resolving data inaccuracies required communication and, ultimately, trust between SEAs and districts and schools.

The ongoing communication between SSIS staff and district and school personnel in the Accelerated State provided the staff with insight into the challenges the latter faced in participating with the SSIS. The SSIS staff reported that they learned how varied districts and schools were in their technological resources and capacities. They noted that in some districts the superintendent had to upload and report the data, while in others secretaries and receptionists did so. It was even more difficult to determine who actually did the data reporting in schools. They also came to see program divisions within districts, and the communication barriers they posed, as obstacles to data collection. Indeed, several SSIS staff noted that the traditional ways that district staff worked in program silos would have to change in order for data to be collected accurately and to flow efficiently through the SSIS. Finally, the ongoing communication with school personnel led SSIS staff to believe that schools had limited understanding of, interest in, or resources for ensuring data quality. Data collection and reporting were "low priorities" for schools.

In order to deal with this variation and uncertainty, the SSIS staff in the Accelerated State established a certification program for district and school personnel who could voluntarily take a combination of online classes and workshops at the SEA. On completion, the SEA issued a certification. The certification program was intended to standardize the skills, knowledge, and practices of the school and district personnel who worked with the SSIS. SSIS staff also believed it would signal to district administrators and principals that this work required skill and training, thus raising the status of the SSIS within these settings. The SSIS staff used certification to establish the grounds for role-based trust predicated on the perception that people who occupy particular roles possess the competencies to do so in a reliable manner.[11] Given the newness of the SSIS, the SSIS staff had to create this role through the certification process.

The SSIS staff in the Accelerated State also instituted a certification program for software vendors and consultants. Given the state's history of local control over schools, the SSIS staff did not want to mandate that schools and districts select particular vendors. This created problems for the SSIS staff as the packages that the myriad vendors and consultants sold districts and schools did not always align with the state's SSIS. Certification, which had to be renewed annually, required vendors to test the operability of their products with the SSIS during the summer. SSIS staff then identified certified vendors and consultants on their Web site. Certification thus standardized the vendors' and consultants' work with the SSIS, reducing coordination costs for the SEA.

Importantly, SSIS staff in all three states also had to work to ensure enrollment in the SSIS among SEA program area staff. The program staff had to submit data to the SSIS. SSIS staff in the Established State provided ongoing training to program area staff, often taking the latter with them to meetings and conferences about SSIS. The longevity of SSIS staff in the Established State also fostered productive relationships with program-area staff. A staff member in one program area noted that because of this longevity and the deep knowledge SSIS staff had of both the SSIS and the educational system, SSIS staff were able to facilitate collaboration among SEA staff. This programmer asserted that SSIS staff had "enough background and experience and respect that people will come to the table." SSIS staff similarly described how their longevity facilitated problem solving across the SEA. One staff member noted, "Everybody around you has hung around a long time. And we do not look at levels. We don't look at tiers in the organizational chart. We look at what we need to accomplish. And we cross over whatever lines to get done whatever it is we need to get done." The longevity of SSIS staff in the Established State thus appears to have enabled history-based trust among SEA staff that facilitated efficient SSIS operation.

For SSIS staff in the Accelerated State, the most challenging area of enrollment was among SSIS staff itself. Though the number of SSIS staff had doubled, there was high turnover among the staff. SSIS staff attributed this mostly to competition from the private sector, which could offer much higher salaries. The SSIS director addressed this turnover by dedicating resources to building the capacity of the SSIS staff. After some initial negative and costly experiences with external consultants and vendors, the director focused on retaining SSIS staff with knowledge of the broader educational system. She provided technological training for these staff and then promoted them to project managers. She then hired new programmers whom she planned to train and later promote in order to maintain a staff with the knowledge of the SSIS and the educational system required to update and expand the SSIS. The director noted, however, that this did not solve the problem of SSIS staff turnover. She still lacked the funds to provide staff with salaries and bonuses comparable to the private sector.

Mobilization and the Importance of Spokespeople for the SSIS

Given expanding demands for data and continual advancements in computer technologies, SSIS will need continual updating. This will require organizational and fiscal resources. Mobilizing support for SSIS is thus part of the ongoing work of SSIS staff. It is essential not only at the implementation stage but also for maintaining, updating, and expanding the information systems. Along with obtaining support from state legislators, district superintendents, and school personnel, mobilization involves identifying spokespeople who can promote the benefits of the SSIS to the people and groups they interact with and whom they represent. These spokespeople are critical to the development and operations of SSIS in two ways. First, their support can help garner critical fiscal resources for system development. Second, they can diffuse trust in the system. Given the geographic distances SSIS traverse, interactions among SSIS staff and all the individuals and groups involved in collecting and reporting data to the SSIS are constrained. Spokespeople can act as critical go-betweens who can provide important secondhand knowledge and transfer expectations to personnel across the educational system for working with the SSIS.[12]

Perhaps not surprisingly, SSIS staff in the Emergent State were not able to mobilize support for the SSIS either within the SEA or beyond. Few people were willing to speak for a system that had failed. SSIS staff in both the Established and Accelerated States, however, employed several strategies to identify spokespeople for the system. SSIS staff in the Established State garnered critical organizational and fiscal support by identifying spokespeople in districts and the state legislature, respectively. As we noted above, SSIS staff in the Established State encountered considerable district resistance to their introduction of the SSIS in the early 1990s. In response, they identified a small group of both large and small districts to pilot the system. According to SSIS staff, the large districts found that the new system increased efficiency while the small districts actually increased their state funds due to more consistent calculations. These districts became spokespeople for the system among the state's school districts. As one SSIS staff member noted, "[We] let them be our stars. They were the ones who carried the flag."

SSIS staff in the Established State also mobilized support for the system in the state legislature. Early in the development of the SSIS, they talked with state legislative staff about the emerging system and invited them to the SEA to see their work. The legislative staff worked to ensure that language requiring school districts to allocate funds to the development of the SSIS was put into a state appropriations act. Interestingly, according to the SSIS staff, two of the appropriations staff had previously worked in the SEA and had been very supportive of the SSIS, and a SSIS staff member had maintained positive relationships with these legislative staffers. The longevity of the SSIS staff again facilitated relationships that proved critical to garnering and maintaining support for the SSIS.

In the Accelerated State, SSIS staff also worked to develop spokespeople for the system among district superintendents. Early in the development of the SSIS, the director and staff met regularly with the statewide council of district superintendents to apprise them of the system's development and to enlist their support. The SSIS director noted that the superintendents on the council then "talked to their districts and to the set of districts that they represent" about the system and its relation to federal and state mandates. The director reported that she made it a policy to "always start" with the council of superintendents because district support was so critical to the success of the SSIS.

Another key group in the Accelerated State comprised the program area leaders in the SEA itself. Because the SEA traditionally collected and reported data by individual program areas, changing to an integrated data collection system represented a significant shift in practice. In order to get buy-in among program area staff for this shift, the SSIS director created a data governance task force comprised of all the program area leaders and the SSIS director and project managers. Because the SSIS was located in the Instructional Technology (IT) division, the director felt it was imperative to get "a group that represented the business of education" involved in the planning and development of the SSIS. If IT was seen as the driving force behind the system, the director felt that SEA program area staff would view the SSIS as a burden rather than as a tool to assist the work of the program areas. Importantly, through her work with program area leaders on the task force, the SSIS director was also able to obtain funds for the development of the SSIS by writing requests for the funds into program-area grant applications.

EXPLORING THE CONSEQUENCES OF STATEWIDE STUDENT INFORMATION SYSTEMS

Statewide student information systems are key components of the infrastructure of accountability. They make available the information that is used to evaluate, monitor, reward, and punish students, teachers, and school performance. As of 2011, nearly all fifty states had comprehensive SSIS in place.

These systems have, however, remained largely unexamined by educational researchers. The goal of this chapter was to make visible this critical part of the infrastructure of accountability by illuminating the work involved in designing, building, and operating SSIS. Drawing on our exploratory studies of SSIS in three states, the chapter shows how the work of problematization, enrollment, and mobilization are critical to installing and maintaining SSIS. Given the rapid nature of technological advancement and the ever-growing demand for educational data, this work will remain vital into the future. As more stakes are attached to data, the issues of trust and distrust associated with this work are also likely to intensify. We consider the implications of both for the development of large-scale information systems in education and for future research.

First, the study begins to document how SSIS are reshaping work and relationships across the educational system. Implementing and maintaining these systems requires building the internal capacities of SEA staff. The hiring and retaining of SEA staff with deep knowledge of the complex technologies associated with SSIS and of the educational system was critical to the development of the most comprehensive systems in our study. As demands for data grow and legislative mandates shift, SEA staff with such knowledge will be needed to update and expand the SSIS. Having staff with insider knowledge of the system will be vital to the success of these efforts. As our study shows, when high stakes are attached to data, breaches in the system, such as occurred in the Emergent State, have major ramifications. They can significantly undermine trust in the information systems, thus increasing their already high coordination costs.

Second, and related to this, our study suggests that internal SEA capacity engenders the development of various types of trust that can facilitate SSIS operations. Such trust is imperative for the operation of large-scale systems that traverse considerable geographic distance and multiple organizational settings. It is never possible to entirely control such systems. They will ultimately rely on the trustworthiness of the individuals who interact with them. Thus, ensuring data quality, a critical assumption for test-based accountability, is more than a technical problem. It is also a social problem that inherently involves issues of trust. Importantly, as our study suggests, while relationships and policies that foster trust are important to data quality, so too are processes for resolving violations of trust. In the Emergent State there were no clear processes in place to resolve the breach created by the testing failure. The result was that the SSIS became a low priority in the SEA, and relationships with school districts remained strained.

Though exploratory, this study highlights the dynamic nature of large-scale information systems like SSIS. Rather than simple technical systems that, once installed, operate with only minimal technical maintenance, SSIS are highly complex sociotechnical systems that both shape and are shaped by the political, fiscal, and organizational contexts they traverse. The work of creating, operating, and maintaining these systems is similarly complex. While our study has begun to specify the properties and dimensions of this work in SEAs, we need to understand this work more fully both within SEAs and across districts and schools.

There are several areas important for future research in this regards. While SEAs have become increasingly active in local schools since the advent of test-based accountability, there have been few studies of how the nature and organization of work in SEAs has changed. Our study suggests that SEA resources are being shifted to fund the expansion of IT departments. In addition, external consultants are becoming increasingly important actors. While the rise of test-based accountability has highlighted the increased importance of testing companies, our study also points to an expanding role of computer and consulting firms. (Chapters 3 and 4 in this volume, also document this expanding market for educational data management and technology services.) A full accounting of the effects of test-based accountability must take into account the rise of these new actors on the educational field. Existing research suggests that these actors have also proliferated at the district and school levels as the demands for data use associated with test-based accountability has prompted the creation of local district and school information systems.[13] Research on how these actors are reshaping educational practice and agendas across the educational system is needed.

Our study also suggests that the implementation and operation of SSIS have reshaped relationships across SEAs, on the one hand, and districts and schools on the other hand. Because our study focused only on SEAs, however, it provides limited insight into these changes. More research is needed to understand how the operation of SSIS has shifted power across SEAs, districts, and schools. These systems centralize power upward to SEAs and federal agencies that can demand that schools and districts collect and report increasing amounts and types of information. The district official we did interview for this study characterized these demands as a form of "micromanagement" of districts and schools by the SEA. We need to understand better how data collection, not just use, acts as a type of management and how people in schools and districts perceive its reach into their work.

Finally, while advocates of data-driven reform extol the benefits of schools and districts utilizing data in order to allocate resources more efficiently and improve practice, the systems that produce these data are not only information systems. Because they are central components of test-based accountability policies that seek to monitor, regulate, reward, and punish schools, teachers, and students based on objective measures of performance, SSIS also serve as systems of surveillance. They require educators in schools and districts to collect the very data that is used to monitor, measure, and, potentially, punish them. Research documents that technologies of surveillance often promote the very behaviors that they seek to punish. They also foment distrust within organizations as individuals being monitored grow increasingly frustrated or demoralized by the dissemination of negative information that casts doubts on their competence and trustworthiness. Importantly, the people who conduct the surveillance also become increasingly distrustful of those they monitor and come to interpret the latter's motives in a negative light.[14] As we assess the full consequences of test-based accountability and the operation of the information systems on which it rests, we need to understand better the potential costs of the distrust that such systems can engender within and across the educational system.

CHAPTER 3

The Accidental Revolution

Teacher Accountability, Value-Added, and the
Shifting Balance of Power in the American School System

CHRIS THORN
DOUGLAS N. HARRIS

Test-based school accountability, introduced by No Child Left Behind (NCLB), has been one of the most influential drivers of policy change in U.S. education history. It has changed what teachers teach, how they teach it, and how they think and feel about their work, while simultaneously transforming the way school leaders allocate resources. NCLB's offspring, Race to the Top, while still a relative newcomer, may be having an even greater impact. Using the more advanced and interconnected data systems spawned by NCLB, it is increasingly possible to evaluate not just whole schools but individual teachers and leaders based on value added to student achievement. This shift in the way we measure success in education represents a sea change, with consequences for the way schools operate as well as for the individual autonomy that teachers came to expect during the past half-century. The balance of power in school decision making has shifted away from teachers, unions, and schools of education—what some call "the establishment"—toward testing companies, data managers, district department heads, school principals, and state and federal policy makers.

The goals of test-based accountability advocates, embodied in, for example, Race to the Top and school improvement grants (SIGs), have been to increase the accountability of individual school leaders and teachers and to provide the analytic tools to help them respond to those pressures and improve learning. But this new push for educator accountability is simultaneously restructuring roles and relationships throughout school districts and yielding entirely new organizations with which districts interact in complex ways. As we show through a series of case studies, this amounts to a major restructuring of the American school system, and one that has been largely accidental.

In a system based on school-level accountability, individual teachers are largely insulated from responsibility for outcomes. The worst case—and very rare—scenario is that a school will be closed and the teachers dismissed. In contrast, teacher accountability not only has an impact on every teacher in every school, but it results in a host of indirect and secondary effects. As any architect knows, pressure on the foundation inevitably spreads up through the whole building. When teacher evaluation lacked teeth, it mattered relatively little what principals thought of their teachers. When teachers are held accountable, those who make school staffing decisions have increased power and also greater responsibility both to ensure that the system is fair and to provide a work environment in which teachers have the capacity to be successful. Many new programs to ensure that the system is fair also create new roles for teacher leaders as master or mentor teachers and peer evaluators. Teacher accountability leads to principal accountability that in turn places pressure on district officials, and so on up to the "top floors" of the educational edifice.

The current reform efforts are forcing traditional actors in the education arena—districts and other agencies—to better coordinate their activities. Educator accountability creates a strong need for fair and accurate measures of individual teacher performance. This has forced an integration of data that was previously either nonexistent or held in silos, including data drawn from assessments, human resources, professional development, and curriculum departments. Integration of data requires coordination that in turn changes relationships. In the past, for example, the assessment director might rarely have spoken with, let alone coordinated with, the director of professional development or human resources. In contrast, one recent federal accountability program, the Teacher Incentive Fund (TIF), requires that teacher and principal professional development efforts explicitly target weaknesses identified by individual teacher evaluations. To accomplish this, different district administrators have to talk with one another. The connection among evaluation results, the selection and assignment of appropriate professional support resources, and the provision of those services to those individuals across many schools requires a level of coordination and cooperation uncommon in the traditional U.S. school district.

The increased coordination extends to teacher preparation. In the past, schools of education (SOE) could largely do what they wished and there was no direct link between their programs and the success of their graduates. Perhaps the most positive role of the SOE was to identify teachers who were committed enough to jump through all the hoops the programs required, even if those hoops did little to prepare teachers for the classroom. Since K–12 schools themselves were not focused on effectiveness in the hiring process, graduates could find jobs regardless of their skills as new educators.[1] But once we can evaluate individual teachers, it takes little imagination, and almost no statistical knowledge, to place teachers into groups based on where they were prepared and to compare average performance across SOEs and other training institutions.

Teacher accountability places greater demands on data systems than most districts have the capacity to provide. This has led to the creation of entirely new—and powerful—data management organizations. Still other groups are creating value-added measures, while others provide professional development to help educators make sense of it all. What has gone unrecognized, however, is that these organizations make consequential decisions that affect not only each teacher's performance metric but the decisions that get made based on them, such as adopting new induction strategies or including new teacher preparation pathways.

While little research into and evaluation of recently implemented reform efforts has been published, in this chapter we discuss several ongoing projects with which we have had direct experience to illustrate how new roles and relationships are reorganizing public education. Until very recently, Chris Thorn worked with a nonprofit organization to which power has shifted: the Value-Added Research Center (VARC) at the University of Wisconsin at Madison, a supplier of value-added measures and professional development to school districts seeking to use it. Douglas Harris works with states and school districts across the country in an advisory capacity as they implement value-added-based accountability. Drawing on these experiences, we are able to provide an up-to-date analysis of what is happening in this fast-moving environment.

In the next section, we discuss the one element that all the cases we detail below have in common: teacher value-added estimates. Because we are interested in how accountability is changing the ways in which schools and districts operate, we leave it to others who have discussed the technical properties of the measures.[2] Instead, we focus on the extreme data demands these measures impose and how this not only changes the roles of existing actors but also stimulates the emergence of entirely new organizations to handle data management and statistical analysis.

In the final section of this chapter, we describe three cases in which efforts have been made to introduce teacher accountability based on value-added. These cases are in their early stages and, while little formal research has been conducted, we draw on firsthand experiences in these and other similar cases across a number of states and districts to generate a set of observations and questions, all of which we believe have important implications for the future of education accountability as well as its effects on the daily lives of educators and on student outcomes. It appears to us that the pressure for individual accountability is leading to a widespread and permanent restructuring of the American school system in ways mostly accidental.

VALUE-ADDED AND THE CHALLENGES OF DATA COLLECTION AND ANALYSIS

At the heart of the educator accountability movement and our case studies are value-added measures of individual teacher performance. While the specific measures produced by a growing number of organizations such as the Center for Assessment, VARC, SAS Inc., and American Institutes for Research (AIR) vary somewhat, the basic concept is the same. Rather than rely on snapshots of achievement at a point in time or on changes in school- or grade-level average test scores, value-added models take into consideration the prior level of achievement of each child. Children come into classrooms at different starting points. Value-added models capture the progress students make given where they start. There are a number of different modeling choices that one might consider—the inclusion of student demographics, multiple years of pretests, classroom characteristics, etc.—but these are extensions of the basic notion of capturing the contribution of the teacher to each student's learning.[3]

There is increasing pressure to expand the footprint of testing beyond the 30 percent of courses (math and English/language arts in grades 3–8) in which tests are mandated by NCLB. Responses have varied. In some cases, existing assessment vendors have been asked to provide end-of-course assessments or end-of-grade tests beyond mathematics and English/language arts. Many districts are also actively engaged in developing local tests and performance assessments across the curriculum. It may be that localized test design including teacher input will become an important trend over the next several years, but it is difficult to see how this will stand up to political demands for standardization and economies of scale, not to mention potential profits that could be leveraged by the large testing companies.

Perhaps the greatest challenge is capturing and maintaining high-quality data about which teachers educate which students in which courses—the problem of attribution. This may sound trivial, but most student information systems are designed to manage scheduling and basic record keeping. If one were to use simple administrative data from the student information system, the resulting value-added results would contain a number of unknown attribution errors that could seriously impact the effectiveness scores of the teachers involved. Many students receive afterschool tutoring or other services that are not traditionally captured in student information system records.[4] The accuracy of the data is absolutely crucial for producing valid and reliable growth measures. It is this requirement for data quality that has shifted power to state agencies and information system vendors as the primary agents of improving and managing longitudinal data.

More generally, there are many key decisions about what data to collect and at what unit of analysis. Value-added measures generally utilize some combination of the student and the course or school year as the relevant unit. That is, each row of the data represents data for one student in one course or year. This choice is important because value-added measures can be no more fine-grained than the smallest unit, and there is a presumption that only one teacher is assigned to any given course. There is also a possibility of direct conflict between the needs of value-added measures and the instructional preferences. A notable example is the recent growth of response to intervention (RTI), in which teachers work in groups to identify and meet the increasingly specific needs of each student. But these needs do not break down along the lines of specific course. It is not clear how one calculates a value-added measure in a school system rooted in RTI, one serving the very different educational needs of individual students. Something has to give.

There are several groups working at the state, district, and school levels to provide tools to overcome the limitations of student information system data. Battelle for Kids provides support for this at the state and district levels through a linkage tool it's developed called BFK•Link®. The National Institute for Excellence in Teaching also provides a comprehensive data collection and linkage system called CODE that supports schools using the Teacher Advancement Program (TAP). Both of these groups are nonstate actors providing a core service to support the validity and reliability of high-stakes measures of individual teacher performance. This provision of a seal of approval of the quality of the state's or district's data quality that it is sufficient for high-stakes accountability is a new and critical role. However, many smaller TIF districts lack such services and are forced to rely instead on simple online or manual student roster verifications without any automated processes to lessen the burden on users. Imagine that teachers are provided with prepopulated course rosters based on the information in the student information system. If a student is missing from the roster, there is no automatic search function to help find that student in a building-level list. The verifying teacher must manually enter the information with the resulting chance of error when that data is compared to online data at a later point—spelling differences, typos, etc., all introducing attribution errors.

At the building level, one of the important roles of the principal is to make sure that no students are "unclaimed" by teachers, or that all teachers have been linked to classrooms to reflect team teaching or other more complex organizational models. These tasks are relatively simple in automated linkage systems. The same tasks are quite labor intensive in a manual system. The other major difference in automated systems is the ability to capture the linkage of support services to individual students. Many students are served by a number of other adults. Dedicated linkage systems can more easily capture these more complex relationships, things that are often not included as features in a student information system. Here we see the first layer of restructuring: teacher value-added measures require data collection that is both more extensive and more complex than ever before. The case studies below highlight additional details about how this restructuring plays out in practice.

CASE STUDIES IN TEACHER ACCOUNTABILITY AND SYSTEM RESTRUCTURING

While all of the cases we consider include teacher value-added measures as a core component, they differ in important respects. Our discussion of Hillsborough County, Florida, highlights the increased data demands, showing that for-profit database management and/or data warehouse companies now play an integral role in schools. Our discussion of Hillsborough County, Florida, and the Maricopa County, Arizona, Educational Services Agency show that the testing companies do not yet have the capacity to meet the demands of these new systems, and this means that, for now, assessments will have to be designed in different ways by other groups. But first we start with the case of the Network of Effective Teaching (NExT), in which participating SOEs provide guarantees of their graduates' effectiveness.

Accountability and Teacher Preparation in the Three Midwestern States

NExT is a partnership of fourteen teacher preparation programs and the Bush Foundation. The initiative is focused on increasing the overall quality of teachers in the three partnering states—Minnesota, North Dakota, and South Dakota—over the next decade.[5] The project will do this by marketing to young adults most likely to be effective teachers, improving teacher preparation programs, creating a more systematic hiring process, and providing adequate support to new teachers to move them from novice to mastery in their first three years on the job.[6]

The Bush Foundation has supported a general marketing campaign targeting high-achieving high school students and undergraduates to encourage them to consider teaching as an exciting and rewarding career as well as examined school district hiring practices to better understand how schools make hiring decisions and how well they are able to select teachers who turn out to be highly effective. Prior research suggests that schools select teachers as much on their affective traits and how well they fit in with school culture as their teaching ability.[7]

The most striking aspect of NExT is that participating SOEs will provide a guarantee of effectiveness for each program graduate.[8] Since the guarantee is based on performance in the classroom, the graduating institution is responsible for providing professional development to all of its teachers, postplacement, to bring them to mastery and satisfy the guarantee. The language used by the Bush Foundation in its original organizing materials was that teachers from NExT SOEs should deliver a "year of growth." Graduates will also receive ongoing support and training after graduation at the expense of the SOE, but what this means in practice is likely to differ by SOE. The guarantee also has implications for the hiring process, though it is unclear whether schools will be much more inclined to hire candidates who have this guarantee over those who graduated from programs without the guarantee.

Most teachers are not teaching in grades or subjects with mandatory state tests. We also know that SOE program goals and student populations differ, making comparisons difficult.[9] One side effect of increased coordination will no doubt be increased standardization across an otherwise decentralized system.

One of the most important aspects of the commitment to a guarantee remains the focus on improving the performance of every student who enters a teacher preparation program. This guarantee has produced interesting interactions with unions and state education agencies outside of an externally imposed accountability framework. One of the most striking examples has been the support of a set of common metrics that has been adopted by all fourteen participants.[10] This process has included engagement with all major stakeholders, since the data crosses many organizational boundaries. All of the groups involved favor the creation of better teacher preparation programs and are generally supportive of the work. This is a novel environment that allows for experimentation and local innovation around a shared goal: creating highly effective teachers.

On the part of SOEs, that has led to substantial program redesign. Preservice students, in most cases, engage in practicum experiences earlier in their preparation (primarily coteaching) and receive support and performance feedback during that period and each of the first three years after their placement as a teacher. There is no single model, but the SOE program leaders spent (and continue to spend) substantial time together in planning sessions sharing insights from their own programs, discussing research on effective teacher preparation programs, and working with the same set of external consultants who helped all participants prepare the proposals.

Some school districts are developing data sharing agreements that will allow them to share local teacher evaluation results (formal observations, walk-throughs, examples of student learning objectives, etc.) with the SOE that graduated each new teacher. These districts have argued that the better feedback they provide to the SOEs, the more likely the SOE is to live up to the guarantee. This is a radical improvement in engagement.

One of the major cooperative activities among the fourteen participating SOEs has been a series of meetings to suggest, craft, and adopt common metrics that will allow programs to gather consistent information on participations and program features through the entire life cycle of the program.[11] Since this large-scale data collection and analysis effort extends across all partners and multiple states, strategies that would leverage the licensure or certification systems of individual states would not be sufficient.

The NExT initiative requires a series of data collection, data management, and analytical innovations that go beyond what is currently fielded by either district or state agencies. It is not that the analytical techniques themselves are that different. The novelty is the self-imposed accountability and the required buy-in from both the SOE and hiring schools to share data to evaluate teacher effectiveness. This partnership will require that SOEs and districts are more transparent and collaborative in structuring their preservices placements and mentoring services after initial hiring if the districts are to take advantage of the support services provided by the SOEs for their graduates. The Bush Foundation acquired the services of a commercial survey vendor to assist the participants in the collection, organization, and analysis of survey results of both teacher candidates and supervisors from various stages of the teacher preparation and placement process for each of their programs, with the ability to compare their own results to the aggregate results of the entire fourteen-member initiative.[12]

The other primary challenge of the NExT initiative is to provide analytical support for creating and using effective productivity measures for the SOE partners. This includes calculating teacher-level value-added results for all program participants using state-mandated and locally adopted assessments. The state has provided statewide assessment data that allows the project team to calculate school- and grade-level value-added. For most of Minnesota and North Dakota, the Northwest Evaluation Association's Measures of Academic Progress is being used as a local assessment. The majority of those districts have allowed VARC to have access to these data to calculate value-added measures as well to provide school- and grade-level value-added for this local assessment. The details of this aspect of the project are still emerging as SOEs finalize their program designs and begin to put the first cohorts through their redesign programs. Where possible, the guarantee of new teacher effectiveness will be in comparison to average value-added in a set of baseline years. VARC is the Bush Foundation's partner in this work. While school- and grade-level value-added results can be calculated using state-level student administrative and assessment data, the ability to calculate classroom and teacher value-added scores requires access to high-quality student-teacher-course linkage data that is currently only available in some districts and requires engagement and verification by individual teachers. The social, technical, and political challenges of implementing these data collection efforts and engaging local staff to expend the effort to achieve the required high-quality data are not trivial.

Consistent with the theme that new actors are playing new and important roles, it is highly unlikely that NeXt would have been possible without the funding and leadership of the Bush Foundation. If the state or federal government had initiated the program, it likely would have been seen as an unwelcome intrusion and a further step down the road of accountability. In the cases we consider next, the governmental role is much more extensive.

Performance-Based Compensation in Traditional Public Schools

The Teacher Incentive Fund was created in 2006 as a competitive grant program administered by the U.S. Department of Education that was intended to allow schools, school districts, state agencies, and nongovernmental partners to design and implement performance-based compensation programs.[13] There were two rounds of grants made under the original funding. The first, referred to by the Department of Education as Cohort 1, allocated a total of $42 million awarded across fifteen grantees in November 2006. The second group of eighteen recipients, Cohort 2, received $38 million in June 2007. There was a third round, with $437 million in funding announced in May 2010 and awards made in September 2010.[14] The grants were awarded to 62 recipients: 50 grantees in the general program and 12 grantees who also agreed to participate in a randomized, controlled trial of their designed program against a simple whole-school bonus treatment. The focus of this program is stated in the press release announcing the most recent call for proposals: "TIF grants support local projects that reward teachers, principals and other school personnel who improve student achievement."[15] This basic notion has been operationalized differently across the three rounds of funding. Changes to the program requirements for Cohort 3 reflect a substantial shift from a reliance on compensation alone to a set of measures (growth on student assessments, proficiency for teachers and leaders on observational rubrics) and interventions (performance pay, new roles for teachers, and targeted professional development for identified needs) designed to achieve the desired core policy goal of improving outcomes for students.

The Rewarding Excellence in Instruction and Leadership (REIL) initiative is a six-district TIF project that targets fifty-two high-poverty schools. The project team at the Maricopa County Educational Services Agency (MCESA), in addition to supporting the development of quality student teacher linkage data for all grades and subjects, is also developing a system for collecting and reporting teacher observation results, building tools for analyzing the budget impact of different teacher compensation scenarios, and assisting in the pilot testing of the state's newly purchased system for linking all secondary education courses to a standard database of National Center for Education Statistics course codes linked to the Common Core State Standards.

The REIL project targets only high-poverty, hard-to-staff schools. Also, Arizona is a right-to-work state but has an active teacher representation group, the Arizona Education Association, which explicitly supports the goals of the project and participates in the work through its members. Teacher leaders are an explicit part of the district-level communication strategy, and they participate in various teams charged with the development and piloting of all aspects of the measurement system—from new assessments to the exemplars used as part of the new teacher practice rubrics.

REIL uses local curriculum experts from across the regional service area to build local assessments that could be used in grades and subjects that are not covered by state-mandated tests. Unlike the more extensive and mature case of Hillsborough, MCESA has pursued a mixed strategy of working with an existing state assessment vendor to help the program accelerate its expansion into other core subjects as well as to other grades. These are all new working groups formed as the result of a series of regionwide meetings to define the assessment requirements and available technical resources and human expertise (subject area specialists and formally trained item writers) across all fifty-eight districts. MCESA has also recruited test developers from WestEd to provide technical guidance and quality assurance to their efforts to create assessments in traditionally untested areas, such as performing arts. The project was expanded beyond the original TIF partner districts to get enough experts across the many curricular areas and levels to provide the required level of expertise and diversity of experience. It may be that MCESA's responsibilities as a regional service agency provide them with economies of scale and access to more partners to support a more complex approach to filling in the gaps in traditionally nontested grades and subjects. The requirements of creating high-quality assessments as well as the required software for item collection, editing, refinement, testing, and publishing are all included in this ambitious effort.

REIL, like all TIF projects, also includes an observational framework for teachers.[16] The regional service agency and the participating districts have collaboratively developed an evaluation rubric and are field testing it during the 2011–2012 academic year.[17] The district is also developing supporting online tools to collect teacher individual observations and provide aggregate reports for school leaders and individual reports back to individual teachers, as well as provide individualized feedback and a basis for the allocation of additional professional support, if needed.

Like many other TIF projects, REIL is phasing in its compensation system. The pilot year focused on the development and field testing of the observational framework and exploration of value-added approaches for the current assessment system. Year two will see the first implementation of the observational system. Highly effective teachers will initially be identified using the observational measures. In year three, teacher effectiveness scores will be a combination of observational results and either classroom or school value-added scores.

Accountability and School-Level Decisions in Hillsborough County, Florida

The Hillsborough project is the result of a $100 million grant from the Bill & Melinda Gates Foundation's Intensive Partnerships for Effective Teaching, but it also includes a combination of other funding sources (including a U.S. Department of Education TIF grant) and leverages strong labor-management engagement, leadership stability, and a thirty-year tradition of developing local assessments to create the program Empowering Effective Teachers.[18]

The district has implemented teacher-level value-added measures based on either state-mandated end-of-grade or district (or purchased) end-of-course assessments. This means that while most states assess students in grades 3–8 in mathematics and reading/language arts, twice in science and math during that period and then again once in high school, Hillsborough assesses student performance in nearly all grades and subjects. The district fields around seven hundred different tests each year to cover all subjects and student electives.[19] To our knowledge, Hillsborough has gone much further in creating its own assessments than any other district in the country. This also means that the district has invested substantial efforts in training some teachers and administrators for these new responsibilities to develop high-quality test items.

Indeed, the data requirements for this work have induced the district to bring in additional skills and to partner with an outside data warehouse and data analytics partner, Convergence Consulting Group.[20] In the past year, the district has improved its student-teacher-course linkages and its ability to deliver reports and has embedded professional development around the reports to support appropriate interpretation. The district also provides a separate Web site with extensive information about the initiative with newsletters, videos, and answers to more than 230 frequently asked questions.[21] This site represents an aggregated approach to dissemination that has targeted material for teachers, parents, and the community at large. The teacher association is politically active and uses the transparency of these systems to build local support in the community for district initiatives. This integration of communication and political action reflects a distributed power base around educational issues. Resources on the site include technical documentation on implementing the rubric for observing effective teaching as well as the entire history of newsletters, press releases, and media coverage of the project.

Teacher value-added measures represent 40 percent of the overall measure of an individual teacher's effectiveness. The value-added result is combined with rubric-based classroom observation scores from principals (30%) and peer and mentor teachers (30%) to create the measure of overall effectiveness. The supporting Web site for the program provides the actual rubrics for teachers serving in various roles and extensive questions and answers about the details of the evaluation process, the role and training of peer and mentor observers, and other critical elements of the implementation of the observational system.[22]

CASE THEMES

While each case is different, there are several commonalities in their implications for teacher accountability and school system restructuring. Clearly, the established institutions—districts, unions, and state and federal agencies— are playing new roles. Silos are breaking down and collaboration among district units is on the rise. In the case of teacher unions, participation is somewhat forced because of the strong political pressure to alter long-established traditions embodied in traditional negotiated contracts. However, the Hillsborough case is distinctive because of the close cooperation between the district and union, including daily conversations between the union president and assistant superintendent leading the project.[23]

New organizations, both nonprofit and for-profit, are also taking on more significant roles. Some organizations, such as VARC, are creating new measures and providing targeted professional development along with them. Other organizations (usually for-profits) are helping create and manage the data that feed into the performance management systems (see also Anagnostopoulos and Bautista-Guerra, chap. 2 this volume). Foundations (Bush, Gates, and others) are also playing an influential role in certain districts, providing funding that allowed them to set the rules of the road.

In the coming years, these structures are likely to evolve further. Each organization will learn through trial and error, common assessments will make it possible to create national systems of teacher professional development and decision support, and the market will evolve from one in which individual districts innovate to one in which many states and districts coalesce around common reforms and seek common—and inexpensive—solutions.

School management and leadership in this new world are likely to be characterized as part of a complex network rather than a bureaucracy. While federalism has always been a part of the U.S. education system, the roles of local, state, and federal agencies are shifting. Combined with the emergence of new markets and vendors and the increasing collaboration among groups within districts, these interactions will be inherently more complex. This makes it even more difficult to predict how the reform movement will evolve.

QUESTIONS GOING FORWARD

Since we are discussing initiatives that are just beginning, and there is unlikely to be any evidence about these programs for several years, we instead use these cases to motivate a set of critical questions about how teacher accountability might proceed. These include policy questions as well as empirical questions that will hopefully engage researchers in the coming years and help policy makers make wise decisions.

Policy Questions

How will the tension between cost and customization be resolved, and to what degree will state and federal governments regulate and/or take over data collection, student assessment design, teacher evaluation, and data analysis tools? With advancements in data management and analytic technology, we are seeing vast improvements in the ability of data warehouse suppliers to customize at a reasonable cost, but there will always be a trade-off here. Some states, such as Wisconsin, are moving toward statewide data warehouses that allow school districts to create and store their own locally determined content as well as data required by state and federal governments. These efforts will eventually reduce technology costs at the local level (e.g., each district will no longer have to hire its own data collection technology vendor without leveraging economies of scale), which may facilitate the customization that districts and educators will undoubtedly prefer.

What will happen if and when federal funding for these initiatives such as TIF dries up? Will states and districts continue to invest in accurate measures as well as in the professional development necessary for educators to understand and appropriately use them? Many of the activities and costs we have discussed are one-time development costs, but other costs are ongoing—and large. The costs of classroom observations can be quite high, especially when the system involves evaluators other than school principals. Also, ongoing professional development will be required in order to help teachers understand the measures and make full use of them, both for understanding their own strengths and weaknesses and those of their students. There is some hope that technology can mitigate some of the costs. The Measures of Effective Teaching study tested the ability to gather classroom video for evaluation purposes at scale. The video approach both reduced the burden on leaders and allowed for the centralized management of observational data and the work of scoring. All of this translates into cost savings and improvements in system quality. It is very likely that state education agencies will need to make strong return on investment arguments for the infrastructure required to support statewide systems. It is only at scale that the cost of these support systems can be reduced significantly.

Empirical Questions

Researchers can help policy makers make better decisions. Given how little we know at this point, one could begin almost anywhere and make a useful contribution, but below we focus on what we see as some of the key questions deserving particular research attention.

How do the new educational organizations fit into the educational governance and management mix, and how will they use their newfound power? Labor unions may take ownership of some elements of accountability and start to self-police. That seems to be what is at the core of the new unionism being promoted by the American Federation of Teachers and National Education Association.[24] What is less clear is how networks formed through collective action will impact the governance and management mix (see also Wong, chap. 5 this volume). Partnerships with private funding agencies and commercial providers create linkages that cross state lines and can provide access to options or technical solutions that are at odds with (or at least quite different than) official government offerings. Indeed, some solutions, such as approaches to educator effectiveness being tested by the Measures of Effective Teaching study might actually call into question the legitimacy of some state-mandated approaches.

How, and how well, will the increasingly complex network of governance and management work? One might see some elements of corporatism in these new constellations of actors—with close collaboration between labor and management and the active participation of state actors. For example, the evolutionary elements and long-range planning of the leadership group in Hillsborough have allowed for the gradual scaling-up of the systems for supporting the collection and analysis of data. All elements of the Empowering Effective Teachers project are also piloted for one or more years before they go into production, allowing for tweaks of the infrastructure, the measurement tools, and the professional development supporting the evaluation tools and the use of the outcome. This strong sense of joint action, shared leadership, and incremental improvement provides both management and labor with the tools and the trust to maintain a sense of shared ownership.

SUMMARY

Reform efforts in educator effectiveness have shifted the balance of power across the sector in unexpected ways. Increasing pressure for common curricular standards, teaching standards, and a shared information technology infrastructure has created new opportunities—and responsibilities—for both old and new actors. In this chapter, we have described the important role of at least nine organizations that either did not exist a decade ago or played quite different or diminished roles in education: American Institutes for Research, Battelle for Kids, Center for Assessment, Gates Foundation, Network of Effective Teaching, Northwest Education Association, SAS, and VARC. And this is only a partial list of multistate organizations; there are hundreds more of smaller groups where these came from.

The incredible adoption rate of teacher accountability in the past few years shows just how powerful the federal government has been with voluntary grant programs. Race to the Top, SIG, and TIF are not required by the federal government. Yet almost every major policy initiative since Race to the Top has adopted the same competitive grant approach (and even the same rhetoric). With a small fraction of its total K–12 budget, the federal government has literally shaken the foundation of the nation's school system in ways that are felt all the way to the top floors.

The cases described here illustrate the emergence of new partnerships in which a network of groups provides analytical support, technical solutions, professional development, and communication strategies. In no case are any of these groups calculating student growth measures on their own. Neither are they trying to single-handedly make student-teacher-subject linkages. Every group is working with state or research partners to develop and test their solutions to this challenging problem. One of the lessons we have taken away from reviewing the challenges of implementing new teacher and principal evaluation systems is that even the most capable actors require outside expertise; some major components, such as value-added measures calculation or data warehousing, may be completely outsourced.

This may change as Race to the Top (and similarly motivated) evaluation systems roll out to districts. Home-grown solutions may be superseded by state mandates. There will also be opportunities for some of these local providers to move up and provide statewide solutions. This emerging market will likely show up first in Race to the Top states. While districts will, in some sense, lose power, they will also gain the power to dismiss low-performing teachers and create powerful information-based tools to guide school improvement, as well as their newfound pursuit of technology, and the data these systems provide, to make a case for tax levies and additional state and local funding.

These partnerships with external actors clearly go beyond anything we have seen in the past. While districts have a long record of working with private contractors for ancillary services such as busing, food service, and textbooks. It has also been common for districts to contract out for technology, and this is perhaps why the phenomena we describe here have gone largely unnoticed. But what we are talking about here is technology of a very different sort. The vast apparatus necessary to collect data involves decisions that directly influence instruction. The information systems are the basis of teacher evaluation, and what gets measured gets done.

In our recent experiences working with school districts implementing value-added measures for accountability, we have also observed a more general crumbling of the walls and silos that separate school districts' administrative activities. While in many cases this has positive implications, since many silos have resisted evaluating their own practices or using data at all to make decisions, the integration and application of new data is often done with little planning or attention to the staff development needs of the actors involved. The combination of new types of data (value-added and observational measures) merged with existing information of dubious quality (administrative data) for novel use (educator evaluation) suggests that decision makers will find it extremely challenging to make sense of this information. Informal discussions with leadership teams across the country suggest that basic assessment and data literacy skills are critical needs, and the lack of these skills leads to uncertainty about how to link evaluation results to concrete action steps. This skill gap stands in the way of schools and districts doing their own research on what works.

It is difficult to anticipate how large assessment, curriculum, and other vendors may take advantage of (and thereby shape) this newly forming market for educator effectiveness services. The market opportunities around the Race to the Top projects alone have brought all of the major vendors of educational systems, materials, and assessments into the mix. Collective action around these policy reforms is generating the specifications for new products and services. Shifts in district organizational structure and access to information are producing changes in the distribution of power and resources. Understanding these changes as they are happening will be a challenge, but those who can navigate these shoals will be better prepared for the coming complexities and challenges of teacher and principal accountability.

CHAPTER 4

Money and Measures

The Role of Foundations in Knowledge Production

JANELLE SCOTT

HURIYA JABBAR

Philanthropists and foundations have been influential in shaping the structure and dynamics of public education in the United States since its origins. Philanthropies have helped to support and expand higher education, provide seed money for scientific discovery, underwrite various forms of artistic expression, provide access to the arts for scores of schoolchildren, and provide schooling opportunities for African American children when the state was slow to live up to its democratic responsibility.[1] While foundations have often supported the expansion of educational opportunity, they have also acted in ways that restricted quality schooling for particular students, relegating African American and Native American children to vocational or remedial schooling forms.[2]

Recently formed venture philanthropies and traditional foundations have underwritten market-based educational reforms that emphasize the use of incentives to improve schooling outcomes and teaching practices and to increase school choice options.[3] These reforms include vouchers and charter schools, teacher merit pay, and pay for performance for students. The availability and use of data are central to these reforms. In relation to these reform policies, foundations have helped to create and sustain an intermediary organizational sector comprised of teacher unions, civil rights groups, think tanks, education advocacy groups, research consortia, and charter school management organizations. Foundations also serve as intermediaries by assuming policy advocacy roles. Through funding, meetings, and other activities, foundations provide the "interlock" between intermediary organizations producing and promoting research and also those implementing reforms.

Foundations' financial and political supports are creating new data systems collection, analysis, and reporting—essential components in the overall infrastructure of accountability. Incentivist reforms rely on the availability and use of performance data on teachers, schools, and students as well as the development of new, intermediary organizations. Foundations are also leading the adoptions of educational policy at multiple tiers of government: federal, state, and local.

In 2011 the J. P. Morgan Foundation, for example, announced a $1 million gift to the Relay School of Education, an alternative teacher education program started in 2010 by the founders of the Knowledge Is Power Program (KIPP) charter school network. Relay certifies and grants master's degrees to teachers who demonstrate measureable improvement in student learning on standardized assessments.[4] In this way, we see the intersection of new data and assessment systems with incentivist educational policies and philanthropic supports. As foundations have seeded and invested in a range of organizations, policy makers have embraced the school reform agenda as well, especially in urban contexts like New York City, New Orleans, Los Angeles, and Philadelphia.[5]

At the national level, two of the U.S. Department of Education's (DOE) signature policy initiatives—Race to the Top (RttT) and Investing in Innovation (i3)—demonstrate the Obama administration's preferences for incentivist educational reforms. The DOE endeavors to reward high-performing models and relies on performance data to determine organizational effectiveness. The administration has tapped former leaders of venture philanthropies to lead and shape these initiatives.[6] Yet, the research evidence supporting the efficacy of incentivist educational policies is highly contested, and the rising intermediary sector's production of research evidence, promotion of such evidence, and utilization of the research to inform policy efforts traditionally performed by teachers unions, researchers, and professional associations stands to provide the evidentiary basis for these policies' expansion.[7]

Despite heightened foundation activity, we lack a comprehensive picture of how foundations' investments inform policy and practice, as well as sufficient consideration of the political and philosophical implications of foundations' influence on public education. This chapter considers how philanthropists are shaping policy and research through knowledge production and the creation of data systems and assessments. Given the centrality of data to incentive-based reforms, understanding the role that foundations play in data production and research use is critical and helps to reconceptualize foundations as de facto public policy actors.

We discuss three key strategic funding areas in which foundations have invested to influence policy making, public awareness, and knowledge production. These include constructing data systems for accountability; the funding of education journalism, media, and blogs to translate data and research for the public; and providing grants for engaging policy makers, state and district officials, and reformers in conferences to share research and allow them to network.

After providing a historical and sociopolitical context for the ways in which foundations have helped shape public schooling, we consider the relationship between foundations and knowledge production. First, we conduct an analysis of foundation spending, relying on 990 Internal Revenue Service filings. After presenting our analysis of the five largest funders of educational initiatives, we focus on the Bill & Melinda Gates Foundation. Analysts consider the Gates Foundation to be a leader in the development and promotion of new data systems, and Gates has also been one of the largest foundation investors in incentive-based reforms. Given this intersection, the Gates Foundation's investments warrant closer analysis.

Second, we draw from interviews from our study of research utilization in the advocacy of incentivist reforms to demonstrate the influence of foundations on data production, knowledge, and advocacy in national and district contexts.[8] We conclude with a discussion of the implications of our findings for research and policy, with a particular focus on issues of power and the ways in which foundations are a part of a broader blurring of the lines between private organizations and public policy makers. A primary way in which foundations are operating as de facto policy makers is in their funding of the knowledge base supporting their preferred reforms and in their investments in advocacy organizations and school reform and management organizations that advance incentive-based educational reforms.

PHILANTHROPIES, FOUNDATIONS, AND EDUCATIONAL POLICY

Philanthropic investments in school and teacher reform efforts have received considerable media attention in recent years, but foundations have a much longer history of creating and cultivating the marketplace of ideas, not simply responding to them.[9] With minimal federal regulation of philanthropy, and longstanding concerns about their advocacy role, foundations continue to have significant influence on public school policy. They have often shaped the public discussion and debate around education reform.[10] Philanthropists have multiple methods of getting issues onto the public agenda and have funded research, pilot programs, and public information campaigns to create momentum that results in policy makers sensing that a specific reform is "an idea whose time has come."[11]

In a pluralistic and democratic society, however, the influence of elite or wealthy organizations can come at the expense of the participation of less advantaged groups or communities in their children's schooling. The history of K–12 education is replete with struggles for control, with African Americans, teacher unions, immigrants, language minority communities, special education lobbies, and groups representing the educational needs of girls, gay, lesbian, bisexual, and transgender students organizing to achieve their visions for public schools. In the politics for control, foundations have assumed adversarial *and* supportive roles in efforts to increase equity or democratic participation.

Lagemann describes the tensions between democratic processes and knowledge funded and disseminated by elites in the context of the Carnegie Corporation.[12] Researchers have also examined how some foundations have circumvented or ignored existing social movements as they influenced approaches to inequality counter to what those movements advocated.[13] Stanfield argues that official foundation histories gloss over the ways in which foundation giving and the research produced by grantees reflected elite beliefs about the social order and the best ways to approach social problems while excluding the perspectives of less powerful citizens.[14]

While the role of philanthropy in the United States has been contested, media coverage has been largely positive, both from a historical perspective and in more contemporary contexts.[15] Early critics of foundations were concerned about their limited governmental oversight and their potential threats to democratic processes in their circumvention of personal and corporate income taxes to support elite policy preferences.[16] More recently, journalists and bloggers have become critical as philanthropists exert more power, and using more aggressive tactics than in the past, in K–12 education as well as in other domains. One example is the funding and control by the libertarian Charles G. Koch Foundation of a free-market economics program at the University of Florida, which some critics believe to have violated academic freedom principles.[17]

Like foundations, elite school reformers' access to media has been important at least since the early twentieth century, when, according to Tyack, "reformers enjoyed nearly total control of the news and editorials in the major newspapers . . . Thereby they could define the nature of the problem in such a way that their remedies seemed self-evident and opposition to reform selfish and misguided."[18] Researchers have found that coverage of contemporary education reformers has been largely positive, rarely critical, and focused primarily on entrepreneurial education efforts.[19] A study of media portrayal of educational philanthropy by major news outlets showed that there were about thirteen positive accounts for every critical one.[20] This positive coverage contributes to foundations' authority and stature, as does the frequency with which the media produces stories on them. For example, despite the relatively small monetary contribution of philanthropy to the funding of public schools, comprising less than 1 percent of the overall budget, philanthropic involvement in schools receives disproportionate coverage in the press, lending increased influence to reform efforts driven by foundations.[21] Another area in which foundations enjoy influence is in their ability to influence the content of education reporting. While the media does not itself create momentum around a political issue, it provides a venue for reformers to define problems in such a way that their proposed solutions follow logically (see Jacobsen and Saultz, chap. 11 this volume).

FOUNDATION SPENDING FOR KNOWLEDGE PRODUCTION

In order to understand the scope and breadth of foundation spending in support of knowledge production, we collected the tax returns (IRS Form 990) and supporting documents from five of the largest foundations contributing to U.S. elementary and secondary education for 2010, the most recent returns that were available. These included: the Bill & Melinda Gates Foundation, the William and Flora Hewlett Foundation, The Eli and Edythe Broad Foundation, the Michael & Susan Dell Foundation, and the W. K. Kellogg Foundation.[22] We recorded and coded all education grants, paying particular attention to funding for data systems, assessments and testing, and research or information. We also draw from qualitative interviews in Denver, New Orleans, New York City, and Washington, DC, to explore how state, local, and national actors are being influenced by the work and efforts of foundations.[23] Our methodological approach allows us to offer a broad picture of foundation spending coupled with a deeper understanding of how local stakeholders are making meaning of foundation investments.

Knowledge Production Funding Strategies

Three key strategies toward information and data collection and analysis emerged from our financial and qualitative data: (1) the funding of data systems and assessment tools; (2) funding for education journalism and media;

and, (3) grants for conferences and workshops that allow district and state leaders, education reformers, and researchers to share ideas and evidence on data use. Across the five foundations whose spending we examined, total expenditures for 2010 were just under $500 million.

In comparison, the DOE's 2011 budget was $68.1 billion, which dwarfs the combined spending of the foundations we consider here. Despite the relatively lower spending by foundations on education in total dollars, we see foundations clustering their expenditures in specific areas related to the infrastructure of accountability. The relative concentration of spending by these foundations in relation to accountability measures is on initiatives aimed at generating data, data analysis, public awareness, or knowledge production more broadly. And when we examine the further concentration of this spending in urban school districts where incentivist reforms are being taken up, the targeted investments become even more substantial and influential in a context where states and school districts are reeling from the continued economic downturn. Table 4.1 provides a display of this spending across foundations.

From this broad consideration of foundation spending, we provide a closer case discussion of the Gates Foundation, an educational philanthropy that many analysts have identified as a central funder of educational policies and a key linker among entrepreneurial education organizations. Moreover, Bill Gates has been a vocal supporter of particular forms of teacher evaluation and accountability systems in which the construction of new data infrastructures feature prominently. In addition to being instrumental in the rise (and decline) of the recent small schools movement, Gates has been an active funder of many charter school networks and a supporter of the development of assessments for the Common Core State Standards. In these ways, a focus on the Gates Foundation helps us demonstrate that the infrastructure of data and accountability being underwritten by major foundations extends beyond student and teacher evaluations and into the creation of new educational organizations, the building of public opinion, and the connection of advocacy groups.

THE BILL & MELINDA GATES FOUNDATION

The Gates Foundation spent approximately $310,650,000 in 2010 on U.S. public education, which included funding areas like teacher assessment tools, charter school management organizations, and civil rights organizations whose work included education. We examined the names of grant recipients and brief statements of purpose of the grant to identify data-related expenses. We acknowledge that this approach has some limitations. For example, some grants may not have been classified as education related or policy and advocacy related without that being apparent from the brief statements, and, as a result, it is possible that we have overlooked some investments. But there are strengths to our approach as well. Analyzing the statements at this closer level helps us see the specific organizations (and their range) foundations like Gates are investing in in order to inform their policy and data use, and this analysis helps us establish the reach of these foundations into particular organizations and policy initiatives.

The Gates Foundation funded several areas of giving related to information brokering. We argue that "information" can be in the form of *hard data* systems—assessments or value-added measures—or *soft data*—the kinds of information produced to move public opinion or to help organizations share information and strategy. Using both data forms, Gates also supports the development and support of policy networks, where information and data are shared through meetings and formal partnerships.

Hard Data

In 2010 the Gates Foundation allocated approximately $80 million to the development of data systems, assessments, measures, and tools primarily related to teacher effectiveness and accountability.

Teacher Effectiveness

Grants for teacher evaluation data systems included financing school systems to use measures of teacher effectiveness and included school districts, intermediary organizations, states, and testing companies. For example, Hillsborough County (FL) Public Schools received $11 million for this purpose. The Gates Foundation also funded the hiring of consultants for a teacher evaluation project, giving Teachscape Inc. just over $8 million. The Educational Testing Service received a grant of $1.6 million to develop measures for teaching effectiveness, and College Ready Promise received $6 million to "use measures of teacher effectiveness to fundamentally alter the approach to recruiting, supporting, evaluating, retaining, promoting, distributing, and rewarding effective teachers." The NewSchools Venture Fund received $3 million to create data systems and develop growth models for teacher evaluation for the Newark (NJ) Public Schools. Gates awarded a $1.6 million grant to Battelle for Kids, founded by the Ohio Business Roundtable, to expand value-added analysis at the high school level; provide support to

TABLE 4.1 Foundation investments in knowledge production, promotion, and utilization

Foundation	Estimated education spending in 2010*	Est. % of education spending on knowledge brokering and accountability infrastructure	Examples of knowledge production, promotion, and utilization		
			Funding performance management and data systems, assessments, and measures	*Communications: media, journalism, online content, organizational communications.*	*Conferences and meetings about data use or incentives in educational reform*
Bill & Melinda Gates Foundation	$310,650,000	42%	Various grants to districts, states, and schools to develop and implement data systems, primarily related to teacher performance Hillsborough County Public Schools ($11 million): For assistance in using measures of teacher effectiveness	Funding for education journalism and documentary promotion Participant Media LLC ($2 million): For a social action campaign in conjunction with the film Waiting for Superman	Convenings of policy makers, practitioners, and reformers The Aspen Institute ($1 million): Support for senior congressional staff and urban superintendents' network to address teacher effectiveness, standards, and assessments
Michael & Susan Dell Foundation	$66,225,167	37.70%	Support for the development of performance management systems in a number of charter networks and key districts Dallas Independent School District ($1 million): For performance management	N/A	N/A

Broad Foundation	$38,967,620	7%	Support for performance management systems as well as miscellaneous grants Board of Education of Prince George's County ($1 million): For implementation of performance management	Support for documentaries on education reform. Arts Engine ($50,000): For documentary on charter schools Participant Foundation ($167,000): For Waiting for Superman social action campaign	Support convenings and symposia for policy makers, governors, and reformers Center for American Progress ($295,702): To support the Teacher Incentive Fund Summit, conferences, and reports
W. K. Kellogg Foundation	$54,675,398	0.4%	N/A	Journalism. The New Press ($221,708): To review, debate, and assess the current state of knowledge on K-12 education	N/A
William and Flora Hewlett Foundation	$28,627,471	17.46%	Strengthening data systems, developing assessments, aligning technology-based education with standards Children Now ($450,000): For efforts to strengthen the state's education data systems	Journalism and public information. Strategic Concepts in Organizing and Policy Education ($800,000): For public education on the need for tax and fiscal reform	Convenings around assessments and education technology State Educational Technology Directors Association ($200,000): To support convenings and research to reduce the cost of assessments

Note: Our estimates are based on the most recent available tax returns and the information contained therein. In some cases, organizations did not provide the purpose of their grant; in others, we had to make judgments about whether the activity counted as "knowledge-brokering." We expect that there may have been some mistakes in our interpretation of the grant makers' activities, but we also expect that these figures provide a reasonable assessment of the types and amounts of grants foundations are making to broker information and create information systems. For the Hewlett Foundation, we used its online grants database. In the case of the Dell Foundation, we were only able to obtain its 2009 Form 990. The foundation told us that an amendment needed to be filed, which is why it was not available yet. For the Kellogg Foundation, we relied on the data reported in its Form 990, which was for the fiscal year 09/2009–08/2010. We included only the grants paid during the year, not those approved for future payment.

accurately and effectively produce, share, and use value-added data; and manage a data warehouse that would be used for research. Over $1 million went to the Celt Corporation to "develop and implement a model common definition of teacher of record and standard business process for linking and validating teacher and student data at the SEA [state education agency] level and a representative sample of districts." State departments of education in Louisiana, Arkansas, Florida, Georgia, and Ohio also received grants for teacher assessment development.

Entrepreneurial educational organizations received funds to develop teacher assessment metrics. Gates awarded Teach for America (TFA) just over $1 million to test for a correlation between the "Teaching as Leadership" rubric and student performance. It gave $722,378 to the National Board for Professional Teaching Standards to score measures of effective teaching videos using nationally validated rubrics and to enhance professional development materials.

The Gates Foundation also invested in school districts, universities, and other research organizations with funding for teacher evaluation. Tulsa Public Schools received $500,000 for an evaluation tool to identify effective teachers; Memphis City Schools received $143,439 to develop measures of effective teaching; Denver Public Schools received $362,969 to develop reliable indicators of a teachers' impact on student achievement; Charlotte-Mecklenburg received $73,263 to develop teaching measures to complement value-added data while helping teachers understand the new measures. Gates gave The Fund for Public Schools, Inc., nearly $900,000 to participate in the measures of effective teaching project. For the same purpose, it awarded the Dallas Independent School District $951,293 and $1.2 million for support of the design of data systems to improve teaching and learning and build district capacity to use data as a tool to improve teaching and learning. The University of Wisconsin received $250,000 to develop a task force to redesign human capital management systems for the teachers, principals, and other leaders in the largest U.S. public school districts. The Brookings Institution received $159,866 to develop criteria for certifying teacher evaluation systems. And Harvard College received $74,998 to examine relationships between teacher performance on The New Teacher Project's performance-assessment tool and student achievement.

Developing Data Analysis Capacities for System Leaders
The Gates Foundation also provided support for state education leaders to use and understand data. It gave the Council of Chief State School Offi-

cers nearly $2 million to increase the leadership capacity of state leaders by focusing on standards and assessments and data systems and another $789,648 to partner with state, federal, public, and private interests to develop common, open, longitudinal data standards. Another Gates grant ($754,550) went specifically to the Georgia Department of Education to facilitate collaboration with district partners in the development of reports and tools with teachers and principals to help them understand and act on available data. Similarly, it awarded the National School Boards Association $133,647 to promote effective use of data in school board decision making by designing training modules, materials, and data tools to be field tests.

Assessments

The Gates Foundation has also invested in assessment development for student learning. For example, researchers at the University of California Berkeley received $2 million to produce and field-test high-quality math formative assessments that reflect "ambitious but attainable" math goals for all students. There were also a number of grants for tying Common Core State Standards to assessments and curriculum—examples include Metametrics, which received $1.3 million for an interactive online tool to focus on implementing literacy common standards, and Research for Action, which received $649,645 to pilot research and validation of instructional tools in math and literacy aligned to the Common Core. Other assessment-related grants included more than $1 million to the International Baccalaureate Fund USA to develop an assessment for its programs; $595,625 to the University of Chicago to fund research on indicators of high school and college readiness; $585,995 to the Center on Education Policy to track state progress on adoption implementation of college-ready standards and aligned assessment through an annual public report; $550,516 to Great Schools to support the planning, design, development, and launch of a series of school scorecards to be launched at NBC's week-long "Education Nation" event and promoted on national broadcasts—an example of the way in which data infrastructure and data promotion intersect.

The Gates Foundation has also invested in organizations developing new assessments for a variety of instructional approaches and curricular approaches, such as assessments to align with the Common Core State Standards; math, science, and engineering assessments; and early childhood assessments. In 2010 it invested nearly $16 million to expand and support these efforts. While these seemingly have little in common with incentive-based reforms, they join such reforms in a policy landscape in which policy makers are demanding assessment-based evidence of the efficacy of K–12 public education. The data infrastructures help create the evidence used to provide incentives to what come to be understood as high achieving and/ or quality schools, districts, or charter management organizations. And given the budgetary constraints governing many states and school districts, it is unlikely that these new data and assessment systems would be developed or implemented without the support of foundations. In addition, we found that foundations like Gates are investing in data and accountability systems for higher education, where we also found significant investments to develop assessments of higher education outputs, such as retention and graduation rates.

Soft Data

In the areas of soft data, our analysis revealed several funding initiatives. We found that the Gates Foundation is funding efforts to inform the public and build constituencies of support for data-driven educational reforms. In addition, it is funding conferences on issues related to data systems and educational reform. These meetings help to create and build strategic approaches to advocacy for data and accountability structures that incorporate the use of incentives to drive improved outcomes.

Public Information and Public Relations

In the realm of knowledge production, Gates funded print and broadcast journalism organizations as well as producers of educational documentaries, including the Education Writers Association; Learning Matters, Inc.; the New America Foundation; NBC Universal, Inc.; Editorial Projects in Education; and National Public Radio. Gates awarded Participant Media, LLC, a producer of the controversial charter school documentary *Waiting for Superman*, $2 million to execute a social action campaign to complement the documentary's message. Gates also funded organizations that would help to advance public engagement on school reform issues through an array of mechanisms: digital platforms, working research papers, the support of blogs, and supporting networks for reform-minded teachers in Seattle and through the New York City Charter School Center. In addition, Gates gave $2 million to the parent information and school rating Web site Great Schools.

Gates provided support to the Charlotte (SC) Chamber of Commerce to build support for the Charlotte-Mecklenburg Schools Strategic Plan, which places strong emphasis on teacher evaluation and assessment, and to the Commission on Hispanic Affairs to support constituency building and supporting the advocacy efforts of the organization. These public engagement and promotion investments connect particular forms of data and knowledge into understandable and actionable information for a broader public, an important aspect of the overall data and knowledge production function of foundations.

Building an Intermediary Network

Another area in which the Gates Foundation has invested is in the support and creation of policy and advocacy networks that advance the use of incentives in public schooling. We identify investments that bring together state, federal, and local policy makers with private-sector actors or with each other for collaboration and information sharing. Conferences about data and research are prime venues for this kind of information sharing to take place, and they represent the second biggest concentration of funding from Gates. In 2010, approximately $12.6 million was invested in such activities.

Examples include a $250,000 grant to TFA in support of its 20th Anniversary Summit, where panels and workshops aimed at sharing evidence on data and teacher incentives and value-added assessments and charter school networks were prominent. Other smaller investments helped districts to share information. Gates awarded a $150,000 grant to the Memphis Schools Foundation to help it share its educational approaches with other southeastern school systems. It gave $6,000 to the Seattle-based Alliance for Education, a nonprofit organization in which Gates has invested significant funding, to support a delegation of Seattle public school district officials to meet with school leaders in Denver to share best practices around initiatives like teacher evaluation and system leadership. The foundation also provided grants to charter management organizations in order to facilitate their collaborations with school districts.

In addition to supporting the conferences and convening of an array of educational groups, Gates has invested in the infrastructure of intermediary networks. It provided the Thomas B. Fordham Institute just over $200,000 to support the Policy Innovators in Education Network. This network brings together policy research groups with state-level education advocacy organizations to share best practices and capture lessons learned around teacher evaluation policy and school choice. The foundation also awarded $1 million grants to the Aspen Institute and to the National Alliance for

Public Charter Schools (NAPCS). The purpose of the Aspen grant was to help support its "human capital framework," senior congressional staff, and urban superintendent networks to address issues of teacher effectiveness, standards, and assessments. The NAPCS award underwrote the organization's federal advocacy, strategic state advocacy and support, and ability to become the "voice of the charter-school sector."

These examples demonstrate the varied, and yet also concentrated, funding that is helping to construct data and information infrastructures as well as a robust policy and advocacy network that is working in coalitional ways across national, state, and local policy settings. Aggregated, these data demonstrate that philanthropic funding is a key piece of the data and accountability infrastructure being assembled around U.S. public schooling.

INTERMEDIARY ORGANIZATIONS, FOUNDATIONS, AND THINK TANKS IN LOCAL CONTEXTS

To date, we have conducted approximately seventy-five interviews with a range of representatives from intermediary organizations (teacher unions, charter management organizations, think tanks, school reform organizations, and foundations) in three school districts and in Washington, DC. We have also interviewed policy makers and their staff. We are following educational blogs and other social networking platforms in order to understand the processes by which intermediary organizations are producing, promoting, and utilizing research and data in the context of their advocacy or reform work and how system leaders and policy makers and their staff are informed by research and advocacy.

These data reveal that foundation support affords new educational reform intermediary organizations legitimacy and provides opportunities for these myriad organizations to network and share research. The research and evaluation produced by think tanks is frequently promoted by intermediary organizations in order to influence policy makers. This utilization is consistent in the state contexts we examined and also in the ongoing deliberations over the reauthorization of the federal Elementary and Secondary Education Act. In the states, such as in Colorado, we have heard policy makers invoke the foundation-influenced intermediary sector over policy initiatives, such as the incentives-based teacher-compensation bill known as ProComp, which allows teachers to earn additional salary based on, in part, demonstration of student growth. According to a Colorado legislative analyst:

I would say that research was the foundation of the argument that we built. The other two pieces of research that I used a lot, and this is from some of the Gates research and some of the others. So we've had a year or so on process on this. And the dominant strain of every conversation has been "show us a structure that you think works and show us a place that you know it works." So it's "let's see what Toledo, Ohio, did and let's see what Houston did with their evaluation system. Let's look at DC IMPACT, let's look at what Louisiana's proposal is, what does The New Teacher Project have to say is the best structure?" So it's not as much "let's look at the Phi Delta Kappan for this month and see what's in it," but it's all about if you have an idea. You have to show us where that idea's been tried before and they've had results on it.

Our data also show the importance of funding for the sustaining of organizations. Many leaders said that without philanthropic funds they would not be able to operate at their current scale. We have seen examples of strategic giving, where foundations joined in their support for the same organizations across multiple school systems.[24] The leader of a Denver-based charter school organization described her organization's funding infrastructure:

> So whether they're donors to our new school development effort or whether they support our advocacy or whatever, we have various—we certainly have at any given time financial support from six to eight, maybe, local or national foundations. Sometimes that's big on one and small here, and it's not—however nice it would be that they would all just write a big check and say, "Use this however you choose," they don't, and it tends to be around specific projects or initiatives and efforts, so there's some fluctuation in terms of who is doing what and when.

In this way, we see evidence of the importance of targeted investments for organizational stability. We also find evidence that foundations' giving is shaping the research agendas of intermediary organizations whose missions include knowledge production. Many organizations reported a need for funding to support technical expertise to collect data and provide analysis and also to develop sophisticated assessments. In this way, we see the rise of a newer cadre of professionals whose technical skills are specifically aligned with understanding and interpreting the new data infrastructures. (See also Thorn and Harris, chap. 3 this volume.) Many intermediary organization respondents felt pulled by what foundations would support in terms of data analysis and research. These approaches typically included the use of quasi-experimental methods informed by economists of education and the use of value-added and growth models to determine academic or organizational outcomes. A TFA leader explained:

> Our 2004 evaluation was a quantitative inquiry, generally about test scores. We learned a lot about our performance, both good and bad. We could see the lack of impact in certain areas, and we were interested in understanding that annually. So it took a long time, people learned a lot about research . . . And so what we did moving forward from that point was to build an internal system of understanding our impact on student learning through test scores and other assessment data that we might be able to get access to. As the economist created value-added . . . it seems that our evolution around the use of student learning data, or student assessment data, has overlapped with that industry.

Intermediary organizations' representatives reported that the foundation support for data collection and evaluation was helping strengthen their credibility in policy circles. A TFA leader indicated that the organization had ratcheted up its evaluation efforts largely at the request of benefactors, who also agreed to fund them. In this area of giving—research and evaluation—we also see the efforts of foundations to facilitate partnerships and collaborations among research organizations (university based as well as those that function independent of universities) and entrepreneurial organizations.

Despite the coalitional aspects of foundations giving to the same organizations, we also have discovered differences in philanthropic approaches to incentive-based reforms such as merit pay for teachers. The philanthropic sector has always been pluralistic and, as such, favors different approaches to policy issues. One of the ways we saw tensions manifest was in the different approaches of local, often smaller, foundations and larger foundations with national funding portfolios. A leader in a Denver family foundation described this dynamic in the context of ProComp:

> We came in and gave them a grant. We were quickly overshadowed by the national foundations, Broad and those folks. So, we had a real interest in it and initially started working on it. It's been an interesting journey, because my take is that it's one of the weakest levers around student achievement out there. And so, is merit pay or pay for performance a good idea? Eh, it's all right. And I think it has some value, but not a lot of value.

While there continues to be much debate and uncertainty about the efficacy of incentivist reforms, policy makers are moving to incubate and experiment with them in key districts, often working in coalition with advocacy groups supportive of incentivist reforms. We see many of the foundations active in funding charter management organizations, new assessments for teachers and principals, and new data systems for student achievement also funding these advocacy groups, which then promote research findings to policy makers and their staff. And legislative staffers are increasingly seeking out new entrepreneurial organizations and leaders for their research expertise. For example, according to an aide for a Republican congressman, "He's not just looking to Heritage Foundation or AEI [the American Enterprise Institute], though he does look to them. He'll also look at what CAP [Center for American Progress] is doing and TFA and Gates and Broad, and we try to keep an open mind to everything that's out there and just meet with everyone." This networked dynamic around research production and policy makers' utilization demonstrates a somewhat closed network that traditional producers of research might be increasingly unable to inform.

FOUNDATIONS AND THE INFRASTRUCTURE OF ACCOUNTABILITY: DEMOCRATIC CONSIDERATIONS

While foundations have historically been active funders and shapers of educational policy, their efforts have been especially geared toward ratcheting up particular aspects of data gathering and knowledge production over the last decade. As we discussed, much of the funding to date has been used to develop new measures of teacher effectiveness, supplemented by the foundations' other grants allotted for the construction of data systems and value-added models, which will test the validity of these new measures, and support for school choice and entrepreneurial organizations. Through these investments, foundations are essential in the infrastructure of accountability and the education reform landscape more broadly.

Foundations have also shaped the types of assessments their grantees use, as well as the kind of research they conduct. The expanding role of foundations has significant implications for policy makers, researchers, and the public, especially since many incentivist reforms are targets of intense opposition from parents, teachers, and students in the very school systems in which they are being incubated.

While foundation leaders no doubt have good intentions for public schools, there is a lack of democratic input by constituencies who might prefer alternative approaches to school improvement, and it is important to note the active opposition to the use of incentives in education by many grassroots community groups that lack a public authority to whom they can advocate. This is perhaps best demonstrated by the eradication of democratically elected school boards in many cities where foundations are underwriting incentivist educational reforms that rely on the data infrastructure. This shift in the governance and management of schooling has the potential to reshape the very publicness of public education. For if the public has increasingly limited ways to voice concerns or vote beyond school choice programs, it is unclear the degree to which citizens without school-aged children will continue to support or feel invested in K–12 schooling.

Foundations have underwritten the data infrastructure with which urban and increasingly rural and suburban schools' effectiveness is being measured. The rise of data collection, management, and analysis helps to determine what types of data governments and reform organizations collect and analyze. They therefore have the potential to both expand and constrain the questions that education researchers address and the conclusions the broader public might reach about the state of U.S. schooling. Through their funding strategies, foundations are influencing not just the types of policies enacted but also the data infrastructure for establishing what works in educational reform and in the public imagination.

PART II

The Infrastructure of Accountability in Districts, Schools, and Classrooms

CHAPTER 5

Governing with Data

The Role of Independent Review Panels in Urban Districts

KENNETH K. WONG

Public school governance is often viewed as an arena of direct democracy where local citizens elect members of the local school board. In many states and communities, public referenda approve the school budget and other ballot initiatives determine major policy changes. In practice, school board elections are decided by low voter turnout and school board meetings are poorly attended. Clearly, much of the control over district administration and resource allocation resides primarily with the leadership of the school system. In urban districts, the institutional boundary between insider professionals and outsider citizenry is substantial. When it comes to control over data and the use of data, professional insiders clearly dominate in urban systems.

To be sure, there are institutional practices that aim at bridging the data divide between the urban school system and its outsider stakeholders. In this chapter, I discuss the role of data in improving accountability in school governance, citing three types of governing practices that promote data-driven accountability. Then I examine a particular type of governing practice, the creation of an independent review panel with national experts, by providing a detailed illustration of the work of the Accountability Review Council in the School District of Philadelphia. The chapter ends with a discussion of the broader implications on independent review panels in enhancing accountability in urban districts.

THE ROLE OF DATA IN DISTRICT GOVERNANCE: TYPES OF PRACTICES

Electoral Accountability

Data can be used as an important tool to improve accountability in the governing of urban school districts. In the current climate of growing public demand for school accountability, data plays a necessary role in broadening public involvement. There are several ways that data serves to improve governance accountability in urban districts. The most common is through the electoral process. This diffused process of data governance offers the electorate an opportunity to assess the overall progress of public schools. To a large extent, local media plays a key role in disseminating and framing the data on school and management performance, especially during electoral campaigns. Using retrospective voting theory, Berry and Howell examined whether or not voters take issues into account in local elections.[1] Specifically, they considered whether or not "average voters hold school board members accountable for the performance of their schools."[2] They analyzed data of more than three thousand school and district achievement trends and precinct- and district-level voting records in almost five hundred races over three electoral cycles in South Carolina. The study found that when the media provided more comprehensive coverage on education accountability issues, voters were more likely to hold local school board members accountable for performance. However, in the years in which the media provided limited coverage on accountability issues, voters were much less likely to hold school board members accountable.

The extent to which data can promote broader electoral participation, however, is constrained by several factors. More often than not, school performance data is not organized in a user-friendly manner that makes sense to the rank-and-file electorate. In England, for example, parents and the general public are able to relate to the school rankings (or league tables), which are publicized in the local media. Further, school performance data lacks detailed information for the electorate to assess the effectiveness of particular reform initiatives. Seldom is the data presented in a timely fashion that coincides with local elections. Equally important is the traditionally low turnout in school board elections where candidates can afford not to engage in debate on school data in their campaigns. Since incumbency remains a key factor for school board election outcomes, data on school performance has relatively low saliency in local school board elections.

In urban districts under mayoral control, in comparison to districts governed by elected school boards, data has played a visibly stronger role in the governing process. In New York, Chicago, Boston, Washington, DC, and about ten other urban districts, mayoral control has created a stronger incentive for the public and key stakeholders to use data to hold the mayor accountable for school improvement.[3] In New York, Chicago, and Boston, for example, the incumbent mayor was reelected in part due to documented improvements in the public schools. In Boston and Cleveland, local citizens approved referendums on the continuation of mayoral control. In New York, Mayor Michael Bloomberg was given an unprecedented third term to govern the city's schools. At the same time, District of Columbia mayor Adrian Fenty was voted out of office after one term due in large part to his lack of communication with the local citizens about the urgency and the direction of his school reform initiatives, including downsizing of the central office and major restructuring of teacher compensation.

Pressure from Outside Organizations

Second, an equally popular practice in using data for school governance is to rely on outside research-based organizations to pressure districts to become more accountable to the public. This practice is embedded in our pluralist political process, where organized interests actively seek to influence decision makers and the policy-making process. In the politics of education, competing ideas and belief systems often result in compromise and incrementalism. Unlike typical interest groups, research-based organizations are keen on using data to shape policy deliberation.

One type of research-based organizations is single-issue oriented. When examining the school dropout problem in California's districts, Jacobsen documented the creation of a new research center, the California Dropout Research Project (CDRP).[4] CDRP was founded to study the problem of high school dropouts in California and to "identify remedies" to the problem. CDRP has a policy committee that works to find quick responses to the group's research findings. The rationale of the organization is that better, more focused research will lead to better data and, in turn, to better policy solutions. In addition to working on California's school dropout problem, CDRP participates in community forums sponsored by Civic Enterprises in all fifty states.

Another type of research-based organizations is more comprehensive in scope. One of the most established research-based organizations to pressure urban district improvement is the Chicago Consortium for School Research (CCSR). Created as part of the 1988 Chicago School Reform Act, the CCSR is housed at the University of Chicago and draws on research expertise from various universities. Over the past two decades, the CCSR has evolved from its original mission of supporting the Local School Councils, which is grounded in the reform model of parental empowerment at the local sites.[5] As the Chicago Public Schools shifted from decentralized governance to mayoral control beginning in 1995, the CCSR has had to manage an uneasy relationship with the district. While CCSR successfully used its research to advocate for and ally with the Local School Councils during its first ten years of operation, it often takes a critical stance on mayoral control and its impact on Chicago students and schools. For example, CCSR's studies raised concerns about college completion of Chicago Public Schools' graduates, school turnaround practices, and the overall impact of mayoral management.

Interestingly, the district leadership in Chicago has not disengaged from the work of CCSR. Instead, the Chicago school system, under Superintendents Paul Vallas and Arne Duncan, recruited key CCSR researchers to work in the areas of research and evaluation. The Chicago Public Schools continues to maintain an extensive data-sharing agreement with CCSR so that the latter can conduct longitudinal analysis on student performance. Clearly, the willingness of the district leadership to make use of CCSR research findings explains why this model of external pressure has worked in Chicago. A good example is CCSR's benchmarking studies on whether students are on-track to graduate in high school. The district leadership has adopted the benchmarking tool as part of its performance management system.

Very few urban districts have seen effective, research-based, external organizations such as CCSR. There are several constraints in this particular practice of using data to influence school governance. First, outside organizations have to raise start-up funds and leverage resources to sustain their research activities. Increasingly, foundations are investing their resources strategically in fewer urban districts that show the promise of reform success.[6] CCSR has the advantage of having several major local foundations committed to public education reform. Second, research organizations rely heavily on districts for data access. Too often district leadership and outside researchers lack sufficient trust to implement a data-sharing agreement. Third, the political climate in urban districts matters. For example, Henig and his associates describe racialized politics in several urban districts.[7] When outside organizations are led by predominantly white researchers and urban districts are led by minority educators, extra attention is needed to manage communication and coordination to avoid misunderstanding.

An Independent Review Panel as a Critical Friend

A third practice of using data to shape school governance is the establishment of an independent review panel within the school system to monitor school performance. Compared to the first two types of practices, this third is not as widely adopted in urban systems. Independent panels serve a unique accountability function. The rationale for this arrangement is grounded in the need for external verification of the overall district performance. Members of the independent panels are not directly associated with the work of the district, but they bring national expertise and outside perspectives. They are expected to use independent professional judgment to assess student performance and advise the district leadership on strategies that may improve district performance.

This type of arrangement is different from efforts to build the data analytic capacity of the district. An example of the capacity building effort is the Strategic Data Project (SDP) funded by the Bill & Melinda Gates Foundation. In sending data fellows in pairs to a selected sample of urban districts, the SDP collaborates closely with the research and evaluation unit of the district. SDP fellows become part of the district team to address district-defined priorities, offer technical resources for the districts, and may nurture a new culture of data-driven decision making. However, they are not likely to be in a position to monitor and report on district performance for public accountability purpose.

In contrast to the SDP, the Accountability Review Council (ARC) in Philadelphia is, in essence, an independent panel that serves as a "critical friend" to the district. The ARC, unlike the CCSR or SDP, is not designed to have a permanent technical staff to gather and analyze original data. Instead, as part of the district governance system, it has full access to district data on school performance and management practices. Its membership is more diverse than simply K–12 educational experts. ARC's seven members include two former presidents of higher education institutions, a former civil rights attorney in the federal education agency, an early childhood expert, a psychologist, a former innovative school superintendent, and a public health expert. The council receives technical support from an executive adviser, who is an educational researcher, and an assessment researcher, whose main area of research is in health care.

Across the urban districts, external review panels have not been popular for a number of reasons. There are very little incentives for urban districts to share data with external experts on an ongoing basis for accountability purpose. District leaders, to be sure, prefer to select what they want to report out to the public. Having an external review panel tends to constrain how and what the district communicates with the public. In fact, once the external panel gains access to student performance data, the locus of data reporting can shift away from the school board or the superintendent's office. Further, it is difficult to sustain a collaborative arrangement between the district leadership and the external panel. High turnovers of school superintendents in many urban districts do not provide sufficient institutional stability to support long-term data collaborative arrangements. New superintendents often move away from actions established by their predecessors, including data sharing and external review. Consequently, independent review panels are largely absent from many urban districts.

The sustaining arrangement in Philadelphia is largely due to the fact that ARC's rationale, namely the need for "an independent and assessment and report center," was included in the 2001 reform legislation. The statutory status of the external panel clearly provides a legitimate claim for ongoing data access on student performance. In 2009, for example, the Consent Decree on racial equity in schools named ARC as an independent entity that is well-positioned to conduct an independent assessment of the policy agreement. Over the years, ARC has been granted full access to the district's data system. It also maintains direct communication with the School Reform Commission and the school superintendent.

I examine the work of ARC in Philadelphia through two lenses. First, as a political scientist with a strong interest in urban school reform, I look at the institutional functions of ARC in the context of Philadelphia's ongoing efforts to improve district performance. Second, I take a participant-observant approach. Since the creation of ARC, I have served as the executive adviser to this independent entity. With the support of the ARC chair and its members, I organized the ARC research and evaluation agenda and put together its annual report on the status of Philadelphia reform for the School Reform Commission (SRC) and for the public. In discussing ARC's role, I am sharing my own perspective and not ARC's view. Clearly, the commitment and the hard work of ARC members have contributed to the integrity and quality of the panel over the years. Indeed, ARC's membership has remained remarkably stable. Since its creation, the ARC chair has remained the same. Two ARC members retired from the independent review panel.

ACCOUNTABILITY REVIEW COUNCIL IN PHILADELPHIA: HOW AN INDEPENDENT PANEL FUNCTIONS

In late December 2001, the state of Pennsylvania formed a partnership with the city of Philadelphia to jointly take over the governance of the Philadelphia school district, ending an earlier attempt by the Republican governor to place the Philadelphia district under state receivership. Following citywide protests from parents and many stakeholder organizations, the reform legislation allowed the governor and the mayor to jointly appoint a five-member SRC, which in turn selects the chief executive or the school superintendent. Regardless of partisan differences between the governor and the mayor, the two offices have worked closely in the SRC appointments over the years.

As part of the 2001 state-city partnership agreement, the district started to implement its "diverse provider" initiative, whereby education management organizations (EMOs) were contracted to manage and operate about sixty of the lowest performing schools.[8] The for-profit Edison Project became the largest provider, managing forty-five low-performing schools. In return for taking over low-performing schools, EMOs were given additional state aid. Clearly, state and local policy makers were interested in finding out if Philadelphia schools were making progress under the new reform. To ensure accountability on this new state and local reform initiative, the state mandated that the district create "an independent assessment and reporting center" to conduct an annual review and report on the district's academic performance. In 2003 the SRC established such an independent entity, ARC, to carry out the legislative mandate. ARC held its first two meetings during 2003 and since then has generally met four times annually. As of September 2012, ARC has produced eight annual reports, and their findings and recommendations have been disseminated to state and district policy decision makers as well as to the public. In meetings with the SRC and the school superintendent throughout the year, ARC engaged in ongoing discussion on policy improvement with the district leadership. Each year ARC fulfills its responsibility by making a public presentation at a SRC meeting on the status of academic performance in the School District of Philadelphia.

From an institutional perspective, ARC has been a source of institutional stability and independence, as its chair and four other members remain unchanged since they were first appointed by the SRC in 2003. At the same time, district and state leadership have changed several times. The district has had five chief executives or superintendents and four chairs of the school board (or the SRC). Further, the city has had two mayors and the state three governors since 2001. Despite these leadership turnovers and political changes, ARC has been able to collaborate with key policy stakeholders. ARC not only visited schools to gather firsthand inputs from educators, it also invited local reformers, parents, and students to participate in panel discussions on reform issues. These local and diverse views have proven to be useful to ARC in its effort to contextualize its report's findings and recommendations.

Over the years, ARC has broadened its research and evaluation activities. At the initial period, ARC's mission was largely defined by the NCLB-like accountability in Pennsylvania. During the first couple of years, ARC focused primarily on the extent to which public schools in Philadelphia met the Adequate Yearly Progress (AYP). Its reports examined the proficiency gap by subgroups as defined by NCLB, including African Americans, Latinos, students eligible for free and reduced lunch, special education students, and English language learners. The reports also tracked the district-state gap in meeting the proficiency goals at the benchmarking grades in the Pennsylvania System of School Assessment (PSSA). In the last several years, ARC has expanded its scope of work by commissioning research studies on key reform initiatives and their effects on student outcomes. This independent entity has engaged researchers to conduct analysis on the effectiveness of charter schools, alternative high schools, and diverse provider initiatives. Findings from these studies have formed an empirical basis for ARC's policy recommendations in its annual reports. Given ARC's remarkable stability and its ongoing contributions to the reform policy deliberation in a politically dynamic context, the Philadelphia case illuminates the design of this independent review panel, its implementation, and its role in district governance and policy changes and stability.

Monitor District Progress

ARC has focused its work to promote accountability through greater data transparency and annual reporting to the public. First, a key annual focus is the district's academic performance. ARC's annual report has examined a key accountability issue: did the School District of Philadelphia make annual progress in meeting the NCLB expectations? To address this question on the district's progress, ARC relied on data and analysis from two sets of metrics: (1) student performance as measured by the state's PSSA exam in mathematics and reading and the SDP's performance compared to the rest of the state; and (2) schools' AYP as measured by the PSSA proficiency targets and other indicators as mandated by the Pennsylvania Department of Education's accountability system.

Using these metrics, ARC reported to the public and the SRC at the end of each academic year on the status of academic progress in the School District of Philadelphia. Its 2011 report found that between 2002 and 2010 the district has made considerable gains toward meeting AYP requirements.[9] According to the report, during this period the percentage of SDP schools that met AYP increased from 9 percent to 59 percent. While the percentage of SDP schools making AYP decreased between 2004 and 2007, steady and measurable improvement has occurred since 2007. As the Pennsylvania Department of Education's NCLB accountability system increases its AYP thresholds in reading and math, an increasing number of SDP schools were able to meet these targets. In 2010, 158 SDP schools made the AYP, an increase of fifty-one schools since 2007. Similarly, charter schools have made substantial gains between 2002 and 2010, increasing the percentage of schools meeting AYP from 12 percent to 70 percent.

From 2002 to 2010, the independent ARC found that schools in Philadelphia continued to make steady progress at all grade levels in the percentage of students that are deemed Advanced or Proficient in reading and math. Although the state, on average, continued to have a higher percentage of students scoring at the Advanced or Proficient levels in math and reading than the district, the district's increase in the percentage of students scoring at the Advanced or Proficient levels from 2009 to 2010 in reading were higher than those of the state for grades 4, 5, 6, 7, 8, and 11. In math, the district's increases outpaced those of the state for grades 3, 4, 6, 7, 8, and 11. Overall progress notwithstanding, the independent panel urged the Philadelphia district to "accelerate its pace" of improvement in reading, especially in grades 4, 5, 6, and 11, where fewer than half of the students scored at the Advanced or Proficient levels on the PSSA. In math, eleventh grade remained a challenge, where only one-third of the students scored at the Advanced or Proficient levels.[10]

Overall district progress notwithstanding, ARC expressed concerns about modest improvement in reducing the racial achievement gap in Philadelphia schools. According to the 2011 ARC report, in both math and reading for 2010, the percentage of Latino students scoring Advanced or Proficient remained substantially below that of white students (a 23.9 percentage point gap in reading and a 22.2 percentage point gap in math).[11] The percentage of black students scoring Advanced or Proficient remained substantially below that of white students (a 22.8 percentage point gap in reading and a 24.2 percentage point gap in math). The 2011 ARC report also found that schools with greater numbers of NCLB-defined subgroups face more difficulty in making AYP.

Engage Perspectives of Diverse Stakeholders

Second, ARC is fully aware of the importance of gathering inputs from various local stakeholders. In addition to conducting school visits to make sure that its work faces the "reality check," ARC has invited key stakeholders to share their views and experience. For example, during its meeting in December 2008, ARC invited stakeholders to share their perspectives on the progress and challenges of school reform in Philadelphia. Among the invited stakeholders were representatives from the city's civic organizations, educational researchers, and advocacy groups. The invited panelists talked about what had worked in the first several years of reform, among which were: public awareness of high school problems, a sense of urgency to address school problems, improvement in teacher quality, better distribution of experienced teachers among schools, early childhood education, public awareness of what works in the diverse service provider model, evaluation of EMO schools, coordination of policy between the mayor's office and the SDP, and implementation of the core curriculum in K–8. The invited panelists shared their perspectives on areas in need of improvement in the SDP, including: a need for stronger transparency, an absence of community engagement, rushed strategic planning, a wide range of problems remaining in high schools, and high school graduates not having the skills to get a job or succeed in college. The panelists concluded with remarks on the next phase in SDP reform in the context of fall of 2008. While the first few reform years had relied on EMOs and other private providers, local stakeholders pointed to the importance of investing in professional capacity of the system.

A recent example of soliciting inputs from stakeholders relates to the test cheating incidents. During the fall of 2011, ARC reviewed the district report and a news account on student testing irregularities in Philadelphia schools. The news report analyzed the 2009 test result files, which were shelved at the Philadelphia Department of Education for two years. SDP was not notified by the state of any testing problems. In the test result files, every response sheet was analyzed. According to the news account, there were 28 schools that showed three or more times of irregularities (such as a high number of erasures) in a single grade. There was a need to conduct further analysis at the individual student level. Further, the district's assessment highlighted similar findings: 28 schools were cited for grade levels with aberrant PSSA data, 13 schools had grade levels with an insufficient amount of data to explain aberrance of data flagged in the state data report, and 6 schools were found to have questionable changes for the purpose of AYP reporting. The district has subsequently developed a close working relationship with the state to institute stronger procedures on test administration.

Focus on Effects of Key Reform Initiatives

Third, as an entity that grew out of systemwide reform, ARC has paid ongoing attention to the design, implementation, and effectiveness of the district's major reform initiatives. For each major reform, ARC asks: What are the conditions that contribute to student success? How can the district use the "what works" evidence to scale-up its reform? What are the areas in need of improvement? As the examples below suggest, ARC is ready to take on controversial reform topics. It has also commissioned well-respected external organizations to conduct in-depth data analysis on the effectiveness of various reform initiatives. Below are two examples of ARC's data-based policy evaluation.

Diverse Provider Initiative Philadelphia Style

Shortly after the state and the city entered into a joint partnership to take over the school system in late 2001, the School District of Philadelphia launched an ambitious initiative that relied on diverse providers to turn around the persistently low-achieving schools.[12] Edison Project, a for-profit EMO, was commissioned by Governor Tom Ridge to conduct an assessment of the academic and financial position of the district in the fall of 2001. The report provided the basis for the legislation that granted the governor appointive power over the school board. Subsequently, the Edison Project was hired as the lead district adviser to manage central administration between March and July 2002. When Paul Vallas was hired as the chief executive officer of Philadelphia schools in July 2002, the Edison Project became one of the seven outside managers that received five-year contracts to manage forty-five low-performing schools beginning in August 2002. By September 2005 there were 19,000 students in grades 1–10 enrolled in schools managed by contracted service providers, and 16,700 students were attending charter schools in the district.

Under the diverse provider arrangement in Philadelphia, EMOs were provided extra financial incentives ranging from $450 to $881 for each student in the designated low-performing schools. In return, EMOs were held accountable for management performance and student outcomes. In April 2003, for example, the school board terminated the contract with one of the EMOs, Chancellor Beacon Academies, for unsatisfactory performance. Among the EMOs, the Edison Project, given its role in the early phase of the district reform, continued to manage the largest number of schools. In 2004–2005, the third year of contracting out, forty-three schools were managed by four private companies and two local universities. In addition, fifty-two charter schools were operating in Philadelphia in 2004–2005.

The Philadelphia Diverse Provider Model has been a source of much research on the effectiveness of EMOs. In this context, the Accountability Review Council decided to conduct its independent evaluation on the effectiveness of this important investment. Using a cross-sectional analysis, the ARC 2006 and 2007 reports observed that the PSSA reading scores for combined grades 5 and 8 varied among different types of EMOs. For the EMOs, the percentages ranged from the University of Pennsylvania's 27.2 percent to Temple University's 16 percent of students scoring at the advanced and proficient levels in 2005. The degree of change among the EMOs from spring 2004 to spring 2005 also varied. Whereas Universal Companies and Victory Schools showed negative achievement trends (–5.8 and –0.1 percentage points, respectively), scores for the other EMOs showed gains, ranging from 4.9 percentage points for Penn to 0.3 percentage points for Temple. In their study on Edison schools nationwide, Rand researchers also found that Edison's performance did not exceed the gains of matched comparison schools.[13] A Rand follow-up evaluation on the EMOs in Philadelphia commissioned by ARC, showed no significant differences in student achievement gains between EMO-managed schools and other district schools after five years of reform.[14] These findings, however, have been called into question by an evaluation report conducted by a team of Harvard researchers.[15]

In light of both ARC's own findings and the commissioned Rand study, ARC determined that four years of student achievement data were sufficient to generate policy recommendations. ARC's key concern was to find out which types of EMOs "added value" to raising student achievement in Philadelphia schools. Given the evidence that many EMO-managed schools were not making substantial academic gains comparable with the twenty-one district-restructured schools, ARC in its 2007 report recommended that the SRC undertake a major review of the schooling and organizational conditions that contributed to the academic successes of the district-restructured schools. Regarding the forty-five EMO schools, ARC encouraged the SRC to take a school-by-school approach in deciding the future of using EMO management as a reform strategy. For EMO schools that persistently performed below the district average over the four-year period, ARC saw no justification for relying on the same EMOs to manage these schools. Finally, ARC encouraged the SRC to rethink the appropriateness and the magnitude of relying on EMOs as a strategy to turn around low-performing schools. The ARC report called on the SRC to monitor the kinds of instructional benefits for students that additional state aid was able to yield in EMO-managed schools. In short, ARC encouraged the SRC to provide greater transparency in its strategy to engage the EMOs and the efficacy of greater resource allocation to EMOs and other district schools. By 2010, with changes in the school superintendent and the SRC, the district no longer relied on EMOs as the primary providers to turn around low-performing schools.

Building on the diverse provider model, Philadelphia school superintendent Arlene Ackerman in 2010 launched a new version of the diverse provider initiative, Renaissance 2014. There were about a dozen underperforming schools in this initiative, including seven being converted to charter school (these charters must serve students who were attending the school) and several Promise Academies to be governed by the school district. All the Renaissance schools were restructured schools, with fewer than 50 percent of the current teachers hired back. Promise Academies were given extra support, including extra learning time (such as eight additional hours of learning on Saturdays each month), enrichment programs in math and foreign language, and additional professional support and resources such as instructional coaches.

To understand the complex implementation process during the early phase of the Renaissance 2014, ARC commissioned Research for Action to collect data on the planning process from March to August 2010 and the early implementation during September 2010 through January 2011. The commissioned Research for Action study examined several questions: How were Renaissance schools governed? What was the role of the school advisory councils? What were the processes and criteria for school and provider selection for the Renaissance schools, and how, and to what extent, did the community become involved? What school-level changes (administrative, teacher, facilities, curriculum) occurred at the beginning of the 2010–2011 academic year? How did the school principals and charter managers exercise their autonomy? How did site selection affect teacher recruitment in Renaissance schools? What were the teacher characteristics?

Based on the study, ARC identified several areas in need of SRC attention. According to its 2011 report, ARC saw the need to strengthen the capacity and the accountability of the school advisory councils in Renaissance schools. While the district pushed hard to promote community engagement in the school advisory councils, several councils had difficulty meeting the 51 percent parental representation requirement. To ensure meaningful parental participation, ARC encouraged greater parental support and training. For example, school principals and charter managers needed to improve their communications with council members. The district also needed to support council chairs' efforts to play a meaningful leadership role in articulating community preferences in the decision-making process at the school site.

Another set of recommendations in ARC's 2011 report addressed the schooling conditions to support student learning. ARC encouraged Renaissance schools to implement a schoolwide strategy for promoting a positive climate where, in some Promise Academies, tardiness had worsened. There were also variations in suspension rates among Renaissance charter schools, including a school with a 27 percent suspension rate. Clearly, ARC was well-positioned to use many of its base-line findings to monitor the Renaissance reform progress.

Alternative High Schools and the Racial Achievement Gap

Keenly concerned about the racial achievement gap in the district, ARC commissioned Mathematica Policy Research, Inc., to conduct a descriptive study of student characteristics and student outcomes in all the alternative schools.[16] The district's strategic plan at the time, Imagine 2014, envisioned alternative education as a viable strategy to reengage dropouts in the school system. ARC was interested in conducting an empirical examination on the effectiveness of this potential strategy to reduce dropout rates. The 2010 Mathematica study analyzed student-level records from 2001–2002 through 2008–2009. In addition to annual cross-sectional analyses, the study tracked cohorts of students from their entry into ninth grade by school types. For example, cohorts that entered ninth grade in 2003–2004 were tracked for a six-year period. Further, the study compared enrollment and student performance between nonselective neighborhoods and the two types of alternative schools. In other words, the study examined three groups of students: (1) those enrolled in neighborhood schools but never attended alternative school (referred to as "neighborhood students"); (2) those enrolled in alternative accelerated schools; and (3) those enrolled in disciplinary schools. The latter two groups were combined to form the alternative education student population.

In spring 2010, ARC highlighted the key findings from the Mathematica report. Only one in ten students enrolled in alternative schools at some time during their high school careers and alternative school enrollees stayed for about one to 1.3 years on average. Most disciplinary students did not return to regular education. Alternative students were less likely to reach the eleventh grade PSSA testing date. While the achievement gaps were present prior to high school, the gaps widened during high school. Further, larger proportions of transition students were male and black. However, the proportion of accelerated students who were Hispanic increased markedly in recent years. More alternative students were socioeconomically disadvantaged.

In light of these findings, ARC asked a key policy question in its 2010 report: what are the key policy conditions at the district level that will improve student outcomes in alternative schools? With this question in mind, ARC made several policy recommendations. As suggested in the district strategic plan Imagine 2014, the district indicated its support for reentered students in regular schools. For students who reentered regular, nonalternative schools, the district was committed to provide guidance counseling and other transitional support services. While these support services were designed to benefit the reentered students, their graduation rate lagged behind that of their peers. While 59 percent of the students in regular schools graduated, only 41 percent of the reentered students did. ARC urged the district to implement more aggressive strategies aimed at closing this graduation gap.

Equally important, ARC encouraged SDP to work closely with alternative schools to develop strategies to improve the pace of sending reentering students to regular schools. The district's alternative education has shown some promise in addressing the academic needs of some of the most challenging students in high school. However, only 32 percent of the students in disciplinary schools reentered regular schools, according to the Mathematica Policy Research study. Even less encouraging was that only one of four alternative students graduated from an alternative high school in six years.

In light of the relatively low graduation rate in alternative schools, ARC recommended a stronger accountability system. More specifically, ARC called for a stronger focus on program quality, student attendance, and academic performance on a school-by-school basis. ARC also called for greater monitoring of the performance of English language learners, with greater coordination of service implementation. For alternative schools, specific performance goals may include percent of students successfully reentering nonalternative schools, truancy rate, suspension and expulsion rate, academic proficiency, course-taking patterns, and graduation rate. These measurable indicators should be disaggregated by various subgroups, such as race and English language learner status. In response to the ARC recommendations, the district strengthened its annual performance contracts with the providers of alternative education.

IMPLICATIONS FOR INDEPENDENT PANELS IN URBAN DISTRICTS

As the Accountability Review Council approaches its tenth year, Philadelphia's efforts to strengthen data accountability face both opportunities and threats. The extent to which Philadelphia handles the dynamic environment will offer useful implications on the interplay between data and governance for other urban districts.

In terms of opportunities, key governing institutions in Philadelphia have begun to work more closely to use data to improve policy decisions. At the institutional level, the mayor's office, the city council, the school board, and the superintendent are sharing their views on school performance and management issues more frequently. Former school superintendent Arlene Ackerman, for example, cited ARC's report findings in her formal testimonies at the city council hearings on education reform. Coinciding with ARC's focus on alternative education and the district's efforts to support urban youths to reenter public schools, the mayor's top education adviser played an instrumental role in integrating student information with data in the juvenile justice system.

Further, ARC has played a constructive role in facilitating data collaboration by persistently pressing for data transparency and stronger accountability for both schools and the district as a whole. Data transparency has gained wider public attention. ARC has also gained visibility in raising issues pertaining to achievement gaps and other equity issues, such as alternative high schools. For example, the Consent Decree signed by the Pennsylvania Human Relations Commission and the School District of Philadelphia in July 2009 specifically mentioned the need for ARC to independently monitor racial equity in schools. Nonetheless, from a broader perspective, data-driven accountability remains a work in progress as charter schools entered into separate contractual agreements with the district. In the longer term, there is a need for greater uniformity in school reporting on a core set of indicators among diverse types of management.

At the same time, the Philadelphia district, like other urban districts around the country, faces major challenges. First, the test-cheating problem has affected public trust on the level of academic progress that the district has actually accomplished. To be sure, ARC has pushed the Office of Accountability to reassess the data on district performance. After much reanalysis, the district's Office of Accountability found that the effects of "cheating" on the overall district academic performance have been modest. If further investigation confirms the localized effect of test cheating, the district will be able to restore its public trust in a timely manner.

Second, the current fiscal crisis has changed the decision-making process. Instead of relying on evidence on school effectiveness, the demand for rapid decisions to cope with fiscal realities may undermine data accountability. Instead of asking which initiatives have the greatest educational benefits, district decision makers have to focus on cost savings. Central office functions, for example, are likely to be reduced given several rounds of staff reduction. Because of these challenging fiscal conditions, there is a need to sustain the critical role that ARC performs in the district. As an independent entity, ARC can use data analysis to raise questions and generate recommendations on the direction, implementation, and effects of major reform initiatives. The absence of such an entity with ongoing access to district data will substantially diminish data-driven accountability.

Based on ARC's experience and persistent contributions to policy deliberation in Philadelphia's school reform, there are clear advantages for other urban districts to consider this accountability arrangement. First, the school board tends to benefit from an independent voice not embedded in local interest-based politics for short-term gains. Second, the public needs to know the status of district performance on an annual basis. Third, the collaboration between an independent panel like ARC and the district Office of Accountability has raised the visibility of data on the critical issue of what works.

In this current climate of heightened accountability, urban school systems will benefit from the work of an independent review panel such as ARC in Philadelphia. Given growing public skepticism on the role of governmental functions, an independent review panel can ease the tension between the professional insiders and the citizens outside of the system.

CHAPTER 6

"The Numbers Speak for Themselves"

Data Use and the Organization of Schooling in Two Florida Elementary Schools

STACEY A. RUTLEDGE
BRENDA GALE NEAL

Test-based accountability has become a taken-for-granted feature of the current public educational environment. Policies that sanction public schools if students do not make annual learning gains and state-level school grading policies that score schools based on different performance measures are now a routine element of schooling. Indeed, with some research showing that some teachers are more effective than others in raising student scores and that these students have stronger educational and occupational outcomes, policies using student test score data to punish and reward teachers and schools only stand to increase.[1]

Studies over the last fifteen years document the impact and mixed success of test-based accountability policies. These studies consistently demonstrate the powerful influence of these policies in schools in the areas of curricular and instructional decisions, leadership practices, hiring, and teacher assignment, with administrators and teachers in schools facing greater sanctions for realigning practices more intensely toward improving student test scores.[2] Studies provide mixed results, however, in the area of improving student achievement, finding that while student scores on state assessments have improved since the implementation of test-based accountability, scores on the National Assessment of Educational Progress (NAEP) have remained largely stagnant.[3]

Despite the intense interest in documenting the impact of test-based accountability, almost no studies have directly explored the data infrastructure that is facilitating this policy effort. While numerous studies have examined the ways in which administrators and teachers use data in their administrative and classroom practices and contextualized these within the larger accountability environment, administrators' and teachers' use of data is rarely framed as part of a larger data infrastructure.[4] Yet, test-based accountability is dependent on an extensive computing and data network that makes possible an increased focus on student achievement centered around student performance measures.[5] Results on standardized tests as well as measures such as attendance and dropout rates become critical benchmarks of student performance used by multiple stakeholders both within and outside of the educational system. School administrators' and teachers' work, therefore, increasingly occurs in a context in which external accountability policies demand and reward improved student test scores. School administrators and teachers can be seen as the engine of the infrastructure of accountability as they make decisions about teaching and learning in schools and provide the student data fueling the system.

As quantitative measures of student performance have become used as indicators of teacher and school effectiveness, a parallel and complementary structure of standardized materials, diagnostic tests, and computer data programs has emerged to prepare students for the annual assessments. Administrators and teachers use these materials and assessments to obtain more data about students—generally by skill domains and curricular benchmarks—ostensibly to help focus instruction on areas of student weakness and to track students' progress over the school year. These data increasingly compete with professional judgment not only as measures of student performance but also to inform organizational decision making at the building and classroom levels regarding resources such as time, students, and curricular and instructional materials.[6]

The combination of external requirements to produce student progress through test scores and other standardized performance data and an increased reliance on local standardized quantitative measures of student performance is leading to an organizational shift that positions the data produced by these assessments as well as the tools that support the assessments at the center of activities in schools and classrooms. In addition to providing information about students and their progress, data provides administrators with the tools to sort and classify students and teachers as well as orient school reform efforts. The production and use of student performance data is becoming a standard and defining feature of schooling.

What are the implications of the increasing centrality of the data infrastructure on the organization of schooling in the high-stakes context of Florida? In this chapter, we explore the findings of a comparative case study of two elementary schools that focused on how school administrators and teachers made data-driven organizational choices as they sought to address state and federal accountability demands to improve student achievement.[7] With its focus on the production and use of data, this chapter casts these organizational choices within the larger context of the infrastructure of accountability. In addition to showing how administrators and teachers use and produce data for internal and external consumption, it also identifies important implications of these choices for students and their learning opportunities. The schools serve as contrasting cases. One served a high socioeconomic student population and did not face state sanctions. The other served a low socioeconomic student population and faced state intervention due to Adequate Yearly Progress (AYP). The cases, taken together, illustrate the dynamic relationship between state and local context in shaping the infrastructure of accountability. While the infrastructure of accountability reshaped schooling practices in the two schools, educators in the schools also reshaped the infrastructure of accountability through their decisions about the production and use of data and the organization of schooling.

THE DATA INFRASTRUCTURE OF SCHOOLS

The empirical and theoretical literature in the social studies of science and technology (SSST) provides a framework through which to explore the interactions between external policy demands and the organizational shifts that resulted from the way administrators and teachers in the case study schools used data. As discussed in the introduction to this volume, SSST is a theoretical approach that highlights the ways in which material technologies such as computer systems, standardized curricular, instructional materials, and diagnostic tests constrain and define routine social practices and knowledge in organizations. At the intersection of human activities and new technologies, SSST contends that infrastructures often become taken-for-granted features of organizational life subsumed in ordinary routines and practices.[8] Infrastructures, therefore, shape relations and communication between individuals as well as define communities, their cultures, and their knowledge. While they are reflections of the larger ecological context in which they are nested, infrastructures need to be understood as relational. One's experience of the infrastructure depends on where one sits.[9]

In this chapter, we explore three essential characteristics of the infrastructure of accountability and the ways it is manifest in our two schools. First, we examine the ways in which the cultural authority of data infuses administrators' and teachers' organizational choices, in turn defining and constraining activities.[10] Second, we look at how the data infrastructure works both to standardize and customize school- and classroom-level activities.[11] Finally, we turn to the classification systems embedded in the data infrastructure and how they shape students' learning opportunities at the two schools.[12]

While studies on test-based accountability provide evidence of ways in which practices are redirected toward improving student assessment scores and studies on data-driven decision making inform how administrators and teachers draw on and use student data, the data and the infrastructure in which they are embedded are often buried in the evidence rather than the focus of research in its own right. Ignoring the infrastructure present in schools risks neglecting the ways in which the production and use of data for accountability purposes and the classification system the process embeds are increasingly defining organizational practices in schools as well as the learning opportunities of students.

THE INTERSECTION OF ACCOUNTABILITY, DATA USE, AND SCHOOLING

To understand the experiences of administrators and teachers at the two case study schools, it is essential to understand the larger Florida accountability context, arguably one of the most stringent in the nation. Since 2002 both case study schools have faced accountability demands from No Child Left Behind's AYP provision as well as Florida's A+ school grading policy. Further, both schools faced state-level pressures from the then-new Differentiated Accountability (DA) initiative.[13] Historically, students at Linden Elementary scored well on the Florida Comprehensive Assessment Test (FCAT), with the school consistently earning an A from the state. Cypress Elementary, in contrast, received inconsistent grades from year to year. Neither school had consistently met AYP due to specific subgroups not making adequate yearly progress. Because of its AYP scores, however, Cypress faced DA oversight involving both state and district intervention the year of the study.

The two schools serve different student populations. Linden serves a mostly middle- to upper-middle-class student population with approximately 10 percent of students eligible for free and reduced lunch. Cypress is a Title I school serving a predominantly low socioeconomic student population with approximately 90 percent of students eligible for free and reduced lunch. Students at Linden are 90 percent white; students at Cypress are 90 percent African American. In addition to different demographics, the schools are located in different areas of this Florida county. While only a fifteen-minute drive from each other, Cypress is located in the high-poverty area of the county, whereas Linden is in an affluent suburban area.

The two schools are nested in the same district context with access to the same mandated data, technology, computers, and curricular and instructional materials. Many of the systems in place at the schools represent district efforts to standardize practices across the schools, such as the district-mandated assessments and curricular and instructional programs to assess and track student progress. At the same time, however, administrators and teachers at each school develop particular organizational approaches to meet local demands and needs. Data production and use at each school reflects assumptions about how to best meet students' individual academic needs as well as school-level issues. Administrators' and teachers' data-driven decisions—and particularly the consequences of standardization and customization—have had implications for student classification.

In what follows, we discuss administrators' and teachers' past use of data with particular attention to how these practices were predicated on the legitimacy of data as a vehicle to improve teaching and learning.[14] We then turn to standardization and customization, specifically, and discuss their implications for the classification of students.

The Authority and Use of Data

The information infrastructure is predicated on a trust in the authority of numeric indicators of performance.[15] Writing about the "lure of quantification" in education, Labaree identifies historical and sociological antecedents of this reliance by multiple stakeholders ranging from policy makers to educational researchers to school-level actors on data.[16] Objective data, like that produced by large-scale state information systems, he argues, "seem authoritative and scientific and present a certain face validity," yet may deflect attention from important educational issues.[17] In the context of this study, the cultural authority of data turns our attention to the ways in which administrators and teachers produced, used, and understood the role of data. It also raises questions about what administrators and teachers neglected as they turned their focus to quantifying student progress.

Those administrators and teachers who participated in our study at Linden and Cypress elementary schools described work practices as defined and constrained by intertwined demands of accountability policies and the production and use of student performance data. While some were more enthusiastic than others about using student data, administrators and teachers uniformly viewed data, and standardized test scores in particular, as a legitimate way to address student achievement. Administrators and teachers at both schools described the strong pressure placed on them for students to meet AYP as well as to improve or maintain the school grade, both measured by Florida's assessment, the FCAT.[18] Administrators also discussed the new demands from DA. Having not met AYP for consecutive years, administrators at Cypress described direct district and state intervention, whereas administrators at Linden described concern about failing to meet DA requirements after the annual FCAT administration. Activities aimed at preparing students for the test-based assessment, therefore, permeated the day-to-day routines at both schools.

Administrators and teachers at both schools also relied on similar district-provided standardized resources to track student data, including baseline and benchmark standardized assessments as well as curricular and instructional materials and assessments directly and indirectly aligned to the state assessment. Students at both Linden and Cypress regularly attended computer labs to use Pearson's SuccessMaker program for math and language arts. Some of these resources targeted specific skills, such as reading fluency, while others disaggregated students' scores by skill area, facilitating analyses for individual students around areas such as "main idea, plot and purpose" and "comparison and cause/effect" for reading and "measurement and number sense" and "concepts and operations" for math. Table 6.1 identifies the accountability policies facing the schools, the standardized districts resources, and school responses.

While the schools shared district resources and a data-driven focus, they pursued different school- and classroom-level approaches. Administrators and teachers at Linden consistently expressed concern and anxiety about meeting accountability demands. While this is perhaps surprising given Linden's school grade and high levels of student achievement, it is evidence of the ways in which the accountability mandates and pressures affected all schools, not just those facing sanctions.

TABLE 6.1 Comparison of external policy demands, district resources, and school responses

	Linden Elementary	*Cypress Elementary*
Federal accountability policies	Adequate Yearly Progress response to intervention	Adequate Yearly Progress response to intervention
State accountability policies	Sunshine State Standards A+ differentiated accountability	Sunshine State Standards A+ differentiated accountability
District resources	Baseline assessments STAR testing FAIR testing SuccessMaker	Baseline assessments STAR testing FAIR testing SuccessMaker
School response	Progress monitoring Baseline testing Six-week benchmark assessments Crunch time two weeks before FCAT ESE & Level 1 & 2 pull-outs Selected removal of special area Accelerated Reader (AR) Incentives for AR goal (parties) Afterschool enrichment	Progress monitoring Baseline testing Four-week benchmark assessments 3rd & 4th grade suspension of science and writing from November to April (FCAT) ESE pull-outs Art and music suspended All-boy classrooms 3rd, 4th, and 5th grade ability grouping 3rd, 4th, and 5th grade disciplinary teaching Grouping by gender

Administrators and teachers identified three main strategies to meet AYP and maintain the school grade. First, they described a system of using students' prior FCAT scores as well as scores on the varying local assessments and computer programs to inform the direction and nature of additional student resources, such as tutoring, extra computer time, and targeted focus on certain benchmarks. Second, drawing on FCAT data, they placed the lowest-performing students in pull-out courses. Finally, they described general enrichment for all students before and after school as well as through teachers' and the school's Web sites. Overall, while schooling at Linden continued to look much like a traditional elementary school, with grade-level self-contained classrooms overseen by one teacher from August to June, building faculty and administrators drew on data to explain student progress and inform organizational decision making regarding resource allocation for students.

When interviewed, the principal at Linden identified data use as his main focus. He described this focus within larger federal policy demands:

> What I'm trying to get this year for the teachers is "Know your goal." So if I have a class of 23, and we need 20 to make our school improvement goal, or 17 to make our AYP goal, then I should be able to walk up to [a teacher] at anytime and say, "How many do you have now, today?" And they should give me a factual data statement. "I have 17 students who are proficient as of November 21st." And so each time, we're working on our goal, we know where we're going and we know who we need to focus on to get there.

According to the principal, every student at Linden needed individual attention, and data facilitated this. Similarly, the assistant principal asserted that through student achievement data, "we get to know them [students], and we get to know them by looking at their data—and figuring out their strengths and skills and their weak areas, the target areas of skills." Administrators and grade-level teams met biweekly to discuss student data. Teachers described using students' FCAT and SuccessMaker scores as well as the six-week baseline and benchmark tests to identify areas of further focus, complementing their regular curriculum. While some teachers complained that this focus competed with their autonomy to focus on students' social skills, for example, none dismissed or were reported as resisting the focus on data. For all participants at Linden, and despite the school's accountability success, student performance data was a given feature of their work.

Administrators and teachers at Cypress Elementary, in contrast, worked in a very different accountability environment. The school had experienced multiple years of intense accountability pressures from both the school grading policy as well as AYP. Because of their poor performance, school administrators were required to report student data directly to the district and the state on a monthly basis. This resulted in a redefinition of the assistant principal's role centered on managing and interpreting data. At Cypress, the assistant principal's main responsibility was monitoring, disaggregating, and reporting data to inform both school and classroom activities as well as meet state and district demands: "We have to give [the state] a full-out plan of what we're doing, and then we have to follow up with the data." She described the expectations from the state as laid out in the original intervention plan: "We had to have objectives, we had to have who's responsible for these objectives. What do the objectives entail? What materials or curriculum resources are you going to use to achieve this objective? How are you going to monitor this objective? And what are the results you are going to expect in the end?"

Teachers were fully aware of the external pressures and the expectation to use data, underscoring the cultural authority of quantification. One teacher described the school's expectations in the following way:

> You have to have the data to show. We're a data-driven school. Our numbers speak for themselves. So you could say that you're doing one thing in your class, but if your numbers aren't showing that, then maybe you need to change something you're doing. We look at data with everything we're doing, any decision we make.

Another teacher explained that, "as a whole, we . . . know what is needed to achieve AYP and to achieve the school grade. So using the data that drives all that, we're able to instruct on a level that the kids need." Administrators and teachers at Cypress reported following the data. Administrators and teachers relied on data-driven conclusions over professional judgment to inform decisions about the school, classrooms, and students.

At both schools, administrators and teachers pursued data-driven approaches through baseline assessments and routine benchmark assessments. To be sure, faced with stronger accountability pressures than Linden, Cypress Elementary pursued a more encompassing response through multiple data-driven strategies that not only shaped classroom practices but also reallocated students, teachers, and time. They engaged in continual progress monitoring and adopted instructional strategies aimed to individualize and monitor student learning. In sum, administrators and teachers at both schools saw the production and use of data as a legitimate way to address school- and student-level problems. While a few complained about the pressure to increase student performance, all identified data-driven decision making as a legitimate way to address student learning.

Standardization and Customization

As suggested by theorists of the social science of technology, technological infrastructure both standardizes and customizes.[19] This tension has been identified as *structuration,* as the implementation of standardized infra-structure leads to local adaptations. Where infrastructure implies rigidity, technologies themselves are inherently adaptable. In the context of schools, therefore, technological infrastructure needs to be understood as both serving a standardizing function while also reflecting and responding to local and individual demands.

In this case study, high-stakes pressures to meet test-based accountability demands coupled with administrative and instructional data use resulted in standardized practices both across and within the two schools. Administrators and teachers at Linden and Cypress elementaries described five shared types of standardization. First, they described standardization in terms of the state- and federal-mandated activities: curricular standards and the related assessment of the FCAT, as well as requirements to meet AYP. Second, they pointed to district textbooks, computer programs, test-prep booklets, and assessments that became the core curricular guidelines and materials for students. Third, all students participated in standardized test preparation, including routine benchmark assessments as well as a district-mandated computer program centered on reading and math. Fourth, administrators and teachers at both schools engaged in routine progress monitoring meetings based on student data. Finally, administrators and teachers at both schools described a common standardized way of referring to students by their FCAT scores, as in "my fours and fives" or my "ones and twos," thus employing the state classification for different performance levels on the required annual assessment.

Administrators and teachers at each school further described particular school-level standardization among teachers and students. At Linden, administrators and teachers described enrichment opportunities for all students that, while not directly related to improving scores, were seen as ways to reinforce academic skills. Administrators, teachers, and the PTA all supported the Accelerated Reader (AR) program in which students were assigned goals based on a computerized diagnostic reading test. Based on their individualized reading goal set by the AR program, students read books with different point allotments and took a computerized test about the books. Students who met their goal during each grading period were treated to a party sponsored by the PTA and had their name publicly and decoratively displayed on the school walls. The school also sponsored other enrichment activities, such a free afterschool program focused on critical thinking and problem solving activities. Teachers also described putting problem solving activities and the addresses of specific Web sites on their personal school

Web pages for extra activities for students. Further, the school Web site devoted an entire page to lists of online sites devoted to enrichment activities. Linden, with its continued accountability success, thus standardized enrichment for all students.

Administrators and teachers at Cypress intensified the existing data infrastructure by adding more standardized data-driven programs and practices for all students. The district implemented regular monthly testing. Further, curricular and instructional materials and activities were aligned more closely to the FCAT. Students were given a baseline assessment at the beginning of the year and then tested monthly with benchmark assessments. Grade-level teachers met weekly with an administrator to monitor students' progress. Students attended the SuccessMaker lab twice a week. The assistant principal at Cypress explained that the school's leadership team regularly reviewed every tested area—reading, math, writing, and science—"to break down 'this is what we're doing, this is how we're monitoring it. This is the data to support what we've been monitoring so far.' We assess our kids once a month, whole school." Students' scores on these monthly assessments were tracked visually in an administrative conference room. Each FCAT tested student was represented by a circular construction paper dot that could be moved above and below the "proficient" line.

Together, these standardization efforts provide a glimpse at the common infrastructure undergirding activities at both schools. Whether through accountability pressures, state standards and assessments, district-mandated curricula and materials, computer programs, common data meetings, or language about students, the data infrastructure facilitated standardization across each of the schools. Each school shared a common data infrastructure, but they also standardized to meet internal needs and demands. Administrators and teachers made decisions about the extent and nature of standardization based on local priorities and goals resulting in the use of data to forward standardized practices across both schools.

While common curricula, assessments, and computer programs served to standardize administrators' and teachers' practices, the nature of the data itself—its numeric indicators of student progress—facilitated customization of activities and services provided to students. Customization involves tailoring educational practices to meet the needs of individual or small groups of students. In the case study schools, customization entailed using student scores to provide students opportunities for enrichment, advancement, and remediation, with students at the bottom receiving particular attention. Administrators and teachers at both schools described closely monitoring students' progress on the FCAT practice materials and skills. After regular practice testing, teams of teachers met regularly with administrators to discuss student scores, identify students in need of particular assistance, and plan a course of action. At these meetings, teachers referred to their progress monitoring binders in which they recorded students' scores on multiple assessments ranging from reading fluency and computational skills to performance on specific state benchmarks and SuccessMaker scores. Stakeholders used these meetings to keep a watchful eye on a student's individual data and areas of need, as well as the combined data of their AYP subgroups.

Teachers at both schools described using the data to tailor instruction to meet individual students' needs. Several teachers at Linden spoke of modifying the curriculum for individual students, and one discussed altering her teaching methods for different learning styles. The majority of teachers interviewed at Cypress mentioned customizing the curriculum by differentiating instruction. The assistant principal at Cypress explained these practices:

> The data that we get back . . . the information that we get back from his assessments is absolutely wonderful. It's an absolutely wonderful tool to drive curriculum. It gives the teachers a clear snapshot on what areas the kids need remediation in as individual students and as a whole class, because our kids are compartmentalized, based on ability, based on what subjects are taught.

Administrators and teachers at both schools, therefore, described targeting individual students, groups of students, and entire classes by drawing on different assessment data.

In addition to teachers' use of data to customize instruction, each school drew on data to customize instructional practices for different groups of students. Administrators and teachers at Linden described an extensive pullout program for students receiving a 1 or 2 on the FCAT. Students scoring at this level attended intensive reading classes with five or six students taught by either aides or Exceptional Student Education (ESE) teachers. Because of the small number of students scoring at this level at the school, all students meeting this criterion were pulled out. While many were students classified as ESE, a number were students with low scores and no ESE classification. In addition to missing classroom activities, these students were pulled from electives such as art, music, and PE. If parents objected to the pull-outs, they were required to sign a waiver indicating that they did not want their children participating in the intensive reading program. Teachers reported that few parents waived their children.

Cypress also customized student learning by reorganizing students. However, unlike at Linden, where the low performers received a tailored curriculum, Cypress reassigned all students by FCAT scores. Administrators ability-grouped third, fourth, and fifth grade students into high, medium, and low tracks and assigned teachers into disciplinary subjects based on teachers' assumed strengths. Students in tested grades, therefore, followed an organizational model more typical of junior high school. Teachers in these same grades taught one disciplinary field in an FCAT-tested subject— language arts, math, or science—tailored to the academic level of the particular group of students. In addition to ability grouping, administrators placed a subset of boys in second, third, and fourth grades into all-boys classrooms taught mainly by African American male teachers, the logic being that the teachers would serve as role models and that the students would benefit from a consistent all-boys environment. Administrators and teachers described stronger disciplinary practices, a dress code, and instruction on social skills for these boys. The assistant principal explained, "It has just made such a difference with these boys. We're not having as many discipline issues with them. Academically they're doing better." So while the same-sex assignments served a disciplinary purpose, it also served to customize students' experiences based on perceived socioemotional and academic needs.

Administrators at Cypress customized several critical elements of time. While not a direct customization based on student scores, this effort represented a way to intensify students' time on task. Due to the disciplinary structure, administrators organized periods into ninety-minute blocks. In this way, administrators extended the state-mandated ninety-minute reading block for Title I schools to math and science. Second, based on a suggestion from the state intervention team as well as on data that the lowest student productivity was during the final nine weeks of school, administrators implemented April-to-April instruction immediately after the administration of the 2010 FCAT. With no advance notice, students and teachers were reassigned to the following year's teachers. As the assistant principal explained, "All of our third through fifth grade teachers have taught all the curriculum for their grade level before FCAT, so why not go to the next level?" She described it as "the first day of school starts the day that FCAT is over." A teacher described the logic in the following way: "I think it helps the teachers to get to know the students, so when the year starts back, the kids kind of know what expectations we have." Customization of the allocation of time, therefore, again altered the organization of schooling for all students in tested grades.

Classification

Schools are resource-constrained organizations aimed at educating large numbers of children in an effective and efficient manner. As a consequence, they face challenges in customizing education for all students and turn to systems of classification that sort students into categories based on similar criteria, usually student achievement.[20] Classification thus entails efforts to standardize while meeting the needs of specific groups of students. It both simplifies demands and increases efficiency. As schools do not have the resources to customize learning opportunities for all students, they classify students to tailor to the needs of the group.

One important way that administrators and teachers in Linden and Cyprus classified students was through their use of the language of FCAT scores. This became the shared nomenclature of classification at each school with level 1 students ("way below" grade level), level 3 students ("average"), and level 5 students ("exemplary"). While actors at both schools used the FCAT classification system in this way, they also pursued distinct school-level classification strategies that had implications on the organization of schooling. Linden, with its history of success and strong academic reputation, maintained the traditional elementary school organization of self-contained mixed-ability classrooms. While grade-level teachers met biweekly to discuss student progress, teachers largely worked independently in their classrooms, classifying students based on feedback from school-level progress monitoring and routine assessments. As noted above, students with low FCAT scores were further classified as needing extra time on basic skills and pulled out of the classroom as well as art, music, and physical education to receive special small-group and intensive reading instruction.

Cypress pursued nonconventional approaches to the classification of students in tested grades. Students and teachers were organized more like a junior high school with students tracked by ability and taught by teachers who became disciplinary experts. Some boys were organized into same-sex classes. Students also attended ninety-minute period classes, and, after the FCAT, third and fourth grade students were put with their fourth and fifth grade teachers. Students at Cypress, therefore, spent their school days classified in like-ability groups and, in some cases, like-gender groups.

IMPLICATIONS OF THE INFRASTRUCTURE OF DATA
ON TEACHING AND LEARNING

At one level, the case studies presented in this chapter can be understood within the parameters of district and school data-driven decision making. They show the central role of data in these Florida elementary schools as administrators and teachers seek to meet federal and state accountability demands. The infrastructural perspective used in this volume, however, casts the work of administrators and teachers in the larger network of data production and use. This chapter illustrates the ways in which administrators and teachers drew on standardized district resources to customize activities and classify students in an effort to maximize student achievement on the state-mandated assessment. It reveals the production of student test scores that are, in turn, transmitted to the district as well as the state and its information system. The public reporting of aggregate student scores by the state in the form of school grades and AYP status leads to a feedback loop that increases pressure on administrators and teachers, further intensifying testing in schools. With all public schools required to report student scores, no school escapes scrutiny and involvement in the system.

In this study, administrators and teachers participated in the data infrastructure on which test-based accountability is based due to a faith in quantitative measures as a tool to inform local solutions and improve student achievement. Indeed, while current research on data use emphasizes how local interpretation of data varies, for many of the teachers and administrators the data spoke for themselves. Quantitative, objective data possessed cultural authority. While such data were open to local interpretation, it is important to acknowledge the fundamental authority and meaning for teachers and school administrators that the data carried.

With their faith in numbers, administrators and teachers were complicit in the larger infrastructure of accountability to which they both contributed to and were defined by. Drawing on standardized curricular and instructional materials, computer programs and routine assessments, they classified students based on ability as they strove to meet federal and state accountability goals. Together, this suggests profound implications of the infrastructure of accountability on the nature of schooling and learning opportunities for students as administrators and teachers both help construct and elaborate the infrastructure of accountability as well as embed it into their everyday practices. It raises important questions about how test-based accountability reinforces the processes of classification, potentially intensifying the sorting of students.

When understood as part of the larger infrastructure, the similarities and differences between the two schools become critical. While the schools shared similar resources and routines, and both schools were required to participate in the larger data system, administrators and teachers at Cypress experienced greater demands and constraints on local practices and autonomy. Not only were the accountability demands greater, including visitors from the Florida Department of Education, but data use and analysis were more intense. To meet data and accountability demands, administrators and teachers at Cypress were more likely to use more assessments and computer resources as well as experiment with innovative, nontraditional organizational approaches. As a Title I school with the majority of its students receiving free and reduced lunch and facing greater accountability sanctions, the experience of Cypress raises questions about the fairness of requiring schools that serve high percentages of students already facing the challenges associated with poverty being more vulnerable to centrally imposed sanctions and accountability than schools with more affluent students.

Interestingly, administrators, in particular, and teachers at both schools expressed the belief that data were going to provide the needed guidance that would lead to improved student achievement. They did not reference notions of best practice. Nor did they lament the loss of professional judgment. These findings underscore how easy it has been for the infrastructure of accountability to permeate administrators' and teachers' activities, despite little knowledge about whether the practices schools adopt in response to the availability of objective data are educationally sound.[21]

The studies on the social science of technology highlight the ways in which systems both external and internal to schools are being built around the production and use of student data. The data and the infrastructure in which they are embedded are often buried in the evidence rather than attuned to the focus in its own right. This absence runs the risk of neglecting the ways in which the production and use of data for accountability purposes and the classification system the process embeds are increasingly defining work practices in schools as well as the learning opportunities of students with critical implications. As data systems become taken-for-granted features of schools, we need to ask how the standardization, customization, and classification systems they are institutionalizing affect the experiences and learning opportunities for students.

CHAPTER 7

New Data, Old Patterns

The Role of Test Scores in Student Assignment

LORA COHEN-VOGEL
LA'TARA OSBORNE-LAMPKIN
ERIC A. HOUCK

In 2008, Henig and Stone wrote that one of the most serious problems for education today is that nationalizing tendencies are in danger of crafting solutions that fit poorly the complexity of the situation on the ground.[1] Such tendencies in the United States are supported by a burgeoning infrastructure of test-based accountability and data systems to make it run. Henig and Stone go on to warn that "shaking things up" at the national level will serve the public interest only if it proves to be a prelude to putting in place something new and better. But putting something new and better into place—that is, generating practical, real-world solutions that fit local contexts—is, according to the authors, difficult, since so much of local actors' time is now spent on "defend[ing] themselves and pursu[ing] support and resources in broader arenas in which clashing dogmas are at work."[2] In the four years since the publication of their article, the nationalizing tendencies to which Henig and Stone refer have, through the Common Core State Standards and Race to the Top, arguably grown stronger.

Instead of signaling an end to local control, however, the burgeoning accountability infrastructure may instead have encouraged a local renaissance of sorts. In Crowson and Goldring's words, "The constraints of increased state and national prescriptiveness are pulling local actors more fully than ever into newly pragmatic responses to state and federal mandates, around the special details and nuances of local contexts."[3] Responsible for implementation, this reasoning goes, school and district leaders are fully engaged in planning and reform even as they refocus their efforts within the framework of state and national accountability objectives. Sometimes, as the editors write in their introduction to this volume, these test-based accountability objectives introduce new technologies and types of work into schools that must be integrated into existing practices; this integration, as we will show, often lends texture to—even reshapes—the nature of the policy itself.

In this chapter, we consider the extent to which test-based accountability is changing the educational landscape. We do so by describing the texture of local responsiveness to test-based accountability policies, with a particular focus on how the accountability infrastructure may be changing instructional arrangements in schools. By *instructional arrangements,* we are referring specifically to student assignment—to schools, classrooms, and teachers. Two key questions guide our thinking: Has test-based accountability and the data on which it is based conditioned the ways school leaders arrange instruction? And, have their responses served to disrupt or deepen the old patterns of student assignment?

Before answering these questions, we briefly consider what we know to date about whether and how test-based accountability has changed local practices in general. Then, focusing in on instructional arrangements, we draw on two cases in North Carolina and California along with findings from a study by Cohen-Vogel and Osborne-Lampkin in Florida to focus on the extent to which student assignment has been reshaped in response to growing accountability pressures. In two sections—on assignment to schools and to classes and teachers, respectively—we describe the ways in which students have historically been placed and whether test-based accountability has disrupted those norms.

CHANGE AND STABILITY IN LOCAL PRACTICE

The ever-expanding collection and use of performance data to measure, monitor, and regulate schools has been buoyed by sweeping claims that holding them accountable for meeting standardized performance benchmarks would finally solve the dual problems of stagnant test performance and wide achievement gaps.[4] But test-based accountability policies do not, for the most part, prescribe the means or "logics" for solving these problems.[5] Indeed, within this context, schools remain, in the words of Spillane, Gomez, and Mesler, "on their own to figure out the particulars of improvement."[6] In figuring them out, schools seem to respond to test-based accountability in ways that both disrupt and reify conventional practices and the assumptions that undergird them, depending on the type of practice under study.

On the one hand, test-based accountability has penetrated schools in ways few of us would have imagined a decade ago. Indeed, schools—particularly those at the lower end of the performance spectrum—have changed remarkably in this climate. Changes in curriculum, teacher hiring and assignment, and instructional time, in particular, seem to be disrupting long-held norms that gave teachers autonomy over curriculum and its delivery, allocated more or less equal time to core academic subjects, and granted senior teachers choice assignments.[7]

On the other hand, there appears to have been little disruption to other, deeply embedded structural forms like organizing the curriculum by subject matter and students by age and ability. Ogawa argues that policy makers, in adopting reforms to improve performance, and educators, in implementing them, have not altered schools' most basic instructional elements, wherein "students are grouped by age, the curriculum is organized by subject matter, teachers instruct classes of roughly 20–35 students, students are categorized by achievement level, and so on."[8] In fact, instead of provoking broad-scale change in these areas, calls for enhanced performance seem to have encouraged schools not only to work "almost exclusively within their existing core structures, but also [to] have relied on strategies that strengthen or expand them."[9]

Because, in addition to sharpening the focus on the academic content tested on state assessments, test-based accountability presumably is intended to concentrate attention on students who are not meeting proficiency standards.[10] This reliance on traditional structural elements is surprising. Indeed, with a focus on lower-performing students, we expect to see changes to core instructional arrangements—and to student assignment practices, in particular—that shake up old "ways of doing" that privilege assigning kids to schools close to home and separating students by ability.[11] Indeed, in the test-based accountability context, we expect educators to disrupt old assignment patterns and create new ones that better align with school performance objectives. Put another way, we expect school systems to be using performance data in ways that assign lower-performing students to "better" schools, "better" classes, and "better" teachers.

In the two sections that follow, we review the norms that have guided assignment practices traditionally and consider whether they show signs of any "give" in response to test-based accountability. By tracing such practices over time, we show that test-based accountability does not appear to have fundamentally disrupted student assignment. It has, however, made available measures of student achievement that people are using in their assignment decisions not as an explicit strategy for improving school performance but to reinforce goals of educational equity and fairness. In the case of school assignment, some districts are using student test scores as proxies for race to support the decades-old goal of racial integration. In the case of class assignment, elementary schools are using performance measures as part of a broader set of information to continue the practice of creating heterogeneous classrooms with the dual aims of better classroom management and sense of fairness.

STUDENT ASSIGNMENT TO SCHOOLS

Perhaps the most visible form of student assignment is the assignment of students to schools. As we will show, residential assignment has been the primary means through which students are assigned to schools in the United States. In residential assignment, the location of a student's home within a specified, geographic "catchment" area determines the school that he or she attends. But two other forms of assignment have also conditioned the way students are assigned to schools: desegregation and school choice. Whereas desegregation plans assign students to schools in an effort to achieve better racial balance, choice plans are designed to give parents more say over the schools their children attend. After describing these assignment practices, we look at two cases—Wake County (NC) and San Francisco (CA)—and examine whether test-based accountability and the data it generates have led to changes in the ways students are assigned to schools. In particular, we are interested in whether lower-performing students are being moved to better-performing schools in an effort to improve individual and school-level outcomes.

Residential assignment grew out of a strong tradition of local control in the United States, a legacy of the Northwest Ordinances that allocated communities a piece of land to be used to support public education. Local control and the use of a one-room schoolhouse model meant that assignment into schools in colonial times was geographically based; communities only had one school that students could attend.[12] Arguably, with the advent of states' involvement in education, the convention of residential assignment became further entrenched. In their funding formulae for schools, many states allowed local communities to supplement state allocations with property tax revenue, encouraging the establishment of large numbers of small, autonomous districts, some of which operated just one or two schools. Over time, fed by concerns for efficiency, the number of school districts in the United States declined dramatically, from 130,000 in 1930 to 15,500 in 1990.[13] This consolidation and the resulting increases in district size placed more schools, and therefore more options for assignment, in the hands of district leaders. Lines around school catchment areas were drawn, and local zoning boards were established to redraw lines when the school-age population rose or fell.

Residential assignment often meant that minorities and white students attended separate schools, since these groups often lived in separate neighborhoods.[14] And, in the South, when African American students resided in proximity to white schools, Jim Crow legislation ensured that students of different races were taught in schools that were separate but, in accordance with the language of *Plessy v. Ferguson,* "equal." Over time, these racist student assignment policies served both to disenfranchise minority students and create strong bonds in African American communities.[15]

Although significantly delayed by the resistance and intractability of southern politicians like Governors Orval Faubus and Ross Barnett, desegregation came to the South and other regions of the country as a result of the *Brown* decisions of the mid-1950s. This move away from residential assignment was implemented amid fierce opposition. Southern opposition to "forced busing" has been widely documented. But race-based student assignment policies faced community opposition in other regions of the country as well.[16]

Desegregation altered student assignment polices across the country. The most prominent form of new, race-based assignment practices used percentage limits or caps for school-level enrollments.[17] For example, the school assignment policy in Wake County, North Carolina, was known as the "15/45" plan because it set a minimum percentage of African American students to be assigned to schools (15%) as well as a cap (45%), commensurate with the overall African American population in the district. To implement these limits, students were bused, sometimes long distances, to schools outside their neighborhoods. "Voluntary desegregation programs" were also offered in many districts; here, themed schools located in traditionally minority neighborhoods were supposed to act as "magnets," attracting students with an interest or talent in a particular subject or emphasis (e.g., performing arts, engineering) from across the racial spectrum. Although it continued until the turn of the century, race-based assignment was beset by litigation, district petitions for "unitary status," and changing attitudes about the quality of American education and the nature of school reform.

Legally, race-based assignment plans were challenged as early as 1955 in the Supreme Court ruling known colloquially as Brown II. In their decision, the high court validated these policies and called for districts to make "all deliberate speed" in the pursuit of integration. But race-based assignment was under attack again by 1974, when the Supreme Court, in *Milliken v. Bradley*, put limits on race-based assignment by holding that such remedies could extend across school district lines only where there was evidence that multiple districts had deliberately engaged in a policy of segregation.[18] Noting that desegregation did not require "any particular racial balance in each school, grade or classroom," the decision effectively relieved suburban districts from assisting in the desegregation of city school systems.

Soon thereafter, political shifts also presented challenges to race-based assignment. The publication in 1983 of *A Nation at Risk* and the subsequent national dialogue around the nation's "declining competitive advantage" placed an emphasis on "excellence" over "equity," or on what some have come to call *the outputs* of the educational process.[19] Despite the attempts of some scholars to cast desegregation as the road to educational excellence, this outcome-based focus had a dramatic, declining impact on policy makers' appetites for continued battles over the racial makeup of schools.[20] An unlikely alliance of actors also emerged to dampen the momentum behind race-based assignment.[21] African Americans, who bore the disproportionate burdens of the policy's implementation, had grown weary of sending their children on long bus rides to attend school across town. Indeed, by 1999, 82 percent of respondents to a nationwide poll opposed busing, and about half of African American parents, said that students should go to their local schools even if it meant that most of the students would be of the same race.[22] Coupled with opposition to busing, a reframing of neighborhood and community as sources of support for student learning built enthusiasm for a return to neighborhood schools.[23] Advocates for the replacement of race-based assignment plans argued that "neighborhood schools must be an option for parents of poor minority children, as such schools can provide stability, contribute to a sense of community, and make it easier for parents to become involved in their children's education."[24]

In this context, urban school districts returned to court in the final decade of the twentieth century to ask judges to lift their desegregation orders.[25] The removal of a mandatory desegregation order is known as a grant of "unitary status." Given that many court opinions are not published, the number of districts declared unitary is unclear. Yet, in an analysis of published decisions, the Harvard Civil Rights Project found decisions granting unitary status or partial unitary status in thirty-five school districts during the 1991–2002 period alone.[26] According to Goldring, Cohen-Vogel, and Smrekar, unitary status typically replaced race-based assignment with "new student assignment plans that largely reassign students to neighborhood schools, or schools that are closer to home."[27]

Race-based student assignment was dealt its final blow in 2007 when the Supreme Court handed down its decision in *McFarland v. Jefferson County Public Schools* and *Parents Involved in Community Schools v. Seattle School District No. 1*, or *PICS*. In it, the Court strongly reaffirmed the value of racial diversity in schools but limited the options available to districts voluntarily pursuing such diversity. Though disagreements over its interpretation remain to this day, the decision was widely understood to mean that only race-neutral student assignment was legal, and many districts responded by eliminating their existing desegregation plans altogether.[28] By the turn of this century, scholars were already documenting a resegregation of the nation's public schools and the attendant implications for resource allocations, including the distribution of teacher quality.[29]

In addition to residential and race-based assignment, there is one other dominant way students have been assigned to schools in the United States: choice. Choice-based assignment is intended to give parents more say over the schools their children attend. Guthrie, Springer, Rolle, and Houck describe a school choice continuum. On one end of the continuum, magnet schools and controlled choice plans provide limited options to all or some parents from among a district-approved set of public schools.[30] On the other, voucher systems provide a government subsidy for all parents to use to send their children to schools of their choosing, public or private. At the midpoint of this continuum are charter schools, public schools provided by a host of charter operators. Students' access to these choice plans vary by the state, city, and/or the school district in which they reside.

TEST-BASED STUDENT ASSIGNMENT TO SCHOOLS: THE CASE OF TWO DISTRICTS

We turn now to how, if at all, test-based accountability and the data system that undergirds it have conditioned student assignment to schools. Have they led to new innovations in student assignment or otherwise influenced the three dominant forms that have to date characterized district practice?

We began this chapter with the expectation that schools would respond to test-based accountability policies by focusing on lower-performing students or students whose performance is below the proficiency threshold used in determining a school's effectiveness rating. In terms of student assignment, we anticipated the emergence of new kinds of policies aimed at boosting student achievement rather than, or in addition to, traditional plans that have, as their primary goals, keeping kids close to home, in integrated settings, or in schools their parents choose. We thought we might find, for example, districts working to calculate and implement a threshold of lower-performing kids in each school at which some optimal performance might be achieved. Or maybe we would see the strategic distribution of so-called "bubble kids" (those on the threshold of proficiency) assigned to schools in a manner that school officials believed would lift them over the performance threshold.

Unfortunately, there has been relatively little published research on student assignment to schools in the last five to ten years, and none that has looked explicitly at changes in assignment practices as the result of test-based accountability. But some studies, and our own review of school district practices, reveal that districts are using student performance data in their efforts to assign students to schools. In the cases we examined, where performance data are being used in decisions to assign students to schools, their use appears to be motivated not by an explicit effort to improve the test performance of schools or particular groups of students but, instead, as a proxy for race.

In their 2011 article, Siegel-Hawley and Frankenberg suggest that the most significant influence on student assignment practices in the last decade was not test-based accountability but the Supreme Court's *PICS* decision. Since the decision was handed down, two approaches to student assignment have been used by districts that want to maintain racially diverse schools: class-based and multifactor plans. It is in the multifactor approach that we see the introduction of performance data in the assignment process. Even as performance metrics have garnered their fair share of attention in student assignment policies, they have taken a back seat to another proxy for race: students' socioeconomic status.[31]

Here we highlight two districts that have attempted to utilize student performance as a factor in student assignment policies: Wake County in North Carolina and San Francisco Unified in California. Each district has used performance metrics differently and with different ends.

The Wake County Public School System (WCPSS) shifted away from a race-based student assignment policy in 1999. WCPSS comprises Raleigh (the state's capital and second-most-populous city) and the surrounding suburbs. The district moved from race-based student assignment on its review of the 4th Circuit Court of Appeals ruling in *Cappacione v. Charlotte-Mecklenburg*. In that case, a parent sued the school system after his daughter was denied a spot in a district magnet school for the second time on the basis of race. In his opinion, the judge declared that the mandate of a unitary system had been met and lifted the court order for mandatory busing.

The new assignment policy replaced racial caps for the purposes of integration with proxy measures—namely, socioeconomic status and student performance. The policy stipulated that no more than 40 percent of students in a school could be eligible for free and reduced lunch and no more than 25 percent could be low performing, as measured on the four-point scale North Carolina uses for its end-of-grade and end-of-course exams.[32]

In 2011 a new school board majority began examining other methods for assigning students into schools and, like its counterpart in Charlotte, adopted a managed choice plan. Like its predecessor, the new plan incorporates performance, but in a different form. Under the plan, parents submit school preferences from a list of "proximate" schools close to their homes. In assigning students to their first-choice school, an algorithm (reportedly in use in a number of other school districts) grants priority to siblings, students residing within a mile and a half of the school, and students who live in an area ("node") designated as low performing. Priority points are also awarded to students from high-performing nodes whose first choice school is located in a low-performing node. No points are awarded on the basis of an individual applicants' own performance.

A similar algorithm is in use today by the San Francisco Unified School District. As a result of litigation in 1979, the school board initially adopted a student assignment plan that relied on busing and used socioeconomic status as a proxy for race. But, as in Wake County, that plan was eventually replaced with a choice-based system that weighed school performance among other priorities. Recently, the original "diversity index" (a composite of several different socioeconomic indicators) used in the choice plan to assign students when there were more applicants than available spots was reduced to one variable: performance. Performance in this instance is measured by whether or not a student resides in a census track with average scores in the bottom quintile on standardized tests; like Wake County, San

Francisco Unified does not utilize a measure of an individual student's performance when issuing priority points.[33]

Armed with an understanding of the history of student assignment to schools and lessons from assignment innovations in two large urban school districts, we conclude that while test-based accountability does not appear to have substantively disrupted traditional forms of student assignment to schools, the performance data it has generated is being used to forward long-standing goals of school integration.

STUDENT ASSIGNMENT TO CLASSES AND TEACHERS

Having argued that test-based accountability has not profoundly influenced patterns of student assignment to schools, we move on to consider student assignment to classes and teachers. Here, we pay attention to how these assignment practices have evolved over time, focusing specifically on the extent to which test-based accountability has emerged as a driver in them. *Student assignment* here refers to the processes that guide school decisions about how students are organized into classes (i.e., *assignment to classes*) and by whom they will be taught (i.e., *assignment to teachers*). These processes are not one in the same. While the assignment of students to classes refers to how students are grouped into classes with their peers, the assignment of students to teachers refers specifically to whom a student or class of students will be assigned. As we will show, there are differences in the norms and assumptions behind student assignment at the elementary and secondary school levels. As revealed in our reading of the literature and our own empirical study of twelve schools in Florida, however, these norms and assumptions do not appear to have fundamentally changed in the context of test-based accountability.

As late as the 1920s, there were in the United States at least two hundred thousand one-room schoolhouses in which all students, for the most part, were grouped together for the purposes of instruction. But the search for a more manageable "structural alternative" began as early as the 1830s.[34] By the mid-1800s we began to see separate classrooms, some of which contained students who were alike in terms of age and achievement, arguably the first "criteria" used to populate classrooms in this country.

Once the age-based, grade level system became the norm, principals at the elementary level used a spectrum of student demographic and behavioral information to create balanced classes within each grade. Burns and Mason, for example, found that students' reading ability, behavior, ethnicity, and gender were used by principals in assigning students to classes.[35] In addition to this information, principals used ratings of students' time demands from their previous year's teachers.[36] Behind the use of these data were commitments to create heterogeneous and balanced classes.[37] Sometimes, instead of marshaling information in their decisions, principals randomly assigned students to classes in their pursuit of heterogeneity.

The process was often described as assigning teachers after classes were formed. But because principals had to consider teacher certifications—such as English language learners (ELL), exceptional student education (ESE), gifted and talented education (GTE)—and because some allowed parent requests, student assignment to classes and teachers sometimes occurred simultaneously.[38] In fact, empirical examinations described a process that blended the two forms of assignment instead of one characterized by two easily separable, consecutive steps. In 1988, for example, Harrison and Sinclair attempted to rank the criteria principals use to assign students to teachers by counting the time in which principals reported using each.[39] They found that gender and parental requests topped the list (eight principals reporting), with the consideration of students' receipt of special education services in assigning students to classes as the next-most-cited criterion (seven principals reporting). Other criteria used by principals included teachers' social skills (six), teachers' assessments of students' ability (five), students' developmental readiness (four), test scores (three), ethnicity (two), teaching style (two), students' bus routes (two), and students' language proficiency (one).[40]

At the secondary level, assignment to classes worked differently. Here the efforts to ensure heterogeneity that characterized student assignment at the elementary level gave way to processes that grouped students by ability.[41] Proponents touted *ability grouping* as a tool that facilitates instruction and increases learning, arguing that the process enabled administrators to assign students to classes in a manner that reduced heterogeneity, providing a better fit of students' ability levels, instructional pacing, and teaching methods. Ability grouping was also the subject of much reproach, with critics highlighting the unintentional effects of these groupings that, some argued, created more favorable assignments for high-ability students, led to racial segregation, and further exacerbated existing inequities.[42]

Still the subject of debate, ability grouping dates back to the early 1800s when schools experienced an increase in demand due to immigration and industrialization.[43] The emergence of aptitude and intelligence tests in the early 1920s gave school administrators the technical capacity to use data gathered systematically (if not equitably) to assign students to classes on the basis of ability. These data, in Hallinan's words, were "originally used to assign students to academic, general, and vocational *tracks*, with the courses within those tracks designed to prepare students for postsecondary education or careers."[44] Over the years, due in part to research that shows the deleterious effects of tracking for some student subgroups and the efforts of advocates in the "detracking" movement, tracking (academic, general, and vocational) has, for the most part, been replaced by a system of differentiated course levels, with students being assigned to Advanced Placement (AP), honors, regular, or remedial courses for each core subject (i.e., English, math, science).[45] In this system, which some critics refer to as "neo-tracking," a student may be on different "subject-to-subject matter tracks," wherein she is enrolled in a different level course for each subject (e.g., Honors Algebra and Regular English, for example).[46] In this way, ability grouping remains a dominant and "lasting structural element in America's public schools."[47]

Ability grouping into classes also has implications for the way students are assigned to teachers. Research has shown that teachers by and large prefer teaching courses that enroll higher ability students.[48] Because rules in union-district contracts and normative routines often mean that senior teachers are given preferences in course assignments, secondary students in AP or honors courses are often taught by more experienced instructors.[49] Experience is the only predictor of teacher quality for which there is consistent evidence and, therefore, wide agreement.

TEST-BASED ASSIGNMENT TO CLASSES AND TEACHERS: EVIDENCE FROM FLORIDA

Historically, then, two different purposes have guided the assignment of students to classes and teachers in elementary versus secondary schools. A preference for heterogeneity and balance in the early years of schooling is eclipsed in the later years as homogeneity through ability grouping becomes the norm. What, if anything, has test-based accountability done to influence these purposes and their attendant assignment systems?

As with student assignment to schools, here, too, we expected to find evidence that the accountability infrastructure is changing school practices. In terms of student assignment to classes and teachers, we expected that schools might respond to test-based accountability policies by reassigning lower-performing students to "better" classes and teachers. In elementary schools, for example, we anticipated that students below the test proficiency cutoff might be assigned to teachers whose previous students had demonstrated the highest gains in achievement. We thought that high schools might experiment with assignment policies that placed lower-performing students in higher-level courses or that employed other means for exposing these students to their higher-performing peers. We even expected some talk of teacher-student matching, wherein principals used their knowledge of teachers' attitudes, strengths, and prior performance along with the instructional needs of students to pair individual students with individual teachers.

Results from the few studies that analyse student assignment to classes and teachers under test-based accountability suggest that schools respond by further sorting students by ability and targeting resources on the bubble kids, on those who appear to have the highest probability of moving into the "proficient" category.[50] This practice, according to the authors, results in schools further marginalizing the lowest-performing students. But findings from a recent study by Osborne-Lampkin and Cohen-Vogel, though limited to elementary schools, suggests that a continuing desire to balance student performance, behavior, and demographics in order to create positive learning environments for students and positive teaching environments for educators may, in most schools, counter sorting tendencies.[51]

The study of twelve elementary schools in six Florida districts considered student assignment practices in the context of the state's school grading system. Since the passage of the A+ Plan in 1999, Florida has assigned its public schools annual letter grades (A through F) based largely on students' performance on the Florida Comprehensive Assessment Test (FCAT).[52] Interviews with district and union leaders, school personnel, and parents revealed that the principals and other school administrators in the study schools used student performance data as they assigned students to classes, but not in isolation. In 11 of the 12 schools, participants reported using student performance data and behavior to assign students to classes. Gender was used by the next highest number of schools (9), followed by student designations for special services (i.e., ESE, ELL), a criterion used in 8 schools. In 6 of the 12 schools, participants also reported that race is factored into assignment decisions. Administrators and teachers in the schools that cited performance as a criterion said they used FCAT scores, student grades, or a combination of measures in their student assignment decisions.

Even as they used performance data in the assignment process, school leaders in both higher- and lower-performing schools in the study appeared to be working to achieve balance above any other objective as they assigned students to classes and teachers. Principals did not report that they had used the assignment process as a strategy for overall school improvement. Nor did they, for the most part, speak of efforts to pair students with teachers who had previously demonstrated success with similar students. Further, principals did not speak of assigning bubble kids to their top-performing teachers.

There was one notable exception. In a few of the lower-performing schools, principals responded to their school grades by replacing typical self-contained classrooms with departmentalized instruction in some tested subjects. One principal, for example, went to a departmentalized structure wherein students in grades 2–5 rotated to different teachers for math, science, and reading when her school's grade dropped from its previous high the year before. Interviews with teachers showed that departmentalization in two of the schools had recently been coupled with ability grouping. At an F school, for example, where student math scores were contributing to a low school grade, the principal had implemented class-by-class tracking in mathematics.[53]

Overwhelmingly, however, principals reported assigning students in an effort to ensure balance among classes. In fact, educators in the study used student demographic and performance information "to populate classrooms that spread high, middle and low performers equally across grade level teachers."[54] In working to achieve balanced classrooms, participants in eight of the schools said that they begin with student performance data. In the words of one principal, "I start with my test scores . . . I begin with students that are level 5s [highest performers] and [ensure that] every class has the same number of 5s." She then repeats the process with students whose FCAT scores are 4, 3, 2, and 1.

Principals' reasons for seeking balance within classes and across teachers were grounded in the premise that balance created conducive learning environments for both teachers and students and was the "fair" thing to do. Principals spoke of fairness to students in terms of ensuring that they were in educational environments that met their academic and social needs. "Fairness" to teachers meant distributing students equally in terms of behavior and academic achievement and was intended to help produce manageable learning environments. Principals also reported that fairness to teachers—conceptualized as balancing classrooms by student performance—had become even more important as Florida was preparing to implement its Race to the Top plan, wherein student outcomes would be explicitly linked to teachers' pay and evaluations. In speaking about this pressure on her assignment practices, one principal, for example, relayed that her teachers were coming to her to argue that achievement growth is hard to show when they have a disproportionate number of gifted or high-performing students in their rooms.

STUDENT ASSIGNMENT: LOOKING AHEAD

We began the chapter with the expectation that school responses to test-based accountability include replacing old patterns of student assignment with new ones that better align with school performance objectives. Specifically, we expected test-based accountability to have disrupted traditional practices that privilege schooling kids close to home and in integrated settings and that separate students by ability with systems that assign lower-performing students to "better" schools, classes, and teachers. We found little to support these conjectures, however.

Test-based accountability does not appear to have substantively disrupted traditional forms of student assignment to schools. In fact, the performance data that test-based accountability has generated is being used not to reassign students in an effort to improve school grades but as a legal and politically feasible alternative to race, which dominated student assignment policies during the latter half of the twentieth century. While the incorporation of performance metrics in assignment algorithms shows some promise for accommodating additional factors such as individual student performance in the future (as data become more available and their predictive capacity more stable), it appears that advancements in technical capabilities alone will not transform student assignment practices. For now, at least, the values of equity and diversity continue to shape the ways students are assigned to schools. Of course, open questions remain about just how effectively performance-based student assignment will preserve broader goals of integration and racial justice.

Test-based accountability has also not fundamentally reconfigured the norms that guide how students are assigned to classes and teachers, at least in elementary schools, where the creation of heterogeneous classes—believed to provide for manageable classrooms and to be fair to both students and teachers—continues to be the primary driver behind assignment processes. There is early evidence that concerns over fairness and equity may in fact have grown stronger in the context of accountability-based reforms. In the accountability environment, fairness in student assignment takes on a new meaning as teachers are being increasingly held individually accountable for student outcomes. Interestingly, the early evidence discussed here suggests that policies which require the use of student test score data in teacher evaluations may be motivating teachers to request a larger proportion of lower-performing students, belying some fears that teachers will further marginalize these students under value-added evaluation policies. A closer look at this issue by future researchers is clearly warranted. Similarly, we will have to wait for the publication of additional studies to answer whether student assignment to classes in high schools—traditionally determined almost exclusively by ability—has changed as the result of the accountability infrastructure.

CHAPTER 8

What Makes a "Good" School?

Data and Competing Discourses in a Multilingual Charter Network

LISA M. DORNER
ANGELA B. LAYTON

ecently, a group of educators, community activists, and parents created the new network of elementary Language Immersion Charter Schools (LICS) in the Midwest.[1] Immersion programs like these teach content material in a foreign language, such as Spanish or French, for at least 50 percent of the school day.[2] Employing a constructivist approach to teaching and learning, LICS proclaimed its main goal to be the development of thoughtful multilingual citizens. The founders of the network also viewed LICS as an opportunity to rejuvenate a beleaguered city; they wanted to offer an innovative educational choice and prepare urban youth to compete in a global economy.

At the same time, the performance-based accountability movement, most notably codified in No Child Left Behind (NCLB), also shaped the organization of these schools. This became apparent in the discourse used as founders designed LICS. The schools' defining document, their charter, included myriad references to data and performance measures. Throughout the schools' first year, conversations among board members became increasingly focused on test score data, a shift most noticeable in the subtle change among leaders' descriptions of children from Spanish-speaking immigrant families: at first they were conceived as resourceful and knowledgeable *bilinguals* enrolling in the Spanish Immersion Elementary School and later as students who needed special assistance to become proficient on standardized tests taken in *English*.

In short, during LICS's creation, founding educators, board members, and parents expressed many notions of what makes a "good" school. These notions were shaped and reshaped as the schools implemented their own versions of performance-based accountability. In line with the goals of this volume to examine the infrastructure of accountability, this chapter analyzes the creation of one local system and the discourses competing throughout its development. Specifically, drawing from a larger ethnographic project that documented the development of LICS, we questioned what happens when different scripts about "good schooling," especially those related to the accountability movement, meet up in the process of creating unique educational and linguistic experiences: What were LICS founders' and founding parents' original goals for their schools? In developing LICS, how did they understand data, use data, and create accountability systems? Most important, how did different discourses about good schooling at LICS match, conflict, or compete with each other? We examine these three questions to understand how the greater accountability context (especially the use of students' test scores to hold schools accountable) shapes how diverse stakeholders understand and use data in the development of charter schools. In addition, we explore how cultural scripts and discourses about accountability can define and actually reshape ideas about good schooling.

Based on ethnographic field notes, transcripts of public meetings, and analysis of LICS documents, this chapter makes the following assertions. Most notably, the press for performance-based accountability and the use of data for ongoing school improvement definitively permeates charter schools, as demonstrated in LICS's impressive array of data systems and the discourse of their school board meetings. However, this greater accountability context may work against the creation of innovative schooling that aims to meet the demands of an increasingly global and linguistically diverse world. Represented most tellingly in the changed discourse surrounding native-Spanish-speaking students, data-based decision making deflected parents' and founders' original goals and facilitated a movement toward a more conventional approach to schooling; their data-inspired approach ran counter to the multilingual and constructivist orientations that led to LICS's creation in the first place. The greater accountability movement has created a challenging and conflicting context in which to implement and sustain innovative educational practices that prepare *all* students for transcultural and translingual worlds.

ACCOUNTABILITY, CHOICE, AND CULTURAL SCRIPTS OF GOOD SCHOOLING

Since the 2002 reauthorization of the federal Elementary and Secondary Education Act, No Child Left Behind, much research on accountability systems has highlighted the effects that high-stakes testing has on the work happening *inside* of schools. From classroom instruction, to principals' decision making, to student outcomes, the majority of research has examined the internal effects of data use.[3] In contrast, this chapter examines how organizational members existing mostly *outside* of actual school buildings—parents and founders—conceived and designed new schools of choice within the greater accountability context. That is, we conceive of the infrastructure of accountability as including all the ways that individuals throughout the system interact with, understand, and use data. Toward this end, this section briefly reviews the discourses that underlie accountability and school choice movements. We also explain how neo-institutional studies frame our goal to examine the variety of discourses and values, or cultural scripts that are employed throughout the infrastructure.

Neo-Institutionalism and Cultural Scripts

Broadly, neo-institutionalists explore the cultural scripts and ideas (e.g., policies) that guide the behavior of members within an organization (e.g., practices).[4] Such perspectives expose the relationships between the macro forces of an institution or desires of an organization and the micro interactions or practices of individuals within that space.[5] In any institution, individuals at all levels of the system will take up—and create—different scripts, work with others, and garner particular resources in their negotiations. Thus, neo-institutionalists call for research on *microprocesses,* or how people "locate themselves in social relations and interpret their context."[6]

In education, researchers have used such theories to understand how school personnel take up or alter policies.[7] For instance, one study examined principals' and teachers' negotiation and contestation of sanction policies (putting schools on probation because they have a high percentage of failing students); the ways that educators mobilized different scripts and resources shaped how school personnel changed their instructional practices.[8] Similarly, a study of a new statewide reading initiative demonstrated that schools' cultures, informal and formal networks, and authority relations shaped how teachers framed and implemented aspects of the reform.[9] We know relatively less about how families or founding members of charter schools apply or create such scripts, although the research on school choice provides some direction.

The "Good Schooling" Scripts Behind Accountability and Choice

Historically speaking, U.S. public schools were designed to be accountable to members of the public, whether through school boards or local councils.[10] Then, in the 1980s and 1990s, as part of the outcomes- and standards-based movements, states institutionalized performance-based accountability measures. School districts now had to submit students' standardized test scores to state agencies. The hope was that standards and testing would act as a hortatory policy, enforcing similar values about what schools should teach across each state.[11] NCLB made such strategies "high stakes" in 2002 when it tied federal funding to test results and required the production and representation of all kinds of data.[12]

Public Agenda polls reviewed in 2003 found that respondents believed that state standards and standardized tests helped students learn; 76 percent of public school parents agreed that publishing data like school report cards showing students' aggregate test results "makes principals as well as teachers work harder."[13] When taught how to understand test score data, experimental studies have shown that parents more often chose schools with higher performance data.[14] In essence, the accountability context has provided a particular script for parents (and teachers, too): high test scores signify good schooling.

At the same time as public education professionals were defining standards, implementing statewide accountability systems, and creating databases, the U.S. system was experiencing another reform: school choice. Reportedly to improve schooling, address issues of racial integration, and increase educational equity, many large urban districts created magnet schools in the 1980s. For similar reasons, in the 1990s many states implemented public charter school laws. While magnet schools are district-run schools that offer a special curriculum and accept students from beyond neighborhood boundaries, charter schools often exist outside of districts altogether. Although the laws differ in each state, such schools usually have more autonomy in structure and curriculum in exchange for direct accountability for student performance to a sponsor, or "authorizer."[15] Thus, schools of choice reflect a similar script as described above, because they must collect performance data in order to remain accountable. Equally important, many view charter schools as one way to encourage innovation in failing districts, so the idea that "good schooling is innovative" is another key cultural script.

Other Scripts: Good Schools as Moral, Social, and Identity-Building Spaces

Thus far we have reviewed at least two scripts available to parents and founders as they create schools: good schools have high test scores/data and they have innovative programming. The ways that parents choose schools, however, demonstrates that other scripts exist. Multiple studies—of magnet and charter schools, of high- and low-income parents' educational decisions—have demonstrated that families choose schools using holistic notions about good education. Often these holistic ideas are related to children's social and emotional development, diversity, and identity. Such cultural scripts are formed and framed through conversations (and other qualitative data collected) within one's social networks.

For instance, a literature review from the 1980s on magnet schools found that parents chose schools based on location and what they imagined about the moral and social upbringing of children at those locations.[16] A more recent study examined how white upper- and middle-income parents in California chose their neighborhoods and thus their schools. These individuals trusted what other high-status parents defined as good schools, which were actually described in contrast to poor schools that had students (mostly of color) who presumably misbehaved and cared little about education; the parents in this study rarely visited schools before choosing them, did not examine their instructional programs, and hardly any consulted test scores.[17] In other research, African American parents viewed certain schools as a good fit for their children partly because they believed different locations would provide particular racial experiences for their children; some wanted integrated experiences with whites, while others wanted to build pride and self-esteem with greater exposure to African American history and identities.[18] In short, school choice sometimes has little to do with the promise of academic progress, innovation, or test score results. Instead, parents often rely on friends, creating cultural scripts of good schooling within their social networks. Some of these scripts highlight diversity or multiculturalism, while others place value on one particular community or identity.

THE LICS NETWORK

Charter school legislation varies across the United States. Some schools are built by interested parents, educators, and/or other community members who want to create a new model of schooling. Others are run by for-profit or nonprofit educational management organizations (EMOs), like Edison Learning, Inc.[19] The LICS network was one of the former, led by a parent educator and activist who was interested in creating language immersion schools for her own children and especially for African American children from disadvantaged school districts.

Guided by a board of racially and linguistically diverse influential community members, LICS opened two elementary schools around the height of NCLB's implementation. They were the first public language immersion schools in their midwestern city. The initial enrollment at LICS was similar to the city's population, with slightly higher percentages of children from multilingual homes and children who identified as multiracial or Hispanic. The first two schools enrolled about 50 percent African American, 30 percent white, 10 percent Hispanic, and 10 percent "other" or multiracial students; 50 percent of the students received free or reduced lunches, and 10 percent were classified as English language learners (ELLs).

THE DOMINANCE OF DATA AMONG COMPETING CULTURAL SCRIPTS

We turn now to explore how the coexistence of competing cultural scripts of schooling shaped and reshaped the mission and organization of LICS. Drawing on our critical discourse analysis (CDA) of field notes, school documents, and interview transcripts collected during a three-year ethnography of LCIS's creation, we show how the press for performance-based accountability and the use of data for ongoing school improvement permeated LICS and often conflicted with founders' and parents' preconceived values and notions of good schooling.[20] First, the sheer number of data systems promised in LICS's charter demonstrates how strongly these schools were shaped by the larger accountability context: the data/performance script competed with and overwhelmed the progressive and multicultural scripts in LICS's defining document. Second, we analyze how the accountability context led to the founders' increasing focus on the English language development of children from immigrant families; this demonstrates a major shift from the schools' multilingual stance (multicultural script) to a focus on English language development (as shown through data on state tests, the performance script). Third, analyses of parents' perspectives provide a glimpse of how some stakeholders actually dismissed data, thus demonstrating the limited power that performance-based measures held in certain circumstances.

Multicultural and Progressive Scripts Meet Performance-Based Accountability in the Charter

Before the schools even opened, the founding president of the network publicly described LICS: "[LICS] students will learn all of their course work in a second language. They will experience a curriculum that challenges them to understand the scope of their communities through a global prospective." While this pronouncement highlighted the school's multicultural orientation, the school's written charter, which established its goals and purposes, was dominated by the discourse of accountability and performance. The following CDA of the charter provides a sense of how the founders navigated the broader performance-based accountability context while also promoting their progressive and multicultural commitments.

LICS's charter defined the important components of the school—language immersion and constructivism—as follows:

> The language of instruction for all subject matters will be the *immersion language* [e.g., Spanish or French] of each school. First, students will learn literacy skills in the *immersion language* and then apply these skills to English Language Arts classes which will formally begin in the spring semester of Second Grade.
>
> [Our program] focuses on the development of the whole child in the classroom as well as in the outside world through meaningful interaction in various environments. In a *constructivist, inquiry-based model*, educators encourage students to create meaning in every phase of their learning and pose multi-layered questions of their world.

These statements define at least two of the intersecting goals and values held by LICS founders and parents: constructivist education (progressive script) in a multilingual environment (multicultural script).

Looking more closely at all ways that *language immersion* appeared in the document, we found that immersion was discussed (1) as an educational model that offers academic success and an international/global education for all; (2) within paragraphs about how to create and support language learning and value multilingualism across all stakeholders (children, parents, and personnel); and (3) in sections about appropriate instructional practices for language schools. For example:

> 1. LICS believes in . . . ending world poverty among low-income and African-American populations through language immersion instruction . . . One of the unique benefits of language immersion elementary programs is that they provide a level playing field for all kindergarten students.

2. LICS will cultivate a partnership with [local international/interpretation agencies] to provide translators for families who speak a third language in their home.
3. During the mandatory school day, all instruction occurs in the immersion language for kindergarten, first and second grade classes.

This kind of discourse highlighted the strong values that LICS founders placed on creating and sustaining multilingual school environments.

Likewise, the constructivist and inquiry-based approaches portrayed in the charter foreground the importance of the progressive script at LICS. These terms were used most frequently in a description of curricular choices and justifications, for example:

> This kind of curriculum works in harmony with constructivist learning (where students build knowledge by finding context in their own experiences and perspectives) and inquiry-based learning (where students question and explore a subject to make meaning and to gain deep understanding of it).
>
> Each unit of inquiry is trans-disciplinary in nature. This means that the subject matter is not taught in discrete classes or even in combination, but instead is integrated into holistic units that address several disciplines or subject matters simultaneously.

While these multicultural and progressive scripts coexisted in the document, their existence was overwhelmed by references to the accountability/performance script. The term *language immersion* was used 73 times, and *bilingual/ism* or *multilingual/ism* only 10 times (see Table 8.1). Mention of inquiry learning and constructivism appeared 28 times. In contrast, words associated with the accountability context—such as *standardization, evaluation,* and *measurement*—occurred 313 times.

Indeed, the LICS charter detailed extensive plans for data collection across various actors, all of which the schools promised to use toward improvement (see Table 8.2). From student testing to teacher performance reviews and parent satisfaction surveys, LICS was embracing and implementing data-based decision making, an important component of the broader performance-based accountability context. Specifically, to measure student achievement, the LICS charter declared that the schools would use an array of standardized assessments required by the state, norm-referenced assessments on language and basic skills, classroom evaluations, and student portfolios/projects. The network also promised to assess every staff

TABLE 8.1   Key terms found in the charter

Script	Key terms	Number of instances
Accountability		Total = 313
	Assess/Assessment	75
	Data	44
	Standards/Standardized	41
	Evaluate/Evaluation	38
	Progress	33
	Measure/Measurement	32
	Achieve/Achievement	28
	Test	18
	Accountability	4
Language		Total = 83
	Bilingual	6
	Multilingual	4
	Language immersion	73
Constructivism		Total = 28
	Inquiry learning	21
	Constructivism/ist	6
	Authorship	1

member through regular performance evaluations as well as evaluate community involvement and parent satisfaction through annual surveys.

A closer analysis of the charter's description of teacher evaluations provides an interesting example of how progressive and multicultural scripts competed with ideas about accountability and data. Besides having to assess their students using a variety of standardized tests and classroom projects, LICS teachers had to assess their own work through the annual 360° Performance Evaluation. This process promised to use student achievement growth data, records of parent involvement, professional development attendance, and teachers' self-evaluations. Teachers had to account for all of their work using many different kinds of data in order to receive a merit-based raise:

> LICS will institute a Performance Pay–based annual compensation system for all administrative and professional staff . . . Using explicit performance

TABLE 8.2 Data systems described in LICS charter

Data systems	Designed to evaluate	Conducted by
International Baccalaureate candidacy and accreditation processes	LICS (administration, teaching/learning, curriculum development, etc.)	International Baccalaureate Organization
President's annual performance evaluation	LICS president	Board of directors
Heads' biannual performance evaluation	Heads of school	President
Teachers' annual 360° Performance Evaluation (performance pay-based annual compensation system) Professional development portfolio aligned with National Board of Professional Teaching Standards Individual professional development plans Student growth scores	Teachers	Heads of school Teachers/Peers Self
Student performance analysis (external and internal formative and summative assessments) Standardized state tests Nationally normed early language and literacy assessments Classroom evaluations Student portfolios Other internal assessments and collection of student work such as: 4th grade summer process journal 5th grade culminating project	Students	Teachers Teacher assistants Resource specialists
Assessment of schoolwide goals Academic progress Socioemotional growth Citizenship Community participation	Students Families/Communities	Teachers
Home language survey	English language learners	Unspecified
Community outreach reports	Service providers Volunteers Neighboring organizations	Assistant head of school
Annual parent surveys	Parent satisfaction	Assistant head of school

goals in at least four essential areas: student growth on internal and external assessments, parent participation, professional growth and engagement, and effective data reporting, the 360° performance evaluation will serve as the basis for determining the percentage of bonus or annual raise that each employee will receive.

In short, LICS teachers were held accountable to their administrators for certain measurable aspects of their practice; these ranged from student outcomes, to their own attendance at required meetings, to their students' family involvement at school events.

Ironically, the performance goals listed above neglect mentioning a critical component of teachers' work per the progressive script, perhaps because it is not so easily measured for each individual: the development of inquiry-based education. As explained in another area of the document, the schools were not going to provide their teachers with specific lesson plans or pre-written curricula. Instead, just like LICS students had to be inquirers and designers, teachers were going to work together to create units of inquiry: "[LICS] recognizes classroom teachers as the authors of their work. Instead of providing standardized curricula, units or external assessments . . . the curriculum team focuses on building capacity within each school's faculty." LICS valued ideas of ownership and local control, its charter calling teachers "authors of their work" and suggesting that LICS teachers should not use "standardized curricula" or "external assessments." However, being an author of one's work was mentioned only once throughout the entire charter, in contrast to the myriad references to standardized assessments, data systems, and testing procedures. While LICS placed a high value on its constructivist approach, creativity, and authorship, other discourse in the charter suggested such ideas were relatively less important than accounting for one's work in measurable, state-sanctioned ways.

In summary, there is a huge struggle in official documents to prove that schools' values and visions of providing children with equitable, multilingual, and global models of education can and will be proven through children's resulting test scores. Standardized data systems competed with LICS's progressive and multicultural approach, where teaching and learning were described as a creation of meaning in local settings. The portrayal of teachers as both authors and accountants exemplifies this first case of competition among cultural scripts.

Valuing Multilingualism Meets Measuring Students at School Board Meetings

The multicultural script essential to the founding documents strongly valued multilingualism. As the charter stated, "Each LICS school will resemble a true multilingual society in which individuals interact in the language(s) that are most comfortable for them." However, analyses of board meetings and interviews with founding board members demonstrate that the performance-based accountability context also shaped an increasingly strong focus on student test scores in English, especially for subgroups like children from immigrant families. Ironically, the charter did not list any specific accountability or performance measures for students' development in the target immersion languages. In short, the performance script competed with LICS's desire to value students' abilities to speak many languages, including the ones that children from immigrant families spoke at home.

While the majority of LICS students came from homes that spoke only English, almost 20 percent came from multilingual homes. About half of these families spoke both English and one or more other languages at home, and about half spoke only Spanish; many in this second group were lower-income Mexican immigrants who enrolled their children in the Spanish Immersion Elementary School. They were interested in LICS for many reasons, but especially because they wanted their children to read and write in both English and their families' language. Juan's mother reported, "Me interesó mucho porque está el español y el inglés, que es lo que más batallo con mi hijo mayor, que no sabe leer en español" (I was very interested [in LICS] because there is Spanish and English here, which is what was so challenging for my oldest son, who cannot read in Spanish). Like many other immigrant parents at LICS and across the United States, she hoped that her children would be fluently and academically bilingual and biliterate. [21]

Many public school districts in the area worked with families like Juan's, but almost none offered any opportunities for studying other languages in elementary school. In fact, other school districts only offered support classes in English as a second language, and most of them called students like Juan "limited English proficient." They focused on what students lacked (English proficiency), in their view, rather than what they had (emerging bilingualism). In contrast, in documents and outreach meetings, LICS placed a high value on serving immigrant families and developing an educational program that valued children's languages.

Despite this focus, throughout LICS's first year, founding board members grew worried about the achievement of ELLs, as they called them. (Newer research uses "English learners" or "emerging bilinguals."[22]) This concern grew out of the accountability context. In the third year of operation, the eldest students at LICS would enter third grade and would be the first group to take the high-stakes state tests. LICS's board knew that students' test performances would be analyzed by subgroup per accountability mandates, and they were concerned about the performances of their English learners. They knew that if each subgroup did not perform better than the local school district, their sponsoring university might close them down. Echoing these concerns, one member said: "In the Spanish classes where there are a couple of Spanish-speaking kids, the English kids are learning Spanish faster and they're learning English faster. It's all anecdotal, of course, the data are all anecdotal, but . . . there's not much opportunity for the kids to speak English, okay?"

Despite all of the testing LICS promised, this board member noted concerns based on "anecdotal" data—observations of the schools and conversations he had with LICS staff and families—rather than on performance data/test results. And he was right about their lack of opportunity to speak English, at least in a formal academic way; students were receiving nearly 100 percent of their regular classroom instruction in Spanish through second grade. While this kind of model has proven beneficial for English learners' academic and linguistic progress (gaining literacy first in one's home language), LICS leaders felt that it might not prepare them to succeed on standardized tests in English by third grade. Indeed, research suggests that it takes until fifth grade to meet and exceed English-dominant, monolingual peers' academic achievement in English.[23] The board member continued: "So we just want to make sure that they don't get lost as we move along here."

To address these concerns about student performance, founders made a change to board meetings; they began to require that principals give regular reports on student test scores. Conversations at these meetings then turned to, "How can we ensure English Learners succeed on the state tests?" These kinds of conversations demonstrate yet another competition among cultural scripts. As an immersion school network, LICS valued multilingualism, and it also provided native speakers of the immersion languages with perhaps the best model for their linguistic and academic development. However, with state tests looming, the discourse changed, focusing on students' abilities in English rather than making sure all students were emerging as bilinguals.

Measuring Family Satisfaction and (De)Valuing Data at Parent Meetings

Here we explore the uncertain power that accountability data held in certain circumstances though an examination of how parents used—and sometimes dismissed—different kinds of performance measures. To do so, we rely on analyses of transcripts from two town hall meetings as well as related interviews on how parents chose LICS for their children.[24]

Studying school choice at this site, we found that LICS parents did not rely on performance scripts. That is, they did not equate good schooling with good academic achievement or the promise of high test scores. While some parents, like Juan's mother, enrolled children primarily for the language instruction, others were interested in the inquiry-based education, the foreign staff, and/or the racially integrated student body. That is, more often than not, they used multicultural and progressive scripts, believing that good schools should value multilingualism and/or constructivist approaches to education. For example, in a conversation about the mission of the schools, one African American mother said, "I honestly believe that it is to make our children better experienced, I guess. Um, more equipped, more diverse. Give them a greater opportunity, because if you notice, you look in a paper, a lot of things are veering toward, it's better to have a second language. So if you're bilingual, that's a plus." And in response to a questionnaire about why he chose LICS, one white father wrote that "the language immersion provides both a valuable lifelong skill and critical brain development, the [inquiry-based] curriculum is a solid proven educational framework, and foreign teachers and a diverse student body offer a diversity of interactions that will serve to broaden children's worldviews."

Obviously, these parents were concerned about education writ large—"equipping kids," developing their "brains"—but they did not say that they chose the network because it would help their children succeed on tests or get into the right middle school. Moreover, like other parents, they did not depend on test score data (from LICS or similar schools) in making these claims. Rather than examine accountability-driven data, most parents formed their opinions about LICS by collecting other kinds of data in a variety of ways, much like prior research has found. They drew from conversations with family members, friends, and preschool teachers; observations of demonstration lessons; and prior knowledge or assumptions they had about what schooling should be and how they wanted to identify.

Professed disbelief of school survey results likewise supports this assertion that some parents did not value performance data to the degree policy makers might expect. In town hall meetings, LICS's president annually reported the Parent Satisfaction Survey, a questionnaire created as part of the schools' attention to NCLB parent involvement policies. In the first year, based on responses from 50 percent of LICS family members (who represented the networks' racial, ethnic, linguistic, and socioeconomic diversity), she presented overwhelmingly positive data:

- 99% of respondents believed that their child's teacher engages their child
- 97% of respondents believed that their child is learning and growing
- 97% of respondents believed that their child's teacher supports child when s/he is struggling
- 94% of respondents believed that parents feel welcome
- 94% of respondents believed that their child's teacher has skills to be successful
- 91% of respondents believed that their child's teacher makes the time to communicate with family individually
- 85% of respondents believed that their child's teacher manages class well
- 81% of respondents believed that their child's teachers use rewards and consequences appropriately

In short, this survey demonstrated that the majority of respondents were satisfied with all aspects of the schools; overall, 91 percent marked that their school met or exceeded expectations. However, the parents who came to this town hall meeting (representing about 15 percent of the parents) had serious questions, especially about discipline, classroom management, and behavior issues.

These vocal and involved family members—most of whom were white or African American middle-class parents—were using other (not performance-related or mandated) data to assess the schools. Just like the families who made the initial choice for LICS, and like the board member who used anecdotal data in assessing LICS, their concerns about the schools were formed in their particular social networks and based on stories they heard, their own interactions and observations at school, and assumptions about other students/families. Given these perspectives and experiences, they did not believe that such a great majority of families could be so satisfied. At one point during the forum, a parent even asked, "Is it just me or does that survey seem unbelievably skewed? Because tonight all the parents are concerned about the same thing [behavior]."

In summary, we suggest here that parents were negotiating among many scripts about good schooling in their decisions and interactions at LICS. They did not primarily use accountability data to make their choices for LICS. Like the research briefly reviewed above, parents made decisions based on fuzzier beliefs about good schooling; they drew on both the multicultural and progressive scripts, among others. Yet, the analysis of the town hall meetings suggests that even when performance data are available, parents may not believe them. They may even dismiss it. In short, other kinds of data and cultural scripts, often unrelated to test scores or survey results, shape schools at all levels of the infrastructure.

DATA AND COMPETING DISCOURSES ABOUT GOOD SCHOOLING

This chapter set out to examine the infrastructure of accountability by exploring how the founders and parents of new charter schools use, implement, and understand performance-based data systems amidst their local goals and commitments. In this case study of LICS, we found that the institutional reach of the nationwide accountability movement is extensive; it can shape the discourse and practices of stakeholders, even those outside of the classroom. In turn, the implementation of local data systems, an offshoot of state-sponsored accountability infrastructure, is not smooth. As such systems are created, performance scripts must compete with local values. Sometimes, such scripts actually reverse initial notions that educational leaders have about good schooling; at other times, people ignore performance data entirely.

The development of large-scale information systems certainly contributes to the proliferation of local systems and assessments. It is significant that LICS thoughtfully planned how to measure success across a variety of actors in a variety of ways. It promised to allow educational leaders to use performance data to assess the academic achievement of students often "left behind"—including emerging bilinguals from immigrant families. And it provided a range of data on teacher performance and parent satisfaction that educational leaders could use to determine new directions for their schools.[25]

Most significantly, however, the development of large-scale information systems also shapes particular discourses about performance that can redefine notions about or practices toward good schooling. One intention of the charter school movement was to spur educational innovation through the creation of schools that endorse new methods and appeal to their local communities. At LICS, parents and founders highlighted the progressive, multilingual education that their schools would provide their diverse student population. Yet, the network's charter placed more emphasis on teachers' measurable outcomes rather than their creation of inquiry-based lessons; and board members questioned how to ensure English learners were proficient in English rather than multilingual. LICS's focus on performance and assessment data reshaped the purposes that founding leaders ascribed to their schools, altering their original progressive and multicultural scripts.

In summary, the case of LICS illustrates how the infrastructure of accountability—as it enters schools through data systems and discourses—reshapes how we practice, organize, and even think about our schools and their proper purposes. While stakeholders have multiple ideas about what "good schools" are and do, these ideas coexist and compete with performance-based accountability scripts, which define good schools as those that produce good data (test scores). This chapter asks us to consider what is lost when our broader goals of creating questioning, global, multilingual citizens are marginalized as we hold our schools accountable to narrow measures.

CHAPTER 9

Technologies for Education and Technologies for Learners

How Information Technologies Are (and Should Be) Changing Schools

RICHARD HALVERSON
R. BENJAMIN SHAPIRO

The revolution in information technologies is changing the way we think about education. This chapter explores the curious ways in which new technologies have and have not been taken up by schools. We propose a contrast between technologies for *education* and technologies for *learners*. The contrast is intended to highlight how the cultures of use in schools and in the world explain the ways that technologies have and have not flourished in schools and point toward productive opportunities for schools to embrace the power of new technologies.

TECHNOLOGIES FOR EDUCATION

The advent of data-driven technologies, such as student information systems, formative assessment systems, statewide school information networks, and computer-adaptive testing, has come to redefine twenty-first-century public education. Technologies for education generate, collect, and distribute information on the degree to which students meet learning goals, while data-driven decision practices organize technologies to create feedback loops that can guide instructional practices in light of student achievement. In particular, the contemporary discussion of data use in schools has been dominated by an accountability logic that uses information to measure the school's ability to produce learning goals. The accountability logic is grounded in (1) clearly defining the common standards toward which learning should be directed; (2) developing assessments that measure the degree to which education systems achieve these standards; and (3) providing feedback to schools on the gaps between current and expected achievement outcomes. Accountability logic guides the design of new tools and practices that, in time, are routinized and establish an accountability culture.[1]

Technology use in accountability cultures focuses on how data systems allow members to monitor progress toward producing outcomes. Data-driven decision making links standards, assessments, and instruction into a system through which data on performance flows. Attending to data-driven decision making practices requires educators to rein in the considerable amount of information generated by assessments and to focus attention on efforts that relate data directly to student learning.[2] Data-driven decision-making practices hold organizational outcomes constant (i.e., learning goals for the system and for the students) and cultivate the ability of local actors and learners to organize and select the appropriate instructional means and assessments. Schools and districts orchestrate new forms of professional interaction to translate data-driven diagnoses into new practices.[3] The role of information technologies is to provide the capacity to collect and distribute information to support accountability.

The multiple layers of information management necessary for successful accountability practices play a central role, using data to improve school performance. Data technologies, such as student information systems, benchmark assessment systems, computer-guided instructional tools and learning management systems, store and distribute assessment information to relevant stakeholders. Taken together, the technologies bind monitoring practices into the resilient accountability systems that have come to define early-twenty-first-century public schools. Schools across the United States purchase information technologies, which originated in the business world, to meet the accountability-driven reform agenda. Schools are expected to furnish and implement information systems that capture, store, and track student performance on standardized tests.[4] In the following sections, we highlight three types of technologies for education that have been used widely in recent public school reforms: student information systems, assessment technologies, and instructional programs and systems.

STUDENT INFORMATION SYSTEMS

The defining technologies for education collect, store, distribute, and provide analytic tools on student performance data. The most ubiquitous type of technology for learning is the *student information system* (SIS). The districtwide data system provides the information technology conduit network through which accountability information flows. SIS are typically third-party, commercial database systems that provide real-time access to student attendance, demographics, and performance; warehouses that store and provide access to information; and analytic tools that allow users to interpret data in various ways.[5] They often also include components that organize curricula and instructional materials, manage financial information, provide planning tools, coordinate scheduling and student services, and open the data system for public access. Because different vendors often provide these components, over 60 percent of school technology leaders continue to face the challenge of integrating information flow across platforms.[6]

The SIS takes information from students, classrooms, teachers, and schools and reports it to state agencies, board members, and policy makers. Thorn described how student information systems are designed to organize data for administrative purposes—that is, for school leaders to measure and monitor the success of the instructional system.[7] In Thorn's view, the function of the student information system is to analyze information taken from the school and classroom context in order to render judgment on the instructional quality. Thus, the SIS reinforces the tendency of technologies for education to support the information needs of systems managers (administrators) rather than system participants (teachers and students).

The focus of SIS has recently shifted toward tools that provide teachers with the information they need to guide instruction. Means, Padilla, and Gallagher note that while 90 percent of districts capture student performance and attendance information, less than half can link outcome data to instructional or teacher practices.[8] Teachers are largely left to their own (typically low-tech) devices to organize the disparate data sources that need to be managed in successful classrooms. In classrooms, educators consider student problems individually, rather than collectively, and think carefully about the relation between interventions and individual student outcomes.[9] And, of course, the only role for students in the typical SIS is to contribute information. Generated by accountability pressures, the contemporary SIS responds mainly to the custodians, not the customers, of the education system.

ASSESSMENT TECHNOLOGIES

Assessments provide the bulk of the performance data in contemporary accountability systems. The assessments required by No Child Left Behind

(NCLB) have transformed the data landscape for local schools and districts. NCLB required all public schools to test students in grades 3–8 and one year in high school in reading, math, and science. The tremendous amounts of data generated by required testing sparked the need for SIS technologies. It also sparked public critique of current testing practices and learning standards.

The widespread implementation of high-stakes assessments has illustrated the inherent (and often tacit) flaws of test-driven accountability practices. The five testing companies that controlled 90 percent of the testing market faced critical problems of quality control as the NCLB-driven market ramped up.[10] The widespread use of standardized tests for accountability has resulted in a press to reform assessments led in two directions: toward reforming what students need to know (standards) and toward developing new approaches to testing. One reform direction was to develop new national standards that could bring together the diverse state-based learning standards. The Common Core State Standards initiative, for example, rewrote K–12 learning standards into statements that are readily translatable into measurement activities.[11] The need to articulate national learning standards into measurable learning outcomes has also led to the development of learning progression research.[12] Learning progressions trace the development of student understanding in a discipline and predict the trajectories students follow to gain knowledge over time.[13] Understanding learning development at the disciplinary level also helps teachers anticipate the misunderstandings that typically arise in the course of learning.[14] Articulating learning progressions affords more targeted assessments that can provide formative data on the microprocesses of learning.[15]

Computer-adaptive assessments present a new form of technology-driven testing that provides timely information to document student learning. Computer-adaptive tests tailor the difficulty of exam items to the individual test taker. This allows for a more efficient test-taking experience, and the computer-based testing provides instant feedback. These tests give new currency to formative assessment research as educators and reformers consider how to generate and use testing data to improve instructional practices. Benchmark assessments, such as the Northwest Evaluation Association's Measures of Academic Progress (MAP) or McGraw Hill's Acuity, provide timely feedback on student learning in terms of content standards. To be sure, the emergence of formative assessment tools has not been smooth. Shepard notes that interim assessment systems narrow the curriculum to the knowledge evaluated by standardized tests, and Blanc, Christman, Liu, Mitchell,

Travers, and Bulkley suggest that successful use of interim assessment technologies requires robust professional capacity to use data for instruction.[16] Still, the widespread use of benchmark assessments—by 2008, 79 percent of U.S. districts had benchmark assessment systems—point toward a significant investment in computer-adaptive testing.[17]

New assessment technologies for education are also being adapted for mobile devices. Early literacy tools, such as DiBELS, served as models for easy-to-administer assessment on student learning progress. Developers have responded to this interest by building handheld versions of formative assessments. Wireless Generation's mClass products operationalize early reading assessments into handheld tools to help teachers manage assessment data and link performance data to the student information system.[18] Classroom response systems, such as clickers, provide another level of whole-class feedback on instruction. The digital interaction of classroom response systems not only provides instant feedback to students; it also leaves a record of interaction that teachers can view as evidence of student understanding and participation.[19]

INSTRUCTIONAL TECHNOLOGIES

Learning management systems (LMS) are the instructional counterparts of student information systems. A typical LMS automates course administration, provides user guides to learning resources, organizes and provides access to learning content, and personalizes learning tools in terms of user preferences.[20] An LMS mediates interaction between instructors and learners through resources such as discussion boards, drop boxes, chat tools, visualizations, and wikis. Online LMS, such as Blackboard and Moodle, are widely used in universities and are growing in popularity in K–12 education. A typical LMS affords "teachers generating content, teachers gathering resources, teachers grouping and sequencing information, and teachers giving the information to students."[21] The controls of the LMS are in the hands of the educators, not the students.

While the LMS is used to coordinate learning activities toward school learning goals, other technologies have emerged to guide instruction in the classroom. Computer-assisted instruction (CAI) structures activities for individual learners. CAI systems can range from page-turning programs that replicate the structures of textbooks to video games that scaffold learning activities toward desired outcomes. Schools have long made investments in comprehensive computer-assisted learning platforms, such as PLATO and Read180, to provide supplemental instructional support for struggling learners. Virtual schools draw on the capacities of LMS and CAI to provide course content for millions of students.

SIS, new approaches to assessment, and instructional technologies are defining types of technologies for education. Each technology supports the goals of educators dedicated to teaching students toward system outcomes. Each takes the disciplinary organization of knowledge as a starting point and assumes that the goal of an instructional system is to organize resources as means toward these valued social ends. Technologies for education define data use in terms of fixed organizational outcomes. The use of data in these contexts comes to define learning in terms of helping students achieve specified learning goals and defines technology use in terms of the information educators use to estimate learning progress and the instructional tools that guide students toward learning goals. In each case, technologies for educators assume that the goals of education are fixed and that technologies should be organized to facilitate means to these goals. We turn next to the kinds of technologies that put the control of the learning environment firmly in the grasp of the learner and that flourish in contexts outside the classroom.

TECHNOLOGIES FOR LEARNERS

Technologies for learners are organized to support the needs of users, not system designers, administrators, or educators. The vast and expanding realm of entertainment and consumer technologies is dominated by technologies for learners. Technologies such as social networking, video gaming, Wikipedia, Google, fantasy sports, and mobile devices flourish by serving the needs of their users. Tools that are difficult to use, have arcane interface designs, limited customizability, or awkward conditions of use are cast aside in favor of tools that give users what they want. Goals are chosen by the learner, not by the system in which the learner participates. There is no successful use, for example, of Facebook. Rather, Facebook serves a wide variety of user goals. Some people use Facebook to network for jobs, others play online games, and others engage in hybrid spaces that allow multiple paths for interaction with friend networks.[22] Instead of information being generated for system administrators to assess system success, here information is generated to serve the interests of users.[23] Technologies for learners give users control of relevant information and provide systems to manage cognitive load so that users can focus on how to facilitate valued activity.

It may seem odd to label these largely consumer tools as "technologies for learners." After all, users are not students, and the motivations for use of new media tools may seem to have little to do with learning. A key point of our argument, however, is that information technologies allow us to reclaim the range of what counts as *learning*. Accountability-driven environments narrow the definition of learning to individual student mastery of school-defined knowledge. This narrowing enables schools to clearly define what counts as learning at the cost of the scope of how learning happens in the real world. Technologies for learners provide tools to recover the inquiry, interest, and social aspects of everyday learning. Many occasions for real-world learning involve finding answers to pressing questions. Information and search resources, such as Google and Wikipedia, are designed to facilitate just-in-time inquiry by answering user questions.

These technologies for learning also rely on user interest to motivate participation. Frequently, users are interested in mundane concerns (e.g., Where is the movie playing? How was the upcoming blockbuster movie reviewed?). However, there is no necessary opposition between mundane and learning, and technologies for learning serve the sublime as well as the ridiculous. At a social level, real-world learning relies on participation in knowledge communities that help users gain expertise and learn which kinds of questions to ask. Many technologies for learners, such as video games and digital media production worlds, generate cultures that invite users to understand complex media and also induct users into knowledge-producing communities. Participation in knowledge communities motivates learners to engage in knowledge creation and sharing and also leads learners to explore new domains of knowing and doing. Technologies for learners revive these issues of inquiry, interest, and community as the defining components of learning. In so doing, they enable us to see the ubiquity of learning outside the school context and how information technologies can recapture this wider world of learning.

The effort to shift the definition about what counts as learning has received considerable comment. Researchers and writers have remarked at how new media distract us from the educational and social goals we value.[24] Because, in many cases, learners would rather participate in new media environments, advocates of schools have dismissed and downplayed the potential of these technologies. We read about the detrimental effects of new media technologies on our students—how Google makes them stupid, how Facebook makes them sad and more likely to become bullies, how Wikipedia leads to plagiarism, and how video games make them violent and poor readers.[25] Seen from the perspective of the technologies for education, new media technologies threaten the motivation of learners to participate in business-as-usual school practices.

The idea of participatory culture challenges the disparaging, antisocial narratives of the effects of new media on users and is central to understanding how new technologies are reshaping ideas about learning. Participatory cultures emerge as the social expression of new media environments in which members use, create, and share content and strategies for engagement. Rather than conceiving of new media participation as an isolating, antisocial experience, the notion of participatory cultures draws attention to the range of social interactions created by participation with new media. Jenkins and colleagues propose that participatory cultures afford four forms of engagement:

- *Affiliations.* Memberships, formal and informal, in online communities centered around various forms of media, such as Facebook, message boards, and game guilds
- *Collaborative problem solving.* Working together in teams, formal and informal, to complete tasks and develop new knowledge, such as Wikipedia, alternative reality gaming, and fantasy sports
- *Expressions.* Producing new creative forms, such as digital sampling, digital media production, fan fiction, and modding
- *Circulations.* Shaping the flow of media, such as remix, mash-ups, podcasting, Flickr, and blogging.[26]

When viewed as positive venues for interaction, each form of engagement in participatory cultures has obvious value to contemporary education discussions. Affiliations, for example, complement the disciplinary focus of schools and engage participants in affinity spaces.[27] Expressions give new ways for learners to represent what they know in new media and to receive authentic feedback on the learning process. Collaborative problem solving highlights how participatory cultures engage users in building knowledge about unknown problems (such as which slugger will emerge on a baseball team [fantasy sports], where the best sushi is in Biloxi [Yelp!], or how crowd-sourcing protein folding can cure AIDS [Foldit.com]). Circulations provide a model of student work as "knowledge assembler" rather than as a single-source content generator. Participatory cultures typically have low barriers to expression and engagement, multiaged membership and informal mentors who pass along experience to novices, a shared belief that contributions matter, and members who feel a social connection with one another.

Together, these forms of interaction provide actual contexts for new literacies that allow learners to engage in socially recognized ways of generating, communicating, and negotiating meaningful content and participating in socially recognized discourse practices.[28]

In short, these examples reveal the contrasts in data use and generation between technologies for education and technologies for learners. Technologies for education generate data for system administrators; technologies for learners generate data for learners. Participatory cultures thrive with data technologies designed to provide users with rich information on their learning goals, learning resources, social interactions, and identity status. For schools to integrate technologies for learners, schools will need to come to terms with the challenges, the costs, and the value of transforming school cultures into participatory cultures.

We provide here three examples of the kinds of participatory cultures sparked by technologies for learners: social networking, Wikipedia, and video gaming. These wildly popular innovations were sparked by new technologies that scaffold user participation, provide multiple channels of data to guide user interaction, and facilitate learning and fun. Understanding the interaction of technology design and user culture point toward how schools might adapt technologies for learners to current education contexts.

Social Networks

Social networks provide the prototypical example of the social dimensions of participatory cultures. It is difficult to grasp just how pervasive social networking has become. As of late 2012, Facebook claims over 1 billion monthly active users, with 500 million active *daily* users. Eighty percent of Facebook users are outside the United States or Canada; and Facebook is available in more than 70 languages.[29] The professional social network LinkedIn has 150 million registered users in 200 countries.[30] People use social networks to maintain contact with friends, relatives, and colleagues and to become aware of new knowledge creation. Facebook and Twitter have become the news feeds for the new media generation, as breaking stories often trend before being released by broadcast media.

Social networks serve as both ends and means of learning processes. Learners develop interests in and through participation in knowledge communities.[31] Members engage with communities of practice to learn how to act and respond to other members.[32] In learning communities, members rely on social interaction to determine what kinds of questions to answer, what counts as an answer, and how knowledge is created and shared as a cultural resource. Thus, active participation in social networks is an outcome that marks successfully acculturated learners. Social networks also operate as means for learning. At a basic level, learners rely on social networks to find answers to their questions. Vibrant knowledge communities motivate learners to participate in knowledge dissemination and creation. In most cases, though, access to knowledge communities is tacitly embedded in cultural practices and closed to most forms of investigation. In other words, the defining contexts for real-world learning are either invisible or off-limits for designers of learning environments.

Social network sites make some of the connections in sociocultural communities visible (by friending and through group membership) and thus provide valuable tools for visualizing and designing social interaction around knowledge access and creation. Studying knowledge dissemination across social network sites and studying how students use social networks for academic and social purposes can provide a window into how learners engage in real-world knowledge communities. Learning environment designers have turned to social network tools such as Grockit.com (homework and academic support), professional networking (linkedin.com), and do-it-yourself affinity-based networks (ning.com, Google Groups) to create and maintain knowledge-building communities. When built around existing affinity spaces, social networks can support users in learning social norms, tastes, knowledge, and culture through expressions of preferences exchanged while hanging out online. For example, RemixWorld, created by the Digital Youth Network (DYN), is a social network used by youth to learn about how to produce digital media products. RemixWorld mentors use the system to support mutual engagement to learn how to create new media art. The Remix-World community is a source of public critique that provides the kinds of feedback from which designers learn to redesign their work and in which youth learn to participate in a community of artists.[33]

Unfortunately, the extremely restricted use of social networks in schools has limited the benefits of networking to out-of-school interactions. It has proven difficult for many of these "designed" networks to take root in existing school structures and result in the kinds of vibrant interest-based social interactions that characterize learning in new media environments. The institutional discomfort (legal, moral, and practical) about integrating students' social lives into the classroom has thwarted efforts to bridge the divide between networks and schools. Facebook use in schools has been stigmatized as a catalyst for sexting, bullying, and sparking inappropriate relationships between faculty and students. Appropriate-use policies and software censors at many schools simply ban Facebook access from school networks. Casting social networking in detrimental terms curtails the extraordinary potential for social networking tools to transform learning in schools. Social networking provides a channel for students to construct and maintain representations of their identity that persist within and outside the institution.

Wikipedia

Wikipedia is the leading example of a collaborative problem-solving participatory culture. Like Facebook, the scope of activity in Wikipedia is astounding. Wikipedia currently has over 3.8 million articles in 200-plus languages. More than 1,000 new topics are added every day. Wikipedia is the world's largest collaborative writing project. Each Wikipedia article is written and edited by some of the 16 million registered users. There have been over 500 million page edits on Wikipedia, with an average of 20 edits per page.[34] Even though the reliability of Wikipedia has been questioned by teachers and librarians, the quality of Wikipedia entries has been shown to rival the *Encyclopedia Britannica,* and the scope of Wikipedia articles greatly surpasses any other encyclopedia source.[35] Like Facebook and Google, the Wiki has spawned a vocabulary and technology of its own as the name for a Web site that supports asynchronous user contributions and collaboration through simple text editors and threaded contributions.

A key to Wikipedia's success as a participatory culture is the systematic integration of formative feedback into the user experience. Black and William argue that formative feedback, which involves direct commenting and coaching on student's work, is among the most effective strategies for improving learning.[36] The Wikipedia community, like the fanfiction and open-source software development communities, is structured for massive communities of practice to correct, suggest, and adjudicate disputes about posted content. Users typically receive feedback on entries within twenty-four hours and are expected to use the feedback to recraft their writing. Crowd-sourcing authorship affords multiple channels of formative feedback on author contributions. Like an enormous massively multiplayer game, Wikipedia users are rated by the success of their contributions and the quality of their challenges. Participation in legendary Wikipedia entry disputes (on topics such as Scientology, abortion, and the correct spelling of Gdansk/Danzig) establishes the status of power users. The Wiki community makes editing decisions and records of participation public as a model of information transparency as well as to encourage new user participation.

Wikipedia is a leading example of how formative feedback practices can be implemented at scale to produce high-quality writing.

Video Games

Video games are the bête noire of formal education. Often taken as diversions at best, and as evil at worst, it is difficult for many educators, and even more difficult for education researchers, to consider video games as a model for how to organize learning. Yet, the video game market is expected to grow from $54 billion in 2009 to an anticipated $86 billion by 2014, exceeding the film market and doubling the music market.[37] The average American child spends over an hour playing video games every day.[38] McGonigal describes how the eleven million *World of Warcraft* (*WoW*) players have collectively spent 5.93 million years in the massively multiplayer online game—roughly the same amount of time that humans have been on Earth.[39] The political and social debates of the value of this extraordinary new kind of entertainment have often degenerated into stereotypes of lonely adolescent boys staying up too late at night, eating junk food, not doing homework, and becoming inspired to commit violent acts as a result of playing violent games. It can seem as though the only cultural "community" to which such players belong is a shared consumer ethos that exchanges isolating diversion for money.

Caricaturing game players, however, leads educators to overlook the extraordinary internal design elements of video games that can serve as models for technology-driven learning environments. As Gee notes, games provide challenges that progress in difficulty or content in order to support the development of players' expertise as they inhabit in-game roles and make decisions.[40] That is, players develop expertise as they discern the underlying rules of the game played.[41] Successful games scaffold player progression seamlessly by moderating the difficulty of in-game challenges and by providing well-designed data displays that offer relevant formative feedback. Games allow players to inhabit alternative realities and to experiment with possible selves. Players can take on the role of pilots or presidents, raise families, design creatures, or to engage in fantasy/role play. In these identities, players make consequential decisions within the game world and receive feedback about the quality of their decisions. Game play can thus develop players' content expertise, computer programming skills, socialorganizational experience, and writing skills.[42] The design of contemporary video games provides the leading model how interface design, task articulation, and assessment design can be used to structure virtual learning tasks.

The third spaces that develop around video game play give rise to several forms of participatory cultures. Many games, such as *World of Warcraft,* immerse players in a shared virtual place where players must actively coordinate with one another to achieve success. *WoW* is simultaneously played by millions of people on a monthly subscription model that provides players access to a rich, multilevel virtual world. *WoW* players interact with other players in guilds (larger, coordinated groups in which players are assigned specific roles) to engage in quests (long missions to achieve specific goals that result in rewards relevant to game play). *WoW* technologies facilitate the game-play process and provide constant feedback to players on the success (or failure) of individual and collaborative play. The technology system in *WoW* is designed to support the transition from individual to group play and to provide feedback for players throughout the game context.

INTEGRATION CHALLENGES

We have argued that the divergent logics of accountability and participatory cultures have resulted in significantly different approaches to technological innovation. These logics contribute to a significant divide in the ways technologies have been used in and out of schools. The demand of accountability cultures presses for all participants to engage in the same content, not just those lured by affinity groups. Custodians of accountability cultures have not accepted this dependence on learner commitment to the disciplinary mastery as a condition for learning environment design. Instead, schools have moved in the direction of technologies that can improve learning for all students in traditional disciplines and have chosen to shun investigating new media technologies, such as video games or digital media production initiatives, with high learning curves and unreliable outcomes.

The appropriate use of data on learning also plays a defining role in the two approaches to technology adoption. Technologies for education generate data on learning to measure and guide system progress, while technologies for learners generate data to guide user progress. Can we shift the discourse toward thinking about how technologies for learners could transform public education? Here we present three areas of possible investigation/design that may bridge the gap between technologies for educators and for learners: (1) orchestrating convergence of administrative technologies, (2) designing participatory media production spaces, and (3) bridging assessment of learning with assessment for learners.

Orchestrating Convergence

The technologies that support student information systems, learning management systems, and social network systems are quite related. Each involves coordinating access to distributed databases; each involves customizable user profiles, querying tools, and context organization. Student information systems are *about* students instead of *for* students. SIS user profiles encode permissions about which *information about others* users are allowed to see. Social networking technologies represent the other extreme of organizing access. Social network systems (SNS) allow the user to create a local information cluster in order to customize who gets to see what kinds of information in the user profile. The persistent agent profile allows users to customize how they appear to others on the network (creating a medium through which users can design the interface for what James calls the "social me").[43] Social network user profiles encode permissions about which *information about themselves* others are allowed to see.

Learning management systems may provide a bridge between institution-controlled (SIS) and user-controlled (SNS) data exchange. LMS connect persistent user profiles with institutional learning resources through technologically mediated opportunities for interaction. Social network profiles could serve as links into an LMS in which content and certain information about learners (course enrollment, instructor, learning goals, etc.) are provided by the SIS. SNS motivation structures, such as customizing presentation of self, point- and merit-based participation rewards, and scaffolded task structures, could inform the learning process and provide multileveled opportunities to coordinate social interaction around learning. Students could retain a self-created, persistent self-image (avatar) across learning environments that would feed information about success and failure back into the (properly secured) SIS. Maintaining a context for persistent interaction among digital selves would provide students with another channel for participation in learning and might well inject a measure of institutional influence (and civility!) into the currently self-policing adolescent social network communities. Research into the next generation of LMS might well create the kinds of technologically facilitated interaction that would produce better information on learning *and* information for learners.

Designing Participatory Learning Spaces

Homework is a traditional school practice that involves the rehearsal, or repetition, of known content as a demonstration that learners have met the learning goals (set by others). Even if it is collaboratively produced, the design constraints in which homework assignments are developed prohibit much meaningful learning production. Meaningful production, however, is a central feature of participatory cultures. If we are to utilize technologies for learners in school contexts effectively, we must revisit the challenge of homework as an opportunity for students to engage in authentic production. How can meaningful production opportunities be designed, in the context of schools, that produce both information on learning and information for learners?

Participatory cultures in technology and the arts provide examples of meaningful production. Youth media arts organizations provide models of how students can develop new literacy skills through making sophisticated media products to share with authentic audiences. Organizations such as ReelWorks, Street Level, Appalshop, and In Progress have already established programs that guide youth through the challenging course of creating, critiquing, and sharing authentic new media products.[44] Reframing media arts or technology development courses in terms of these vibrant participatory cultures may present a viable option for high school program design. Similarly, technologies for learners are transforming civic participation around the world. The majority of youth already gets political information, hears and voices perspectives, and learns norms of public interaction and participation in online spaces.[45] Online participation in nonpolitical participatory cultures provides youth with models for public interaction that can be leveraged to support engagement in traditional political and social arenas. Situating civic education in participatory communities, such as Wikipedia editing, can help teach students norms for appropriate public interaction with authentic audiences that can be carried outside the school experience. Exploring the (relatively) unmonitored subject areas in the typical school program provides a unique opportunity to experiment with technologies for learners in schools.

Assessment

Assessment for accountability focuses on summative assessment of the quality of system outputs; assessment for participation focuses on formative assessment to guide the learners' process. The similarities in underlying assessment technologies, however, suggest ways in which new practices can emerge if we can change the cultures in which practices are embedded. Video games provide the most compelling examples of how information technologies organize data for learners. The typical game interface is a dashboard of essential system information organized to produce direct feedback on game play. The connection between action and outcome is so tight in games that the ability to proceed to the next challenge *is* the evidence of successful learning. The tight connection between action and outcome is also the problem with assessment in video games. When we want the learning process to lead to distal outcomes (e.g., standards), it is difficult to generate the information necessary to provide evidence for learning gains.

The MacArthur Foundation's 21st Century Assessment project explores how technologies for learners can be structured to yield the information relevant for learning and also how technologies for learners can begin to reshape technologies for education.[46] A key design challenge in this work has been the exploration of "data-channels" that convert in-game play processes and outcomes to out-of-game learning goals. The goal of this work is to create data structures that translate evidence of player/user mastery of learning goals within the game/environment structure into representations that are convincing to nonparticipants. Badges have played in important role in thinking through this "evidence translation" process.[47] Traditional badges, such as diplomas, certificates, and degrees, serve as legitimacy markers that communicate the value of achievement across domains. New media badges seek to serve a similar function in communicating the quality of in-environment achievements to out-of-environment audiences. For example, a reliable badge system would allow out-of-game observers to use badged in-game accomplishments as evidence of successful learning or skill development. The Digital Youth Network platform iRemix creates a multifaceted badging system to certify student efforts to make, critique, and share new media products. The next goal for learning design would be to validate whether (and how) badges can support inferences about the mastery of learning goals outside the system.[48] Research on building badge-based assessment "bridges" that translate the value of in-community achievement to out-of-community audiences points to new areas for how educators can integrate participatory cultures in to everyday schooling activities.

AN AGENDA FOR TECHNOLOGY INTEGRATION

Technologies for education produce information that provides feedback to guide the work of system managers. Technologies for learners produce information that provides feedback to guide the work of technology users. The apparent chasm between technologies for learners and learning, displayed as the separation between education and information technologies, is mainly a question of for whom information is produced. We have argued that the current preoccupation with technologies for education has limited school reformers/designers from exploiting the incredible variety of technologies used to support the interests and goals of learners. We argue that the exclusive focus on technologies for education in the contemporary accountability culture is effectively shutting out the tremendous potential of technologies for learners to reinvigorate the learning experience in school. The systematic push for "what works" *despite* student interests is at considerable odds with the widespread success of participatory cultures defined *by* student interests. What is now a forbidding gap between education and entertainment technologies should, in our view, be transformed into a complementary partnership between those who run schools and those who learn in schools. Developing new designs to integrate technologies for learners into public schools may help bridge the gap and demonstrate how digital technologies can reshape learning in and out of schools.

PART III

The Infrastructure of Accountability and the Public Good

CHAPTER 10

A Tale of Two Tests

Test Scores, Accountability, and Inequality in American Education

JENNIFER JENNINGS

HEEJU SOHN

For the last two decades, American education policy has relied on test-based accountability policies to improve student achievement and to close achievement gaps between advantaged and disadvantaged groups. The most consequential of these policies has been the No Child Left Behind Act (NCLB), which sought to narrow achievement gaps by requiring states to test students in grades 3–8 annually and to disaggregate scores by race, ethnicity, poverty, special education, and English proficiency status. In its original form, schools were held accountable for improving the performance of students in each of these subgroups so that all students would reach proficiency in math and reading by 2014. Though the Obama administration has recently relaxed this 100 percent proficiency requirement, the theory underlying test-based accountability continues to be that educators will channel more time, resources, and attention to minority students, poor students, and students with special educational needs when their performance is made public and schools are held accountable for results.

The effects of NCLB remain hotly debated. What is uncontested, however, is that state test scores have increased dramatically across the country since its implementation.[1] Because increasing student achievement was a central goal of NCLB, many observers believe that the federal accountability system is working as intended. Complicating this picture, however, is students' performance on a national test not used for accountability purposes: the National Assessment of Educational Progress (NAEP). Recent studies conclude that progress on state tests has significantly outpaced progress on the NAEP, a finding that has been relatively consistent since the first accountability systems were designed in the mid-1990s.[2] Substantial differences in gains on different tests raise important questions not only about which of these two sets we should believe but also about the larger implications of these conflicting views of educational progress for public deliberation about the state of American public education.

While a substantial body of literature has now accumulated about the effects of test-based accountability systems on student test scores, less attention has been paid to how the test score data produced through accountability systems shape the way we conceive of the purposes of public education, as well as how we understand and seek to address educational inequality. This is an important oversight, because measures themselves play a central role in constructing social problems. Considering the use of measures in fields outside of public education is helpful in understanding this point. For example, poverty rates and unemployment rates are social metrics that affect how we understand the impact of economic and social policy. Because poverty and unemployment measures have important implications for the resources that poor or unemployed people receive, the policies we adopt, and the success or failure we ascribe to our public officials, how they are measured has been contested since they were first reported. Multiple versions of these measures exist, and policy makers and researchers advocate fiercely for the use of one measure versus another precisely because they are so important to framing policy debates (and thus the allocation of scarce resources).

For most of the history of American education, no standard measures existed for every school in the country. Weick wrote three decades ago that "schools are not like other organizations . . . Much of their uniqueness derives from the fact that they are joined more loosely than is true for other organizations . . . only a limited amount of inspection and evaluation occurs in schools."[3] This depiction of the unevaluated school appears deeply removed from the last two decades of American education policy, during which decisions about which schools to close, which policies are effective, and increasingly how teachers should be compensated and evaluated have been based on students' test performance. In addition, education and policy researchers now rely heavily on these scores to evaluate a range of policies. When we hear that a study demonstrated that an intervention worked, or that a program was effective, what this generally means is that it was effective at increasing test scores.

In this chapter, we consider how the use of state test scores to measure student achievement and inequality may affect both how we distribute resources to students and the ways in which we seek to address inequality in our public education system. We begin by describing patterns on recent high- and low-stakes assessments using two cases: the Houston Independent School District and the state of New York. These two cases represent two very different parts of the country, but in both places test scores have assumed a prominent role in public and political debates about educational equity. We show that high-stakes tests used for accountability purposes and low-stakes tests that measure similar skills often paint very different pictures of educational performance and of progress in reducing between-group inequality. We then turn our attention to how data produced through accountability systems affect the way we understand the issue of educational equity. We focus our attention on how the proliferation of test scores measures shapes our perceptions of what goals public schools should accomplish, how we define educational inequality, how resources should be distributed between students, and how the political deployment of test scores may affect the reproduction of educational inequality.

A TALE OF TWO TESTS

We begin by providing descriptive evidence about the extent to which state test gains generalize to other tests of student achievement. Many have charged that state tests results are "inflated" by "teaching to the test." Score inflation occurs when test results overstate students' skills in the tested area and thus do not provide a valid measure of students' knowledge and skills in that knowledge domain. Tests are based on a sampling principle whereby only a fraction of the full knowledge domain of mathematics or reading is tested each year. State test results can become inflated when only a small fraction of state standards are tested and the content and form of test items is predictable across years. The predictability of tested content may lead teachers to teach to the test, to narrow their instruction to focus only on the state standards represented on state tests and to teach these skills in the specific format that appears on the test. As a result of score inflation, it is difficult to make inferences about students' proficiency in the larger domain—the state standards—which the test is intended to capture, as students appear to have made more academic progress than they truly have.

Score inflation has at least five major consequences. First, when scores are inflated, students have learned less than their scores suggest. Second, because schools serving poor and minority students face the most pressure to quickly increase test scores and greater barriers to doing so, inflation may disproportionately affect these students, for example, by changing instruction in these schools to focus more narrowly on the test or by changing students' exposure to nontested subjects like social studies. Third, because inflation varies across schools, *relative* improvements become difficult to evaluate, and researchers and policy makers may misidentify effective and ineffective schools and teachers. Fourth, accurate data on how students are performing is necessary for policy makers to identify and implement interventions that improve students' long-term outcomes. In the absence of such data, we may pursue interventions that are not effective or fail to implement policies that could improve student achievement. Finally, inaccurate perceptions of how students are performing may feed back into the political process and potentially affect the debate about how to improve schools.

Measuring Achievement and Inequality Between Groups: Houston and New York

Houston Independent School District

The Houston Independent School District (HISD) is the seventh largest school district in the country and the largest in the state of Texas. Approximately half of its students are Hispanic and about a third are African American. Eighty percent of its students are considered economically disadvantaged and about a quarter are classified as "limited English proficient."

We analyze longitudinal student-level data from 1998 to 2007 that includes students' annual scores on the Texas Assessment of Academic Skills/Texas Assessment of Knowledge and Skills (TAAS/TAKS) and the Stanford Achievement Test in both reading and math. The TAAS/TAKS is considered the district's high-stakes test, as it is used to evaluate districts, schools, and teachers. Under NCLB, the TAAS/TAKS scores are used to identify which schools did not meet Adequate Yearly Progress (AYP) as well as which schools and districts are labeled "exemplary," "recognized," "acceptable," or "low-performing."

The Stanford can be considered HISD's low-stakes test, in that it is not tied to the state accountability system. However, this test plays several important roles in the district and is not a no-stakes test. For example, it is used as one criterion for grade promotion in grades 1–8. HISD students are expected to perform above a minimum standard on the Stanford (e.g., one grade level below average or above) as well as the TAKS. In addition, the Stanford is used to place students in gifted, special education, and other programs.

We first provide a broader picture of test score trends in HISD. High-stakes test scores have increased substantially over the period of NCLB implementation (2003–2007). In math, students' scores have also improved on the low-stakes tests, though gains are four times larger on the high-stakes test used for accountability purposes. The story is somewhat different on reading. While high-stakes reading scores increased at a similar rate as math scores, low-stakes reading scores actually went *down* over the period that we study. In short, a substantial fraction of the gains on high-stakes tests does not generalize to another measure of math and reading achievement.

The patterns above suggest that test scores are inflated in HISD, but they do not tell us whether scores are equally inflated across all demographic groups. Figure 10.1 answers the question of whether our inferences about progress in closing achievement gaps vary across high- and low-stakes tests. On the one hand, it could be such that score inflation is uniform across demographic groups if, for example, all students' scores are inflated by the same amount. On the other hand, we know that schools serving high proportions of black and Hispanic students generally face the most accountability pressure. As a result, we might expect that scores would be most inflated for these students, which would create a greater narrowing of the gap on the high-stakes test than on the low-stakes test. Our data provide support for the unequal score inflation hypothesis. Figure 10.1 demonstrates that the black-white achievement gap appears to be closing on the high-stakes test but is unchanged or widening on the low-stakes tests.

New York State

We next analyze data from the New York State tests and state-level aggregate data from the NAEP exams in math and English language arts administered in 2005, 2007, and 2009. The latter are audit tests; neither student outcomes nor teacher or school evaluations depend on the results of these exams. The NAEP also differs from the state accountability test in that it is matrix sampled; students receive one of many possible test booklets, with each booklet containing a subset of all the questions asked in a given year. This allows NAEP to test a broader range of material than is typically possible in state test settings where all students receive the same test.

We begin by describing standardized gains on the New York State test and the NAEP over the period 2005–2009. The general patterns mirror those presented above for Houston. State test scores increased approxi-

FIGURE 10.1   Black-white gap on high- and low-stakes math tests in Houston, 1998–2007

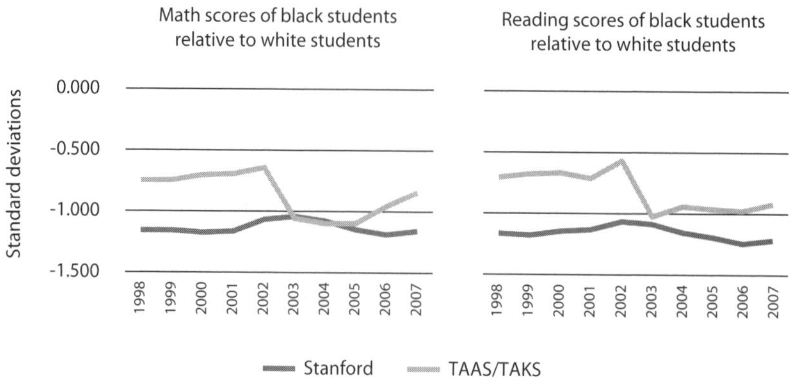

mately six times as much on the state math test than they did on NAEP, while state reading scores increased about three times as much.

Figure 10.2 reports black-white and Hispanic-white achievement gaps on the state and NAEP math tests. In all cases, results on the state test create the appearance of substantial gap-closing, but the NAEP results tell the opposite story: we observe no changes in achievement gaps.[4]

Inequality Between Lower- and Higher-Achieving Students

We now turn our attention to another domain for which the choice of measure may substantially change the conclusions we draw. Until very recently, the sanctions associated with NCLB have been based largely on proficiency rates. This threshold-based system potentially influences how educators distribute instructional resources between students, since schools get no credit for raising the achievement of students already above the proficiency bar; and in cases where the proficiency bar is set high relative to the achievement of students, schools may neglect students far below passing. For example, teachers may focus on "bubble kids," those students close to the passing cut score.[5] Since sanctions are doled out based on passing rates, slightly increasing the scores of a small number of students can positively impact the school's accountability rating. This focus could affect the achievement of both high- and low-scoring students relative to the cutoff. Because the lowest- and highest-performing students are not equally drawn from all racial and socioeconomic groups, this may have important implications for social stratification.

FIGURE 10.2   Mean achievement by race on eighth grade state and NAEP math tests

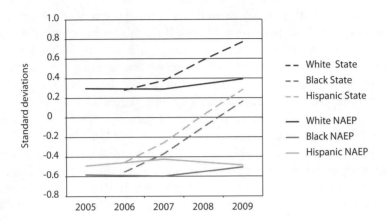

A large body of evidence addresses the issue of distributional effects and provides insight into the extent to which teachers are using data to target resources to students close to passing state tests. The evidence is decidedly mixed. In Chicago, Neal and Schazenbach found negative effects of accountability pressure on the lowest-performing students, while Reback in Texas found larger gains for marginal students and positive effects for low-performing students as well.[6] Four other studies identified positive effects on low-performing students, while four found negative effects on high-performing students.[7] We suggest that this literature is mixed in part because of differences in accountability systems across states. In states where the bar for passing is higher, very-low-performing students may be more likely to lose out under accountability systems, and these students are often poor and minority students. In states where the bar is set low, low-performing students may be more likely to benefit, while high-performing students will be negatively affected.

One issue that has been ignored in this literature is the extent to which gains on high-stakes tests transfer to other measures of achievement. When resources are targeted toward students close to passing, teachers may focus on test-specific skills that will not generalize to other measures of achievement. It could thus be the case that the positive or negative effects on low-performing students that have been reported in prior studies do not show up on low-stakes measures of achievement. In other words, high-stakes measures may overstate the effects of accountability on inequality.

Figure 10.3 illustrates this problem using data from Houston. Here we display the consequences of the implementation of the NCLB on both high- and low-stakes tests for lower- and higher-performing students.[8] We show results for the math test, where students at the bottom of the distribution were very unlikely to pass the math test. If teachers were maximizing passing rates, they would focus their attention on middle to higher-achieving students in HISD. Conversely, if teachers were focusing their attention equally on students across the distribution, we would expect figure 10.3 to be a straight line—all students gaining or losing equally.

We show results for the math test in Houston, which has a high proficiency cut score relative to the distribution of Houston students' performance. There are two important points in figure 10.3. The first is that students closer to the passing cut score are making the largest gains on the high-stakes state test. These results suggest that students at some parts of the distribution seem to benefit more from the implementation of NCLB, and a plausible mechanism producing this finding is the time and effort that teachers and schools dedicate to these students. Put simply, higher performing students make larger gains on the high-stakes test, while lower-performing students are negatively affected by the initial implementation of NCLB.

The second finding presented in figure 10.3 is that the consequences for inequality are not the same across both tests. On the low-stakes test we do not observe any differences in students' gains across the distribution; in fact, all students make relatively similar gains on the math tests. The mean difference between predicted and observed scores remains close to .06–.10 for students across all five performance quantiles, and the differences between these groups are not statistically significant.

Taken together, figures 10.1–10.3 drive home our central claim: the conclusions that we draw about between-group inequality and the effects of accountability policies on lower- and higher-performing students are strongly dependent on our choice of outcome. Improvements in achievement and reductions in achievement gaps on high-stakes tests do not consistently hold when we consider low-stakes tests in Houston and New York State.

HOW THE USE OF TEST SCORES TO MEASURE PERFORMANCE SHAPES OUR IDEAS ABOUT ACHIEVEMENT AND INEQUALITY

We now turn our attention to the potential indirect consequences of the rising use of test score data to evaluate educational performance. These consequences are not experienced directly by the student population as a result of

FIGURE 10.3   Distributional effects of implementation of NCLB on low- and high-stakes math tests in Houston

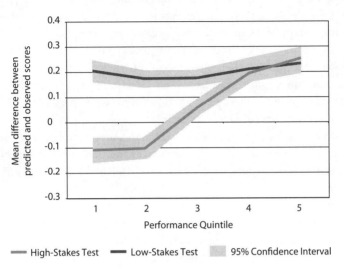

schools' responses to accountability policy. Rather, these effects may unfold in two major areas in the public sphere over a longer period of time.

First, accountability systems may reorient educators around one set of metrics: proficiency on state reading and math tests. Ultimately, this may change the way that educators think about the purposes of schooling and how resources should be distributed among students. Decisions that were previously viewed as moral and ethical decisions—how we should allocate scarce resources between students—may be transformed into technical ones. Second, the proliferation of test scores may influence public debates about public education and educational inequality.[9] While the large-scale use of test scores has many implications for students, here we focus on the consequences of the use of test scores to track systemwide achievement and inequality.

What Should Schools Do, and for Whom?

Issues of inequality have historically been at the center of debates about the goals and purposes of public schooling. This is summarized nicely by Labaree: "Schools occupy an awkward position at the intersection between what we hope society will become and what we think it really is."[10] What do we want our schools to do, and does the implementation of accountability systems reorient the historical mandate of public schools?

Schools, like most organizations, have many goals. These goals often compete with and displace each other. Following Labaree, we frame the educational accountability debate by discussing three enduring goals of American schools—*social efficiency, democratic equality,* and *social mobility*—and the perspectives on educational accountability they imply. While they are not mutually exclusive, the three goals introduce different metrics of educational success. We then introduce a fourth goal of American schools in an era of accountability, *organizational legitimacy,* which has the potential to displace the other three goals and interfere with our ability to determine which schools are, in fact, successful.

The first goal of American schools, social efficiency, is to prepare children to be successful in the workplace. We often hear this goal espoused by elected officials and business leaders, who stress that students' human capital must be developed to maintain a competitive economy. In this view, public schools are a public good. Each citizen's welfare is enhanced by the existence of a strong economy, and the nature of that economy is a function of the skills of its workers. Increasing students' academic achievement, as measured by their test scores or educational attainment, is the gauge of our educational success. Schools' function, then, is both to increase overall achievement and sort students of varying ability into different jobs. While these two goals may at first seem at odds with each other, proponents of the social efficiency goal focus as much on levels of performance as on differences in outcomes among groups; the view here is that a rising tide lifts all boats.

For those concerned primarily with the social efficiency goal, test scores are viewed as an adequate measure of schools' effectiveness because scores are seen as measuring capacities highly correlated with success in the workforce. Adherents to this view also generally believe that it is difficult to increase test scores without increasing learning and skills. We see this perspective most clearly espoused by those who argue that there is nothing wrong with teaching to the test so long as it is a test worth teaching to.

A second goal of public schools is to achieve democratic equality. It was this goal that propelled universal elementary education in the nineteenth century. The republic could not persist, Horace Mann argued, if students lacked a shared socialization experience that initiated them as members of a common polity. According to Labaree, democratic equality has two signature components. First, it demands that schools prepare children to become active citizens in a democratic society. Students, at the very least, must have the tools necessary to serve on a jury, vote, and understand the rights and responsibilities implied by our social contract. This includes both cultivating a range of cognitive as well as noncognitive skills, behaviors such as engagement, motivation, and ability to work well with others. Second, ensuring equality in the political arena requires that we place some limits on social inequality. This does not suggest that schools must produce equal outcomes, but it charges schools with attenuating, rather than exacerbating, preexisting inequalities.

Schools' achievement of the first component of the democratic equality goal proves more difficult to measure than social efficiency, because these outcomes are not observed until well after students leave K–12 education. The second component, relative equality, can be quantified for outcomes like test scores and has been incorporated into the achievement gap provisions of NCLB. For other outcomes, however, our progress toward achieving this goal is more difficult to quantify. Many advocates of using test scores to evaluate school effectiveness tap into the democratic equality goal and argue that doing so will close the achievement gap. Others concerned with educators' behavioral responses to these measures argue that strategic responses to accountability by teachers serving primarily disadvantaged students may increase scores without increasing learning. If true, this would create the perception of increased equity while achievement gaps are either unchanged or growing.

A third goal of public schools is social mobility. One perspective on the social mobility goal sees schools as breaking the link between parents' current status and children's future status. In this argument, schools level the playing field by providing a neutral venue in which each student can showcase his natural talent and merit. Because all students have an equal opportunity to succeed in this contest, the unequal rewards attached to positions in the social structure are fair and legitimate. A less optimistic view of the social mobility goal conceives of education as an object of struggle. In the contest to maintain or enhance one's relative position, educational credentials are a powerful weapon. Scholars writing in this tradition stress the role of the school in reproducing inequality by rewarding those who inhabit class-specific status cultures or possess cultural capital. The idea here is that children of the dominant class thus benefit from the alignment of their dispositions with those valued by the educational system. Privileged parents teach their kids to seamlessly express their preferences, to respond to questions rather than commands, and to look adults in the eye. Schools, in expecting the same behaviors, give upper-middle-class kids a leg up on their peers. Still other scholars argue that schools are a "great equalizer"—that is, they play a compensatory role—as gaps between disadvantaged and advantaged students increase more quickly during the summer than during the school year.[11]

Irrespective of one's take on the efficacy of schools in promoting social mobility, both sides agree that the social mobility goal is achieved when one's family background is not a strong predictor of one's educational and labor market outcomes. Put simply, the child of doctors should be no more likely to make it to graduate school than the child of construction workers. As with the democratic equality goal, advocates of using test scores to measure school effectiveness often draw on the social mobility goal of public schooling to support their argument.

We suggest that new goals beyond social efficiency, democratic equality, and social mobility come into play when we measure school performance and inequality based on test scores. Schools, as organizations, have an additional goal: to be recognized as legitimate by the surrounding community and, in an era of accountability, by the state. Historically, schools gained legitimacy through looking and behaving "like a school." Schools that adopted these rituals achieved legitimacy. But schools going against the grain (e.g., by outlawing letter grading or trying out "fuzzy" instructional techniques) risked losing public confidence.

The era of soft legitimacy is over, and it is no longer enough to behave like a traditional school. The current accountability climate emphasizes quantitative indicators with a focus on standardized test scores. By succeeding on these indicators, schools can attain legitimacy and avoid state sanctions. As the results presented earlier suggest, high-stakes systems like this, in addition to promoting intended behaviors of the policy, may lead schools to fundamentally change their activities or manipulate information to produce more favorable organizational statistics; and in doing so, important goals of education may be displaced, and it may become more difficult to determine how schools are really doing. We believe that the results presented earlier suggest that organizational legitimacy may be currently overtaking a focus on the other three goals of public education.

In describing these goals, we draw attention to the persistent absence of agreement about what American public schools should be doing. The question of "Who gets what and why?" is central to these debates. Accountability systems offer a solution to this thorny distributional problem because they circumscribe the problem and make it tractable. The central goal—increasing math and reading scores—is explicitly defined, as is the responsibility of schools for raising students to a prescribed level of proficiency and ensuring that this happens across racial and socioeconomic groups.

Accountability systems thus have the potential to redefine and transform the meaning of educational inequality; a qualitative, multifaceted construct that encompasses both inputs and a range of outputs is reduced to the proficiency gap between advantaged and disadvantaged groups on a single measure. We next highlight the most prominent accountability measure in use today, a threshold measure indicating the percentage of students proficient on state tests. Since the proficiency gap can be narrowed or even closed as advantaged students remain the same distance ahead of disadvantaged students on standardized tests, we raise the possibility that accountability systems may ultimately lead political actors—and, more broadly, Americans—to believe that they have adequately leveled the playing field for poor and minority children while leaving them just as far behind.

HOW SHOULD WE DISTRIBUTE RESOURCES BETWEEN STUDENTS?

Proficiency-based accountability systems recast the social mobility and democratic equality goals of public education by positioning achievement as an absolute, rather than a relative, outcome. Educational inequality has historically been conceived of relationally because most coveted opportunities—jobs, college admission, a good grade in a college course, or a positive evaluation in the workplace—are not divvied up based on students crossing an arbitrary line of proficiency or competence. Educational institutions and workplaces do not have an unlimited number of positions or slots; rather, individuals are competing against one another for access. Everyone who has passed a basic reading test is not assured a job, nor are all students scoring more than a 450 on the verbal SAT assured admission to the flagship university. These decisions are made by comparing the performance of applicants in a pool and choosing applicants who perform better relative to their peers. Accordingly, the test score achievement gap has been defined and discussed as the difference in average scores between, for example, white and Asian versus black and Hispanic students, or the difference in scores at different parts of the distribution.[12]

When we instead use proficiency rates to measure inequality, we can close achievement gaps using this measure even as disadvantaged students remain as far behind in their average scores. Primarily, the problem is that proficiency rates do not differentiate between students who just made it over the proficiency bar and those who scored well above it.

Imagine two classrooms of students: Classroom A is made up of students who start out as high achievers, and Classroom B is made up of students with middling performance. If every student in both classes answered two more questions correctly than she had in the previous year, we could say that both classrooms made equal amounts of academic progress. If 95 percent of the students were already proficient when they entered Classroom A, then the additional two questions each child got right is unlikely to have much impact on the passing rate. But in Classroom B, where only 50 percent of the students entered as proficient, the additional two questions answered correctly might boost Classroom B's proficiency rate from 50 to 70 percent. Comparing proficiency rates from these two years would make Classroom B look more effective than Classroom A, even though the students in both classes actually made the same amount of progress.

Now, imagine that Classroom A is composed of white or Asian students, whereas Classroom B is comprised of African American or Hispanic students. The gap in proficiency rates between the two classrooms at the beginning of the year is 95 − 50 = 45 percentage points, and at the end of the year is 95 − 70 = 25 percentage points. It might appear that Classroom B substantially closed the racial/ethnic achievement gap, but this is only an artifact of the threshold-based proficiency measure. In reality, all students made the same academic progress. In short, proficiency rates can increase substantially by moving a small number of students up a few points, just enough to clear the cut score. Applied to the case of racial achievement gaps, African American and Hispanic students may still lag far behind their peers even as their proficiency rates increase.

HOW DOES THE PROLIFERATION OF TEST SCORE MEASURES FRAME PUBLIC DEBATES ABOUT PUBLIC EDUCATION?

> It is hard to pick up an education article these days without reading about some excited governor or mayor who is busy closing the achievement gap. Test scores of minority children go up a few points, and there stands the politician on the 6 o'clock news declaring that merit pay for teachers or laptops in the classroom or the federal No Child Left Behind law is closing the gap between white and minority children.
>
> Michael Winerip, *New York Times*, December 15, 2005

Social scientists have a long-standing interest in the role of schools in reproducing and legitimating inequality through maintaining a veneer of equal opportunity. The practice of keeping track of educational inequality via test scores raises new questions for researchers about whether and how the reproduction of educational inequality changes when schools are publicly held accountable for closing the achievement gap.

Political actors of all stripes now use accountability measures to make broad claims about improvement in students' academic achievement and the reduction of racial and socioeconomic inequality. This represents an important shift. Historically, scholars and policy makers approached the question of whether inequality in educational outcomes by race, socioeconomic status, and gender is increasing, decreasing, or unchanged by observing outcomes of the education system (e.g., educational attainment or test scores) that were not used to evaluate schools. With the advent of accountability systems, the metrics by which policy makers and researchers keep track of educational inequality are now those that schools have the greatest incentive to manipulate.

Today, many political actors have argued that accountability systems decrease the "achievement gap," education policy's shorthand for racial and socioeconomic inequality in educational outcomes. In making these claims, they rely on accountability measures, such as the percentage of students passing state tests, and assume that these tests provide accurate proxies for the underlying math and reading skills these tests measure. But as we have discussed, there is a great deal of evidence that organizations respond strategically to accountability systems. This begs the question of whether these responses create the illusion of reduced inequality even as inequality is unchanged or growing.

We suggest that the two goals of accountability systems—to incentivize and to accurately measure—are, to some extent, at odds with each other and pose challenges for measuring between-group inequality in outcomes. These systems are intended to alter behavior and change the way business is done in organizations, particularly those serving disadvantaged populations, and the consistent side effect of this process has been the corruption of the measures themselves. Despite these known distortions, many view accountability data as clean measurements that track how students are doing and how much inequality there is among racial and socioeconomic groups. The result of this tension is that accountability systems, intended to provide more transparency about student performance, may interfere with our ability to accurately measure educational inequality.

At the level of cities, districts, or states, educators' actions aggregate to allow political actors to argue that they have dramatically reduced inequality, even as other assessments of student outcomes demonstrate this is not the case. Such results have been used to substantiate particular approaches to reform; largely those that do not focus on out-of-school inequalities but hold teachers and schools accountable for students' results.

In the political arena, perceptions matter. If policy makers and voters believe that inequality has declined when in fact it is unchanged or growing, the political will to implement policies that act on schools or on the family context to address these problems is potentially undermined. In sum, the portrait of schools' performance and of educational inequality provided by accountability measures matters because it shapes the actions taken to address these inequalities in the future.

We conclude by recapping the central claims presented in this chapter. First, using data from HISD and New York State, we demonstrated that gains on high-stakes tests often outpace those on low-stakes tests. Second, and most important for our argument, we show that black and Hispanic students, as well as lower-performing students, are more affected by score inflation than their peers; that is, their gains on high-stakes tests are less likely to generalize to their performance on low-stakes tests. As a result, different tests provide very different pictures of our success in closing achievement gaps.

We suggest that at least two different narratives about inequality and the role of schools in addressing it can arise from apparent declines in the size of achievement gaps. The first narrative is a "beating the odds" narrative. In this view, whether gains are real or not is irrelevant. The fact that we can show decreasing gaps, when they have been difficult to close for so long, may spur and legitimate investment in disadvantaged children. The second narrative is a "mission accomplished" narrative. From this perspective, our current policies have been successful at reducing inequality, and we need not look for or invest in new education or social policy solutions. The prescription for further progress is more of the same.

Which will ultimately dominate remains to be seen. We nonetheless conclude that policy makers, voters, and researchers would benefit from a more nuanced understanding of how test score increases are generated, as well as from more reflection on how the widespread use of these measures may shape our understanding of the role of schools in addressing inequality.

CHAPTER 11

Do Good Grades Matter?

Public Accountability Data and Perceptions of School Quality

REBECCA JACOBSEN
ANDREW SAULTZ

Fueled by demands for greater accountability of school performance, data production in education has grown in both amount and detail over the past two decades. Schools, districts, and state departments of education now collect, assemble, and report on more performance data than ever before. While previously data were mostly developed for and used by school and district personnel, accountability data are increasingly being produced specifically for the broader public. Because our education system is a public institution that must demonstrate to its citizens and elected officials that it has wisely spent public funds on effective educational programs to ensure ongoing support, disseminating data are a logical way of informing the public.[1]

To ensure that people have access to accurate and timely data on which to base their judgments, policy makers now require that education performance data be disseminated to the public. Across states and districts, releasing data (often in the form of school report cards) for public review has become a common practice in education. In part, the No Child Left Behind Act (NCLB) drives the new "publicness" of school accountability data because it requires all districts to publicize performance data annually. Further, recent statements by educational leaders imply that they plan to further increase the amount and type of accountability data available to the public. For example, Secretary of Education Arne Duncan said, "Let's put out data on dropouts, college enrollment, college completion, loan default rates, and every other kind of data that can help us highlight our many remarkable success stories and help us better understand why too many of our children are unprepared and undereducated."[2] As a result, an ever-increasing amount of data about the quality of schools is made available to the public.

Whereas a large body of research exists on how schools, districts, and educational leaders use and respond to data, only recently have scholars examined how the broader public uses or is influenced by accountability data.[3] Currently, researchers in this area are working with a relatively simplistic understanding of how data may lead to improved educational outcomes. Many assume that availability is the key to school improvement and therefore focus solely on increasing the availability of school performance data without questioning whether and how data may be interpreted and used. Policy makers and scholars hope that availability of data will cause some people to "act as a catalyst, actually triggering the causal process" behind improved school performance.[4] It's assumed that making data public will produce change because the public will demand improvement from its schools if the data show that performance is unsatisfactory. However, little work has documented whether people do, in fact, use performance data to take on this role as catalyst. Moreover, sparse research has expanded this theory of action to consider the many other, and possibly competing, sources of information people use to inform their decision-making process. The lack of theory and scholarship on public use of accountability data is not limited to education. As one scholar of performance management noted, "The wealth of performance data contrasts with the poverty of the theoretical and empirical justifications for performance-reporting requirements."[5]

Overall, while people are a critical voice to consider in education policy, there is little understanding of whether or how this voice is activated or shaped by accountability data, yet the theory of change rests on the assumption that data are influential. Therefore, to better understand how people use and understand school accountability data, this chapter examines whether and how accountability data influence perceptions of school quality and whether other sources of information, such as newspaper reports during the release of the school data, shape how data influence public opinion regarding school performance.

To examine these issues, we use performance data and parent satisfaction data from New York City elementary schools and newspaper coverage of School Progress Reports in New York City. Because new systems may take time to become effective or be embedded in the decision-making process, or because initial newness may eventually wear off, we examine multiple years of data. We restrict our analysis to elementary schools because, when compared to middle and high schools, there is less variation in the curricula and school structure, making cross-school comparisons more meaningful. Our sample includes between 490 (2008 school year) and 552 (2011 school year) elementary schools.[6] For each of the elementary schools in our sample, school-level data are drawn from public sources.[7]

We use the data from New York City to examine two underlying assumptions of data use that may be inaccurate: the "if you build, it they will use it" assumption and the "truth in numbers" assumption. While we find evidence that accountability data do influence perceptions, we argue that to simply assume that this is always the case, as the current theory suggests, is too simplistic. Rather, we demonstrate that the influence of data on public opinion can vary depending on mediated messages provided by newspapers regarding the quality of accountability data. Ultimately, this chapter contributes to our understanding of the way the infrastructure of accountability now reaches far beyond the schoolhouse walls; indeed, the entire citizenry is now participating in the infrastructure as they become increasingly exposed to and make decisions about school quality based on accountability data reports.

FRAMING IDEAS

The Push for Public Accountability Data in Education

With U.S. school districts spending approximately $500 billion annually, it is not surprising that the public wants to be informed about how effectively schools spend this money.[8] As a public institution, the school system derives its legitimacy from the electorate, making it particularly sensitive to public satisfaction and support. The average citizen makes important decisions about whether, and to what degree, to support the public education system.[9]

However, the public often lacks the necessary information to hold its schools accountable and is notoriously unaware of many policy issues.[10] As recently as 2010, almost a quarter of people in the United States responded that they heard "only a little" or "nothing at all" about NCLB.[11] This lack of knowledge may be due to the fact that many citizens have no direct interaction with schools. Even parents may have little more than informal interactions with a small handful of teachers on which to judge the quality of the school or the whole system. This asymmetry of information hinders the ability of people to apply pressure and voice demands for change, ultimately leading to worse educational outcomes as schools and their faculties face little pressure from people to improve.[12] Until NCLB mandated public dissemination of data, most school data reached a limited audience, and conversations about the quality and accuracy of the data remained mostly within academic research and education policy circles.[13]

Disseminating data to reduce the asymmetry of information and empower people to make more informed assessments of school performance[14] has become a popular policy strategy. Public dissemination of data uses political pressure—or the threat of it—from people as the pathway to improve educational outcomes and is popular because publicizing accountability data appears to be a relatively simple policy solution compared to alternatives.[15] Performance report cards, which are not unique to education, are a "regular effort by an organization to collect data on two or more other organizations, transform the data into information relevant to assessing performance, and transmit the information to some audience external to the organizations themselves."[16] Report cards can be powerful policy instruments because they can both "enlighten and embarrass."[17] Often, education leaders focus on the embarrassment power of publicly available data. For example, the release of individual teacher value-added scores was even compared to a "public shaming" by Bill Gates in his op-ed piece in the *New York Times*.[18] But in addition to providing people with data so that they can point out weaknesses in the system and demand improvement, publicizing data can have a positive impact on perceptions as well. Accurate and timely information can build trust and confidence amongst the public who is then more likely to support their institutions if they are able to see what they are getting for their investment.[19] Consequently, performance data can actually boost public confidence in and satisfaction with schools and may in some instances reverse the downward trend in confidence of the past forty years.[20]

The passage of NCLB, coupled with technological advancements that enabled widespread data dissemination, resulted in a sudden increase of public data both in terms of quantity and detail. Today, the infrastructure of accountability includes extensive school data reports (sometimes up to twenty-one pages long) that can be easily Googled for nearly every school in the country. Such extensive data have never before been so readily available to the general public.

Assumptions Underlying the Push for Public Accountability Data in Education

The "If You Build It, They Will Use It" Assumption
While it is clear that the amount of publicly available accountability data has expanded over the past decade, most policies supporting the expan-

sion of data systems operate under the assumption that data availability is the key to improving education accountability. Much like the *Field of Dreams* character Ray Kinsella, who builds a baseball field in his Iowa cornfield because he believes that "if you build it, they will come," many states and districts are investing heavily in data reporting systems as part of their accountability infrastructure under the assumption that if they put data "out there," the data will influence public perception of school quality. If the data show that performance is low, they hope the public will be dissatisfied and demand improved school performance. Improved outcomes result as school districts and faculty respond to public opinion and work harder to improve. Put simply, the current theory "assumes that the availability and quality of performance data is not just a necessary condition for use, but also a sufficient one."[21]

Yet, there is limited and mixed research regarding whether people actually use any of the education accountability data currently being produced, and outside of education, there is evidence that people simply do not use data provided.[22] It is not hard to imagine that in this age of information, school performance data are short-lived in the minds of most citizens. For example, Pride found that it was not school performance data that influenced public judgment of schools but, rather, key, focusing events such as school shootings that overshadowed the data in the minds of the public.[23]

Conversely, we have evidence that parents do use school performance data when selecting a school for their child.[24] However, parents who actively seek information may not be reflective of parents more generally or the broader public. In a recent study using New York City data similar to the data considered in this chapter, however, Charbonneau and Van Ryzin found that measures of student performance for elementary and middle schools were statistically significant and substantive predictors of aggregate parental satisfaction.[25] Therefore, given the limited and mixed evidence of performance data use, we must question the assumption that data availability alone will influence public perceptions of school quality.

The "Truth in Numbers" Assumption

When accountability data are released to the public, they do not stand alone. Rather, the public receives both the actual accountability data and a wide range of information about the data through both formal and informal mechanisms. While some may consider only the data by carefully reviewing the actual school report cards, such information seeking can be costly; it takes time and background knowledge to locate and review the actual data, resources many people lack. Thus, people often use secondary sources of information such as friends and neighbors, school principals, and teachers or formal news reporting as a heuristic for the actual data.

As education rose on the national policy agenda, newspaper reports began to pay more attention to education reporting. National newspapers now cover education topics regularly, as education is no longer confined to small, local newspapers. The *New York Times*, for example, dedicates an entire online section to local, state, and national education coverage. Reporting on accountability data is particularly popular. For example, in the summer of 2010, the *Los Angeles Times* released individual teacher quality scores for more than 10,000 teachers in Los Angeles Unified School District, which sparked a national debate about the quality of the data and the ethics of publishing teachers by name.[26] Even after much criticism, the *Los Angeles Times* continues to make these data public through their Web site, noting that this decision is based "in the belief that parents and the public have a right to the information."[27] New York City recently released similar data for its public school teachers, again sparking interest in and debate about accountability data. As this type of coverage increases, newspapers, both online and in print, are important sources of information about accountability data.

Previous work has documented the powerful influence that the media can play in shaping public perceptions on many policy issues.[28] Media shape public perceptions not only by telling people *what* issues to think about but also *how* to think about the issues. The agenda-setting function, or telling people what issues to think about, can significantly raise the importance of particular policy issues in people's minds.[29] In this way, greater attention by the media can heighten the importance of the policy issue. The second function of the media, framing, provides an interpretation of the issues and gives people a way to make sense of the issues at hand.[30] While sometimes criticized as "spin" or "slant," frames are not intended to deceive the audience; rather, frames are necessary tools "for presenting relatively complex issues . . . efficiently and in a way that makes them accessible to lay audiences."[31]

Previous research in education has found that news coverage can play an important role in shaping the education agenda and influencing public perceptions about issues on the agenda.[32] Because people may not be able to sort through and interpret the vast amounts of public data being produced by the extensive education data systems, they likely turn to the media to help them decide if they should be thinking about the data and, if so, how to think about it. In particular, we suggest that because accountability data have become popular topics in the news, the framing of the data may be key to determining whether and how public perceptions are shaped by accountability data. For example, when studying education data, McDonnell found that when questions of reliability became widespread, people no longer trusted the public performance data.[33] Thus, the faming of data in the news may be critical to understanding how data are used and perceived by the public.[34]

INVESTIGATING THE INFLUENCE OF PUBLIC ACCOUNTABILITY DATA

Public Accountability Data Use in New York City

New York City (NYC) has one of the most extensive and complex accountability systems in the country. Mayor Michael Bloomberg described the system as "the most sophisticated achievement data system in the nation," an opinion perhaps confirmed by the fact that other cities, states, and even countries have studied New York City as a model.[35] To develop this complex data system, the city paid $80 million dollars to IBM and a group of subcontractors.[36] Since its inception, education leaders presented NYC's data system as a catalyst for academic improvement through public pressure.[37] For these reasons, NYC serves as an exemplar system that can inform our understanding on whether and how publicizing accountability data impacts public perceptions of school performance.

Public Performance Data in New York City

Beginning in 2007, the NYC Board of Education began issuing graded report cards for every school in the system as part of its larger accountability and data system. The NYC Progress Reports, as the graded reports are known, combine multiple measures of school performance. Similar to letter grades that students receive to assess their performance in various academic areas, Progress Reports provide letter grades (A–F) to evaluate each school's performance. Schools receive an overall letter grade as well as environment, student performance, and student progress grades. Progress Reports are released each fall, and in past years the mayor and the chancellor held a joint press conference to announce the release of the data. The event was widely covered in the local media, often with multiple articles written immediately after the release. Additionally, Progress Reports are sent home with students and are available online through the NYC Board of Education Web site.

NYC's mayor and the schools' chancellor and chief accountability officer have each been explicit about the "public information tool" role that Progress Reports play in their accountability system.[38] Indeed, as James Lieb-man, former chief accountability officer for NYC schools and chief architect of the Progress Reports, stated when the first set of grades was released in 2007, "The purpose of grading these schools and making those grades pub-lic . . . is to generate pressure to get them [the schools] moving forward, to improve."[39]

Perceptions of School Performance in New York City

Ideally, we would examine satisfaction data for all citizens of New York City to understand whether and how these public Progress Reports are used. Indeed, since the data are intended for all city residents, not just parents, they are available online to any interested citizen. Unfortunately, broader pub-lic perception data are collected only at the city level, making it impossible to examine whether changes in a school's Progress Report grade influenced broader citizen opinions in the neighborhood surrounding the school. How-ever, the NYC Board of Education collects parent satisfaction data every year (since 2007) through a survey administered each spring to all parents in both paper and online versions. School-level results are publicly available on the NYC Board of Education Web site, and these data can be matched with Progress Report grade changes at the school level.[40] We use these data to understand whether and how the specific grade changes schools experi-ence in the NYC Progress Reports influenced perceptions of school quality.

UNDERSTANDING HOW PUBLIC ACCOUNTABILITY DATA INFLUENCE PUBLIC PERCEPTION

"If You Build It, They Will Use It"

While there are many sources of information that influence perceptions of school quality, we first examine the influence of Progress Report data in isolation. In three of the four years of their publication, we find that the Progress Report grades do have a statistically significant and positive rela-tionship with parent satisfaction. During the 2007–2008, 2008–2009, and 2010–2011 school years, parents were more likely to report that they were "very satisfied" with the quality of education their child received when their child's school garnered top Progress Report grades. These findings reinforce the literature that indicates people use data to inform their perceptions of quality.

We do find some indication that the predictive power of Progress Report letter grades diminished over time. In the first year Progress Report grades were released, the overall model explained just under 18 percent of the variation in parental satisfaction with school performance. Over time, the percent of explained variation decreased. For the most recent school year we examined, 2010–2011, the explained variation is just slightly more than 9 percent, or roughly half of what it was in the first year, suggesting that the impact of the data may be fading with time. These findings imply that the "if you build it, they will use it" assumption appears to be, at the very least, partially correct.

The assumption is only partially correct because there is an anomalous year in our analysis: the 2009–2010 school year clearly deviated from the other school years in our data set. For that year, the letter grade a school received had no statistical influence on the average parent satisfaction level. This finding is surprising considering the strength of the relationship in the other years examined. One possibility is the Progress Reports were released with much fanfare initially, which led to increased attention and use and once the newness wore off, parents quit using the data. But our data do not suggest this trend. We find that after the 2009–2010 school year, Progress Report grades again become significantly influential. Thus, the anomalous year suggests that something unique must have occurred to account for the sudden and short-term decline in the impact public accountability data had on parent opinion of school performance.

Other sources of information about the accountability data may explain why the 2009–2010 school year was unique in our data set. The following section examines the second underlying assumption to demonstrate how other mediated narratives interact with accountability data to shape their influence on public perceptions.

"Truth in Numbers"

Education accountability data do not exist in a vacuum. Rather, they are released into a larger discussion about school quality that includes information about the accountability data themselves. While the current theory on public accountability data assumes that the data speak for themselves, our finding that the data temporarily faded in importance suggests that other information must also be shaping public opinion on school quality. We examine newspaper sources for narratives about the public accountability data to inform our understanding of how data, once released, interact with other information to shape public opinion.

In New York City, the press remains an important source of information with three major newspapers—*New York Times, Daily News,* and *New*

York Post—that have a combined circulation of nearly 2.7 million online and print subscriptions. When Mayor Bloomberg and the acting chancellor release the Progress Reports each fall, a press conference is held and each of these papers covers the events. Over the four years examined, a total of sixty-five articles were published about the Progress Reports, including articles in each local paper on the day of the release.

Beyond simply covering the release of the Progress Reports, the media highlighted both positive and negative aspects of the data. While the grades have received both positive and negative coverage across the years, it is evident that the issue cited, or the frame applied to interpret the problems with the grading system, varied greatly across the years. In fact, we found fourteen unique problems cited across the coverage with the data themselves (see table 11.1). But unlike the other years, the 2009–2010 coverage converged on a single problem that received the majority of attention across all three newspapers. Repeatedly, the three newspapers interpreted the citywide Progress Report grades as "inflated" during the 2009–2010 school year. Headlines used this phrase and similar terms to describe the citywide data immediately after they were released.

During the 2009–2010 school year, newspaper coverage reported that the grading system had become "too easy" and that nearly 97 percent of the schools received an A or a B. Parents looking only at the Progress Report for their child's school would never know that their A school was just one among hundreds. Half of the newspaper articles from this period reported this huge grade inflation and included phrases such as "vast majority of schools," "huge increases," "lost all meaning," and "debacle" to frame the grades as useless tools for informing perceptions of school quality. As one *Daily News* article reported, "The dramatic grade inflation has rendered the 2009 reports nearly meaningless to thousands of parents who look to the summaries for guidance to which schools serve kids best."[41]

Whereas in other years a variety of problems with the grades were cited, during the 2009–2010 school year the interpretation of the data became highly focused on grade inflation. The convergence in the news coverage on this prominent frame likely led parents to disregard the data, a finding consistent with prior research that found news coverage of technical issues and quality concerns led to public skepticism of test score assessments and their ability to accurately reflect student learning.[42]

This framing was not an inevitable outcome of the numbers. Newspapers could just as easily celebrated the rising grades as evidence of an improved school system and successful education reform. The multiple narratives

TABLE 11.1   Media coverage of problems with Progress Report grades in New York City, 2007–2011

Year	People paid attention	Number of problems cited in the media	Most commonly cited problem	Percent of articles citing most common problem	Frequency of "inflated grades" or "grades too easy" in newspaper coverage	Percent of articles citing "inflated grades" or "grades too easy"
2007–2008	Yes	13	Too much focus on testing	44%	1	3.8%
2008–2009	Yes	13	Instability of grades from year to year	29.4%	1	6.3%
2009–2010	No	9	Grade inflation	58.3%	20	58.3%
2010–2011	Yes	11	Problem with the formula used to calculate grades	36.4%	0	0.0%

that could have been developed demonstrate that the "truth in numbers" assumption, or that numbers are able to "speak for themselves," is simply inaccurate. While "scientific measurement pursues the ideal of objectivity," such an ideal cannot be obtained.[43] Numbers can be powerful in policy debates, but they derive their power from the larger narrative constructed about them. Thus, newspapers and other media sources play an important role in the infrastructure of accountability because they have the power to construct and disseminate widely different narratives through which we make sense of the data.

LESSONS FROM NEW YORK CITY FOR THE INFRASTRUCTURE OF ACCOUNTABILITY

What can we learn from the efforts New York City policy makers made to highly publicize their school accountability data? On the surface, the evidence supports the assumption that if you make data widely available, people will use it to inform their judgments of school quality, an assumption that underlies the reason policy makers are investing heavily in data systems. As this chapter shows, parents appear to use NYC Progress Report data to shape their perceptions of school performance. Whether and how this leads to increased pressure for improved educational outcomes still remains unknown, but the potential exists for the public to act as a catalyst for this improvement.

We also show that people can just as easily dismiss the accountability data. Using the four years of publicly available data regarding parent satisfaction and letter grades, we find that letter grades do not always have an influence on parental satisfaction. This is because the data do not stand alone. When the data enter the public sphere, they become just one of many pieces of information. In New York City, the media provided important information about the data that shaped how they were understood and used. The year in which parental satisfaction was not influenced by the data was the year in which the news narrative in the NYC newspapers converged on a single, highly salient criticism of the data: the data was not reliable because of grade inflation.

While accountability data may be a particularly salient piece of information due to popular notions about numbers and what they represent, school accountability data do not represent an absolute truth that is beyond debate. Multiple and competing interpretations of the data can exist in public discourse about school performance. As we demonstrate in this study, the media play a powerful role in developing and disseminating both the data and a narrative about how to make sense of the data. As more and more data become public through our ever-expanding accountability infrastructure, the public may not have the sufficient time, energy, or knowledge to determine the validity and meaning of the actual data. Rather, reliance on other sources of information, including readily available narratives provided by the media or educational experts about the data, will likely increase in this context. As a result, significant power may lie with those who are able to offer narratives about the data.

The Role of the Public and the Infrastructure of Accountability

While education leaders and policy makers continue to support increasing the amount of public data available on school performance, we must pay careful attention to how the data shape public perceptions. Since education is one of the largest public institutions, the public plays a critical role in providing support for improvement. Often, advocates of data focus only on the promises publicizing data hold for improving educational outcomes. But just as data can rally the public to demand improvement, it may also erode faith in our public schools. Therefore, future research must continue to examine how data are used and interpreted by parents and the larger public. We highlight areas for which we believe further inquiry is especially needed.

First, how perceptions, once shaped, influence political action is an important area of future inquiry. Thus far, we have only been able to show that perceptions are influenced. More active measures of engagement, such as attendance at school meetings or voicing issues to school principals, are needed to really understand if declining satisfaction leads to pressure for improvement. While unlikely, it may be that the impact of data stops there. Education leaders, however, invest heavily in data systems and reporting mechanisms on the presumption that at least part of the public will take action and mobilize to apply pressure on its schools to improve. Whether and how this occurs remains unknown. One can imagine that some individuals may appear at the principal's door, with the school report card in hand, armed with demands for improvement. But while activating these individual voices may be important, is this enough to prompt school improvements, or must people organize collectively around the data for change to occur? If collective action is required, do accountability report cards prompt individuals to come together collectively to seek change and improvement?

Secondly, advocates of publicizing accountability data assume that individuals will act in ways that foster improvement. But individuals who become dissatisfied with school performance may also act in ways that limit the ability of the system to improve. For example, individuals who believe that public funds have not been used wisely may decide to withdraw this support. Without resources for reform, schools will only further decline. Beyond examining how individual schools respond to public dissatisfaction with accountability data, we must also consider how perceptions of school quality impact support for the larger public education system and how such impact may have harmful consequences. As public confidence in the education system continues to decline, do increased data and media reporting on data provide additional fuel for this decline? As this volume has shown, the infrastructure of accountability reaches far beyond the schoolhouse walls. We must also consider how data impact our belief and faith in our public education system such that they may threaten the very system itself.

The Infrastructure of Accountability

Tensions, Implications, and Concluding Thoughts

STACEY A. RUTLEDGE

DOROTHEA ANAGNOSTOPOULOS

REBECCA JACOBSEN

est-based accountability has focused educators and the public alike on using performance data as the primary means to reform the nation's schools. In this volume, we make visible the information infrastructure that undergirds test-based accountability. The chapters in this volume explore different parts of this infrastructure, from the large-scale information systems managed by state education agencies, to the data and information systems districts and schools use to make decisions about the organization of teaching and schooling, to the teacher value-added evaluation and compensation systems funded by foundations, and the public reporting of school performance grades by districts and newspapers. As they examine the production, dissemination, and use of data across and beyond the educational system, these chapters, taken together, provide one of the first maps of the information infrastructure of accountability.

In this final chapter we revisit the infrastructural perspective we described in the introduction to look across the chapters. We then explore a set of critical tensions that we see emerging from the expansion and growth of this information infrastructure: tensions between equity and effectiveness, outputs and outcomes, standardization and customization, and trust and distrust. As Henig suggests in the foreword to this volume, these tensions have deep roots in the American educational system and our longstanding debates about it. The interdependence of accountability policy and information technologies, however, reframes these tensions in new ways. We conclude by identifying the implications of these tensions and the interdependence of accountability and information technologies for educational policy and research.

MAKING VISIBLE THE INFRASTRUCTURE OF ACCOUNTABILITY

Though the chapters in this volume employ diverse perspectives, when we look across them using an infrastructural perspective, they make visible the practical, political, and moral contours and consequences of this infrastructure. Practically, as the chapters identify the new tools, actors, and relationships the infrastructure of accountability has given rise to and how it has reshaped established ones, they illuminate the constitutive nature of this infrastructure. State education agencies, districts, and schools have begun to use new tools and technologies to collect, process, and utilize performance data. These include the teacher value-added evaluation and compensation systems, with their myriad assessments, evaluation rubrics, and data management systems, that link with and extend statewide student information systems. These new tools and technologies also include the new algorithms districts and schools use to assign students as well as the new assessment and information systems that schools are using to guide their decision making.

The introduction and adoption of these new tools has been accompanied by the rise of new actors and the development of new relationships. Within urban systems, large-scale information systems have given rise to independent review panels that use their access to district data systems to monitor district performance and inform district policy. New organizations, both nonprofit and for-profit, have been created to assist state education agencies, districts, and schools in meeting the data demands of test-based accountability. Foundations have served as a key interlock among the multiple actors involved in advocating test-based accountability policies and building its information infrastructure.

The infrastructure of accountability has also affected relationships among established actors. Building, operating, and managing the statewide longitudinal student information systems that constitute the core component of the infrastructure of accountability require new levels of cooperation among state education agencies, districts, and schools. In some cases, unions, districts, and states are working more collaboratively, and data use has increased cooperation among urban school district leaders, community organizations, and city hall. But in other cases such cooperation is highly fraught. Under test-based accountability, state information systems are not neutral technologies. These systems implicate districts and schools in collecting the information that state and federal agencies use to monitor, regulate, and sanction them. For districts and schools, data collection as well as use can be seen as a type of state and federal micromanagement. While the information infrastructure can spur new collaboration among established actors, it can also reinforce tensions.

The introduction of new tools, actors, and relationships is thus infused with issues of power. We argue that the infrastructure of accountability has given rise to a type of informatic power that combines incentives and sanctions with measurement and computing technologies. As an informatic regime, test-based accountability extends the power of state and federal education agencies over districts and schools by positioning the former as centers of calculation. State and federal policy makers direct student, teacher, and school performance from afar by controlling the collection, processing, and dissemination of data and attaching sanctions to them. Districts and schools shift their practices and goals to align them with the performance metrics of test-based accountability, and school administrators and teachers subordinate their professional judgments and commitments to the cultural authority of data. At other points, however, they use data to meet local goals and priorities. Districts use performance data to preserve their goals of racial integration in the context of legal challenges, while school administrators and teachers incorporate the data into long-standing student assignment practices. In such cases, district and school actors interpret and use data to reinscribe rather than alter existing local practices, goals, and perspectives.

Informatic power also circulates beyond the educational system as it operates through the infrastructure of accountability. A growing number of organizations, firms, and foundations are involved in building, installing, and managing the different components of this infrastructure. This work places them in new positions of authority. The decisions they make build into the data and data systems of test-based accountability particular visions of education and give primacy to particular purposes and practices. While this work often extends the calculative power of the state, these external organizations can become competing centers of calculation. As the market for their products and services expands, these organizations can offer models and systems that embed different visions of education and valorize different purposes and practices that can challenge those embedded in state-sponsored systems.

Finally, the chapters illuminate how the processes of quantification, standardization, and classification operate in and through the information infrastructure of accountability. These processes are central to the production and deployment of informatic power. It is through them that the information collected from classrooms and schools gets abstracted from the particularities and complexities of those contexts and transformed into standardized quanta and performance categories used to evaluate and reward or punish schools, teachers, and students. When the classification systems embedded in test-based accountability converge with local classification systems, they alter how school administrators and teachers think about and respond to their students. For example, pressure to meet performance targets on standardized test scores lead school administrators and teachers to reenvision bilingual students as English speakers with limited proficiency and to identify students by their test scores, as 1s or 3s. Such reclassifications are consequential as they justify particular ways of allocating resources and learning opportunities to students. Local practices and ways of thinking are narrowed and alternative visions of schooling marginalized. Yet, district and school administrators and teachers can also use the classification systems of test-based accountability strategically to preserve and extend multiple goals and the practical knowledge rooted in the particularities of their classrooms and schools. They incorporate standardized test scores into existing student assignment practices to sustain goals of racial integration and to create heterogeneous classrooms that enable teachers to create productive learning environments for students. At these points of divergence, local commitments and competing narratives challenge the cultural authority of numbers.

TENSIONS

As they illuminate the practical, political, and moral work and consequences of the information infrastructure of accountability, the chapters in this volume reveal several deep-seated tensions about how we practice, participate in, and ascribe purpose to our nation's schools. While these tensions are hardly new, the rise of test-based accountability and its information infrastructure both raises new tensions and changes the nature of existing ones.

Equity and Effectiveness

President George W. Bush heralded No Child Left Behind (NCLB) as challenging the "soft bigotry of low expectations" that had contributed to the long-standing racial and economic achievement gaps among the nation's youth.[1] NCLB would compel schools not only to improve student achievement among all students but, more specifically, to close achievement gaps, thereby securing educational equity. The central means for doing this was requiring schools to disaggregate average test scores by race, ability, socio-economic status, and language classifications. Schools would no longer be able to ignore the low performance of students of color, low-income students, students with special needs, and English language learners. In this way, NCLB and the test-based accountability policies that it typifies utilize student scores on standardized state assessments as indicators of both school effectiveness and measures of equity.

As discussed throughout this volume, the dual use of standardized test scores as measures of effectiveness and equity raises challenges. As individual schools, and increasingly individual teachers, are held accountable for raising test scores, schools "teach to the test." Indicator corruption arises, reducing the validity of the test scores as objective measures of school and teaching effectiveness. Rather than redress issues of equity, the emphasis on standardized test scores recreates inequity in a new form. It places pressures on states to control the rate of school failure and success through focusing state assessments on a narrow set of basic skills and content. Improvements in state standardized test scores can, thus, obscure the narrowing of the curriculum. While test scores improve, the learning opportunities that schools provide students can be diminished. Schools that serve predominately low-income, racial minority, and special-needs students are disproportionately affected by this narrowing. These schools have been the targets of the negative sanctions attached to standardized test scores; they comprise the majority of schools placed on probation, reconstituted, and closed by state and federal policy makers.[2] In efforts to avoid such consequences, these schools have altered curriculum, instruction, and student assignment to raise test scores. Increases in test scores in schools that serve mostly low-income and linguistically and racially diverse students can thus reflect restricted rather than enriched learning opportunities for the nation's most vulnerable students.

The dual use of standardized test scores as measures of effectiveness and equity therefore has practical, political, and moral consequences. Practically, it can prompt schools to direct resources and efforts to a diminished rather than enriched curriculum. Politically, it can obscure the persistence of continued inequality. Morally, as it reduces issues of equity to growth in standardized test scores, it buries much deeper questions about the causes of achievement gaps and the relationship between educational equity and broader social and economic inequality. These points are particularly pressing given recent studies on growing income disparities in the United States.[3] By reducing issues of equity in schools to test scores, we risk obscuring the effects of rising economic inequality and locating responsibility for redressing it solely on schools and, increasingly, individual teachers. Improvements in standardized test scores can therefore impoverish rather than enrich the debate necessary to address issues of equity.

Outputs and Outcomes

Related to the tension between equity and effectiveness is the tension between outputs and outcomes. Research on test-based accountability has shown how such policies have led schools to alter how they allocate instructional time to particular subjects, such as math and reading, and away from others, including science, social studies, and art, and how they target time and resources on tested skills and content. In addition, districts and schools, in response to the emphasis on performance data, have increasingly installed local assessments and information systems. This has increased the number of tests administered in schools as local educators seek to measure and monitor student performance on an almost continual basis. Testing comes to stand in for teaching.

Such responses reflect a tension between outputs, as measurable goals, including standardized test scores, and outcomes and valued goals, such as providing a broad-based, high-quality education to all students. Americans have historically ascribed a broad range of goals and purposes to their public schools—ensuring basic academic skills, developing critical thinking and reasoning skills, shaping character, ensuring students' physical and emotional well-being, providing social opportunity, transmitting culture, fostering new ways of thinking, and preparing citizens committed to and capable of sustaining a vibrant and just democracy. Attempts to measure learning through standardized tests fall short of capturing many of these goals. Further, given the tension between equity and effectiveness, low-income and racial minority youth are most in danger of being denied rich learning environments that extend beyond basic skills.

As districts, states, and parents come to rely on and expect numeric indicators of performance, the demand for student outputs only increases. By quantifying learning, such measures threaten to marginalize broader goals of education. These numeric indicators of student performance provide simplified representations of the complex processes of teaching, learning, and schooling. In short, the reliance on quantified performance measures can compel educators and policy makers to focus on producing and recording quantified increments of learning while displacing efforts to provide youth the learning opportunities necessary to maintaining a democratic society.

Standardization and Customization

Standardized educational practices have long been a feature of schooling. District and school administrators and teachers have relied on standardized curricular materials including textbooks, lesson plans, and student assessments for decades. States and districts have collected standardized information about schools and students since the inception of public education in this country. The rise of large-scale information systems, however, has intensified standardization. Through test-based accountability, state and federal policy makers have extended their reach into local schools and classrooms. Districts and schools have turned to standardized test-preparation materials and computer programs. As discussed in this volume, administrators and teachers use these materials to prepare students for the standardized measures of performance needed for state information systems. Standardization processes are thus centralizing control over core educational processes.

Yet, control over the information systems themselves can never be truly centralized. Because they stretch across vast numbers of organizations and geographic distances, these systems are always being reconstructed in light of local practices, conditions, and contingencies. As the growing literature on data use in districts and schools indicates, data, in themselves, do not hold meaning.[4] Local educators construct the meaning of data in light of the particularities of their local schools and classrooms. Parents, students, teachers, and local administrators make sense of the data to inform district and school reform approaches, to hire and fire teachers, to press for resources and form partnerships with nonprofits, universities, and foundations. They thus use data to address local concerns.

In short, tensions between standardization and customization are inherent in the collection, processing, dissemination, and use of performance data across and beyond state educational systems. Ultimately, the tension between standardization and customization plays itself out in how we use the very computer technologies that have enabled the creation of large-scale information systems and test-based accountability policies in education. Our current use of computer technologies to monitor and regulate student, teachers, and schools by measuring their performance on a small set of standards parallels our use of computer technologies for a small subset of their potential. Much as the focus on standardized test scores has prompted a narrowing of the curriculum that marginalizes many of the capacities and qualities that we value and that are necessary to maintain a democratic society, our current use of computer technologies as tools of surveillance and long-distance control obscures the potential of computer technologies to radically alter how we practice and organize teaching and learning and how we define the "educated" person.

Trust and Distrust

A third set of tensions that tracing the infrastructure of accountability illuminates revolves around issues of trust and distrust. The tension between trust and distrust is deeply rooted in American democracy. In a democracy, some public distrust of institutions and elites is healthy. It leads to more critical and effective oversight of elected representatives. However, as distrust grows, it can lead to disengagement and the eventual breakdown of public commitment to and support for the public institution and its elected leaders. The information infrastructure of accountability intensifies these tensions.

On the one hand, the standardized performance data and the information infrastructure that produce these data are technologies of trust. By producing and publicly reporting numeric indicators of school and student performance, states and districts share information about the health of the system as a whole and of individual schools and districts in particular. The public release of school and teacher ratings provides parents and the broader public with information that they can use to monitor the nation's schools. School administrators and teachers use student performance data in their discussions with each other as well as with parents to convey student progress. The information infrastructure of test-based accountability can thus not only enable informed public oversight of and democratic participation in the nation's public schools, but it can also provide professionals and the public common language to describe and monitor student academic performance.

On the other hand, the trust in numbers that test-based accountability and its information infrastructure engender can counter this oversight and participation. Improvements in test scores or other standardized performance measures can obscure enduring inequalities and the narrowing rather than enrichment of public schooling. Further, though they appear objective, the performance measures of test-based accountability are the products of both expert knowledge and professional politics. Trust in the performance measures of test-based accountability, in this case, obscures rather than resolves the tensions between democratic and professional control of the nation's schools.

Tensions between trust and distrust also arise within the educational system. The performance measures and information systems of test-based accountability are not just technologies for collecting, processing, and disseminating information on the nation's schools. They are also surveillance technologies; they allow state and federal policy makers to monitor and intervene in the performance of students, teachers, and schools from afar. Organizational research has documented how surveillance technologies often erode trust within organizations.[5] Importantly, it impedes the sharing of information upward as the people being monitored feel threatened and seek to avoid sanctions. This is especially relevant to test-based accountability. States must ultimately rely on districts and schools to submit accurate data. While states can install auditing technology, data quality remains a challenge. The incidents of cheating on standardized tests among district and school educators are perhaps the most dramatic examples of how sharing information upward is impeded in relation to surveillance technologies.

Importantly, the reliance on surveillance technologies can also foster distrust among those who use the technologies to monitor the work of others. Such distrust is reflected in the tendency of proponents of test-based accountability to characterize teachers' resistance to or questioning of such policies as attempts to escape being held accountable or as an espousal of low expectations, especially for low-income students and students of color. Indeed, test-based accountability and its information infrastructure have enabled state and federal policy makers to locate the responsibility for school failure solely on schools and teachers while depicting themselves as taking action to address this failure. The long-term costs of this erosion of trust within the educational system are not yet clear.

Ultimately, the public must trust that policy makers themselves are not compromising the measures that they are using to monitor schools. Policy makers can alter cut-off scores, producing more or less school, teacher, or student failure or success. If too many schools receive high grades, the grading system becomes suspect. The public must also trust that testing companies are constructing quality assessments and scoring them fairly. The shift from trust in educators to trust in numbers thus requires the continual manipulation of data. This creates a paradox for the nation's schools in which too much success is seen as manipulating the numbers while too much failure raises doubts about the very legitimacy of the system itself.

IMPLICATIONS

The information infrastructure in education is in its infancy. Its full impact on the educational system has yet to be determined. While it is already reshaping work practices across the system, the degree to which it will standardize practices and reinforce current institutional relationships or, instead, foster a diversity of innovations in practice and redefine power dynamics remains unclear. Given its growing centrality in policy and practice across the educational system, it is critical to include the information infrastructure and its effects on educational policy and goals in the larger educational discussion. We identify several issues in this regards that we hope policy makers and researchers will consider.

Issues for Policy Makers to Consider

While the role of testing in holding students, teachers, and schools accountable has been at the center of educational debate and policy, the role of the broader information infrastructure of test-based accountability has received much less attention. As the chapters in this volume show, this infrastructure is both technically and politically complex. It stretches across geographic distance and organizational boundaries and involves people and organizations both within and beyond the educational system, thus defying central control. Managing any part of this infrastructure requires a complex mix of regulation, political mobilization, technical expertise, and persuasion. The power of information systems to affect behavior across and beyond the educational system in ways that can easily be overlooked further make managing and utilizing these systems challenging. While information is essential to meeting core goals of efficiency, effectiveness, and equity, information systems can also prompt behaviors that run counter to these goals, including the gaming strategies and performativity that several chapters document.

The complexity and potency of these information systems raise several issues for policy makers to consider. First, to date, policy makers have largely used these information systems to monitor and regulate school, teacher, and student performance. Yet, these systems can also be used to foster collaboration both within and beyond the educational system. Research on data use in schools shows that when administrators and teachers create cultures of inquiry, information systems can facilitate collaborative efforts to assess and improve schooling practices. Building and utilizing information systems can increase collaboration among established actors—schools, districts, state education agencies, university teacher preparation programs, and teacher unions—and give rise to new partnerships that cross district, state, and organizational lines. The willingness of policy makers to share information has been critical to fostering and sustaining these collaborations and partnerships. This willingness marks a shift away from using the information infrastructure of accountability as a surveillance technology and toward using this infrastructure as a way to include schools, teachers, and other actors in building as well as utilizing this infrastructure. Such a shift recognizes the importance of recognizing teachers, schools, and districts as data producers as well as data users or data targets. While building the mathematical models and technical devices will require expert knowledge, developing partnerships that provide avenues for participation by teachers, principals, and district officials in shaping the content and usability of these models and devices can help create the feedback loops through which policy makers can learn from local schools and districts.

Similarly, these systems can be used as tools to build student and teacher capacity beyond the narrow goals of improving test scores. As states implement teacher evaluation systems, attention should be made to link teachers' value-added scores to effective teaching practices, broadly defined. As schools are identified as successful based on value-added scores, attention should be paid to the multiple activities that improve student achievement—such as personalization between adults and students in schools and students' socioemotional learning—and not just direct classroom outputs. Put differently, improving student achievement is a much broader endeavor than just preparing students for high-stakes test. As we gain more information on the broad range of effective practices in schools, they should be relayed to teachers and school administrators. In terms of student capacity, schools should experiment with computer technologies in ways beyond those that reinforce and assess basic skills—ways that encourage more constructivist ways of thinking and learning.

Second, there is a need for broader public participation both in using data and in understanding how it has been constructed. There are a number of approaches that can be used to involve more actors in data production and use. Educational consortia and university partnerships with districts and states represent an important way to make data more public. The case of partnerships such as the Accountability Review Council (ARC) with the School District of Philadelphia is an example of ways in which districts can facilitate public involvement and data transparency.

In the United States, processing the vast amounts of information being collected on the nation's schools currently rests almost exclusively in the hands of state and federal education agencies. While there are nonstate actors that provide technical support, such as the National Institute for Excellence in Teaching and Battelle for Kids, which provide "seals of approval" for data systems, their use is not widespread. England and Wales provide an example of making data more public through creating multiple centers of calculation. In addition to conducting their own analyses of school- and student-level data, as is done currently by most states in the United States, the British Ministry for Education allows several entities, including nonprofits and universities, to conduct independent analyses of student data. While the value-added algorithms and mathematical modeling are still being done by technical experts, school administrators and teachers are given access to the different findings about their schools. They are then able to compare these findings to those produced by the ministry's high-stakes inspections and, when discrepancies arise, challenge the latter. This, again, creates feedback loops from schools and districts to state and federal agencies that can facilitate the sharing of information for systemwide improvement.

Multiple centers of calculation such as nonprofits and for-profits that provide audits of data systems and analyses of data can provide quality control and make data more accessible to multiple stakeholders. Yet, they also open it up to multiple interpretations and competition. Perhaps ironically, to date states and districts have succeeded in keeping educational data contained. As time goes on, the effects of multiple centers of calculation should be examined, since they have important implications for the transparency of information as well as for school governance and management and the faith the public places on these potentially competing sources of data.

Greater transparency and open access to data as well as informed discussion also require building the public's capacity to understand educational data. As has been discussed extensively, currently data production and use largely rests in the hands of technical elites. As we move forward, more discussion needs to be paid to making data more generally available and user friendly. For example, policy makers need to be more transparent in the decision making behind calculations such as school grades and value-added scores. Including teachers and school administrators in this decision making might also assist in translating the data to the public. When states publish school-level data, they should go beyond the reporting of scores and give breakdowns by academic skills, thereby bringing curricular content more directly into the public debate. Giving the public access to data *and* the decision making informing the data can help facilitate deliberation on the broader purposes of schools and on the tensions we have raised here.

Further, policy makers need to recognize the trade-offs of relying so heavily on numeric indicators of performance. Often, data systems are advanced as relatively cheap and easy ways to reform education. Other approaches, particularly those that seek to strengthen the ties between schools and their communities to develop comprehensive supports for student achievement, are viewed as too costly and too difficult to coordinate and thus are dismissed as viable policy alternatives. Yet, as this volume reveals, vast resources (human, technological, financial), both within and beyond the school system, are being harnessed to develop and grow the information infrastructure. An accurate understanding of the vast resources required to support the information infrastructure is needed in order to evaluate whether the current system is cost effective when compared to other policy alternatives.

Finally, while standardized test scores and teacher value-added estimates provide some measure of school and teacher performance, they remain simplifications. Like all measures, they provide only partial insight into the knowledge, skill, and commitments critical to producing the types of school and classroom environments conducive to quality learning. They also do not capture the full range of goals and purposes that Americans have long ascribed to their schools. It is important for policy makers to reinvigorate the debate about our nation's schools and to recapture the broader goals that Americans have for them.

Issues for Researchers

By making the infrastructure of accountability visible in this volume, we have sought to reframe educational research on data use and test-based accountability to take into account the information infrastructure that facilitates both. Current research has largely focused on the growing role of data in different parts of the system and its promise to improve educational practices. Less attention has been paid to the information infrastructure that produces and disseminates that data both across and beyond the educational system. A small number of studies have examined the challenges state education agencies face in building the large-scale information systems required by test-based accountability and have explored the technical capacities and affordances of the information systems districts and schools have begun to adopt.[6] This volume builds on these efforts by expanding the focus of research to explore the larger information infrastructure in which these systems are embedded. This more expansive research agenda will contribute to a fuller understanding of the consequences of test-based accountability on the broader educational field, including, but going beyond, schools and districts. It will also contribute to a fuller understanding of how information technologies are changing the field.

This volume provides both conceptual tools and substantive starting points for such research. Several chapters describe how building, managing, and using various parts of the information infrastructure of accountability is reshaping work practices across the educational system. While a growing body of studies has examined how the use of data in districts and schools is altering work practices in those contexts, there have been few studies of how the information infrastructure is reshaping work in state education agencies. Further, little research has focused on the coalitions and relationships built among actors and agencies in the construction and use of data systems. These agencies are responsible for building, installing, and managing the information systems that produce the core performance data of test-based accountability. They merit further attention and scrutiny as the work of state administrators, foundations, nonprofits, and education corporations is often conducted in closed offices. As these actors gain increasing influence over schooling purposes and practices, this scrutiny becomes more critical.

In addition to examining the new relationships that the information infrastructure of accountability gives rise to and how it redistributes power through and across these relationships, more research is needed that explicitly examines the tools and technologies that comprise the growing information infrastructure. As we note above, researchers have examined state and local information systems for their technical capacities and affordances. Drawing on the infrastructural perspective we delineate in this volume, we call for more research that specifically examines how classification systems get built into these information systems and into the myriad algorithms, programs, and data files linked to these systems. One goal of this research is to recapture the practical politics through which these classifications systems were constructed. Another goal is to examine the moral order these classifications construct. Addressing both goals will require research into "boring things"—data manuals, mathematical models, user guides, etc.— the work involved in creating them, and the ideologies and interests invested in them. Studies of how the classification systems built into information infrastructures, including policies as well as computing technologies, get interpreted and linked to local classification systems are further needed to understand the moral import of information infrastructure as it traverses state and school contexts.

Finally, the volume points to the need to examine the role information infrastructures play in knowledge production across and beyond the educational system. An infrastructural perspective helps illuminate the networks across which information moves both within and beyond the educational. Research is needed to explore how people not only use this information at the different nodes of these networks but also how they produce and disseminate it and how the decisions they make in doing so shape what can be learned from the information and what cannot. In addition, research is needed to understand how the information made available by state-sponsored and controlled information systems interacts with local, practical knowledge to inflect, reinforce, displace, or erode it. This is particularly important in relation to schools and classrooms as it affects what gets taught, how, and to whom. Studies of how the use of computing technologies to measure and monitor school achievement interacts with the use of computing technologies to foster student engagement and knowledge construction through social media and virtual environments can shed light on the potential of information systems to be used in ways that can support as well as monitor student learning.

The broader focus we advocate here will bring greater attention to the winners and losers of the infrastructure of accountability. While the uptake of computing technologies has been integrated into educational practices, we call for a greater understanding of who is winning and who is losing as these new information systems become embedded into the educational system and field. As schools gravitate toward certain technologies over others, which groups are being privileged over others? Which goals of education or perspective on what and how young people should be taught are becoming the new norms in our education system?

FINAL THOUGHTS

The infrastructure of accountability is having a profound effect on educational practices across the educational system. In this volume, we have sought not only to provide a first map of this infrastructure but also to identify its practical, political, and moral consequences. We have also sought to raise important questions around the tensions it raises as well as larger implications going forward.

As we conclude, we raise the concern that test-based accountability offers a diminished vision of our nation's public schools. The relentless focus on standardized test scores and the production of ever more precise performance metrics threatens to displace efforts to fulfill the broad-ranging goals that Americans have historically ascribed to their schools—building character, ensuring physical and emotional well-being, providing social opportunity, transmitting culture, fostering new ways of thinking, and preparing citizens committed to and capable of sustaining a vibrant and just democracy—with a singular focus on raising standardized test scores as a means to promoting individual and national economic competitiveness. By illuminating the contours and consequences of the vast information infrastructure currently being built to support this narrowed vision, we hope that this book will contribute to a renewed conversation about the purposes of our nation's schools, one that promotes a richer vision of what truly counts.

Notes

Foreword

1. Theodore J. Lowi, "Machine Politics: Old and New," *Public Interest* 9 (1967): 83–92.
2. Raymond E. Callahan, *Education and the Cult of Efficiency* (Chicago: University of Chicago Press, 1962). I don't want to overstate the differences. Early-twentieth-century Progressives also believed that differential rewards were necessary to motivate top performance. Bonus systems based on task performance were an important component of Taylorism. The distinction rests more in the fact that educators broadly have been more deliberately and effectively pushed to the margins of the contemporary effort to design the assessment and incentive systems. There was plenty of antieducator hostility expressed by business-oriented reformers in the earlier era, and classroom teachers (mostly women) had little, if any, influence on the key decisions of the time. But leading reformers included journal editors, scholars of education and psychology at prestigious universities, and state and district administrators, some of whom were true believers and some of whom adopted the language of efficiency out of concern that failure to do so would allow noneducators to dominate.
3. Karl E. Weick, "Educational Organizations as Loosely Coupled Systems," *Administrative Science Quarterly* 21 (1976): 1–19.
4. Bill Gates, "Shame Is Not the Solution," *New York Times*, February 22, 2012.

Introduction

1. While test-based accountability in education reflects a larger movement toward performance-based or outcomes-based accountability (see Mintrop and Sunderman, chap. 1 this volume), we use the term *test-based* to emphasize the focus on assessment, standardized testing, and test scores that characterizes the accountability policies currently dominating education in the United States. For a discussion of test-based accountability as it relates to other types of accountability in education, see Richard Rothstein, Rebecca Jacobsen, and Tamara Wilder, *Grading Education: Getting Accountability Right* (Washington, DC: Economic Policy Institute; New York: Teachers College Press, 2008).
2. There is a considerable body of research on test-based accountability. See Mintrop and Sunderman (chap. 1) and Cohen-Vogel, Osborne-Lampkin, and Houck, chap. 7 this volume, for reviews of this literature.
3. See, for example, Jeffrey C. Wayman, "Involving Teachers in Data-Based Decision-Making: Using Computer Data Systems to Support Teacher Inquiry and Reflection," *Journal of Education for Students Placed At Risk* 10, no. 1 (2005): 295–308; Kerri A. Kerr, Julie A. Marsh, Gina Schuyler Ikemoto, Hilary Darilek, and Heather Barney, "Strategies to Promote Data Use for Instructional Improvement: Actions, Outcomes, and Lessons from Three Urban Districts," *American Journal of Education* 112, no. 4 (2006): 496–520;

Richard Halverson, Jeffrey Grigg, Reid Prichett, and Chris Thomas, "The New Instructional Leadership: Creating Data-Driven Instructional Systems in Schools," *Journal of School Leadership* 17, no. 2 (2007): 159–194; Amanda Datnow, Vicki Park, and Priscilla Wohlstetter, *Achieving with Data: How High-Performing School Systems Use Data to Improve Instruction for Elementary Students* (Los Angeles: University of Southern California, Rossier School of Education, Center on Educational Governance, 2007); Cynthia E. Coburn, Judith Toure, and Mika Yamashita, "Evidence, Interpretation, and Persuasion: Instructional Decision Making in the District Central Office," *Teachers College Record* 111, no. 4 (2009): 1115–1161; Cynthia Coburn and Erica Turner, "Research on Data Use: A Framework and Analysis," *Measurement: Interdisciplinary Research and Perspectives* 9, no. 4 (2011): 173–206.

4. Maris A. Vinovskis, "The Changing Role of the Federal Government in Educational Research and Statistics," *History of Education Quarterly* 36, no. 2 (1996): 111–128.

5. Alan B. Henkin and C. Dennis Ignasias, "Planning Public Education: Lessons from Horace Mann and Henry Barnard," *The Clearing House* 51, no. 9 (1978): 430–435.

6. Ibid., 431.

7. National Forum on Education Statistics, *Traveling Through Time: The Forum Guide to Longitudinal Data Systems.* Book 1: *What Is an LDS?* NFES 2010-805. (Washington, DC: National Center for Education Statistics, 2010).

8. Data Quality Campaign, "State Analysis by Essential Element," http://www.dataquality campaign.org/stateanalysis/elements/. Linking student and teacher information systems is not merely a technical matter; it has been contested by teacher unions in many states. One of the keys to getting federal Race to the Top funds was to pass state legislation that enabled this linkage. It is likely that in those states in which linkages between student information systems and teacher information systems have not been made the issues are political rather than technical.

9. Jeffrey Wayman, "Involving Teachers in Data-Driven Decision Making: Using Computer Data Systems to Support Teacher Inquiry and Reflection," *Journal of Education for Students Placed at Risk* 10, no. 3 (2005): 295–308; Richard Halverson, Jeffrey Grigg, Reid Prichett, and Chris Thomas, "The New Instructional Leadership: Creating Data-Driven Instructional Systems in Schools," *Journal of School Leadership* 17, no. 2 (2007): 159–194; Halverson and Shapiro, chap. 9 this volume.

10. "About the SLDS Grant Program," National Center for Education Statistics, http://nces.ed.gov/programs/slds/about_SLDS.asp.

11. It is difficult to determine how much money has been spent on building statewide longitudinal student information systems. The federal SLDS Grant Program awarded states a total of $547,575,973 between 2006 and 2009 ("About the SLDS Grant Program"). States, however, have been the primary funders of these systems. There has not been, to our knowledge, a comprehensive study of these expenditures across the states. Given the systems' complexity, increasing data demands from state and federal mandates, and the rapid advances in computing technologies, these systems require continual updating, making it necessary for states to allocate further funding beyond initial installation. We have found it difficult to track state funding for the state information systems in part because, as the state officials we have interviewed in our research noted, states often link funding for these systems to other grants and program areas. A systematic analysis of the costs of these information systems at the state and the local levels is needed, especially given the persistent budget constraints local and state school systems face. Such an analysis will help

identify the full costs of these information systems, what groups and companies are benefiting from these expenditures, and how these costs are being weighed against other costs.

12. "What Is CEDS?" National Center for Education Statistics, https://ceds.ed.gov/whatIs CEDS.aspx; "CEDS Consortium," National Center for Education Statistics, https://ceds.ed.gov/consortium.aspx.

13. Research has examined the technical design and affordances of state and local student information systems. See National Center for Educational Accountability, *Results of 2006 NCEA Survey of State P–12 Data Collection Issues Related to Longitudinal Analysis,* 2007, http://www.dataqualitycampaign.org/survey_results/; Jeffry C. Wayman, "Involving Teachers in Data-Based Decision-Making: Using Computer Data Systems to Support Teacher Inquiry and Reflection," *Journal of Education for Students Placed at Risk* 10, no. 3(2005): 295–308. A few studies have examined the challenges that state education agencies face constructing statewide longitudinal student information system. See Regional Educational Laboratory, "Getting the Evidence for Evidence-Based Initiatives: How the Midwest States Use Data Systems to Improve Education Processes and Outcomes," http://ies.ed.gov/ncee/edlabs/projects/project.asp?id=29; and Anagnostopoulos and Bautista-Guerra, chap. 2 this volume.

14. Research in the social studies of science and technology is grounded in numerous intellectual traditions, including ethnomethodology, symbolic interactionism, activity theory, and poststructuralism. It shares a focus on the mutual constitution of the social and the technical through which material technologies inscribe the practices, social relations, and knowledge used to create them and simultaneously mediate the production of new practices, relations, and knowledge. See Wiebe E. Bijker and John Law, eds., *Shaping Technology/Building Society* (Cambridge, MA: MIT Press, 1992); Adele E. Clarke and Joan H. Fujimura, "What Tools? Which Jobs? Why Right?" in *The Right Tools for the Job: At Work in Twentieth-Century Life Sciences,* ed. Adele E. Clark and Joan H. Fujimara (Princeton, NJ: Princeton University Press, 1992), 3–46; Steven Epstein, "Culture and Science/Technology: Rethinking Knowledge, Power, Materiality and Nature," *Annals of the American Academy of Political and Social Science* 619, no. 1 (2008): 165–182; Bruno Latour, *Reassembling the Social: An Introduction to Actor-Network Theory* (New York: Oxford University Press, 2005).

15. Susan L. Star, "The Ethnography of Infrastructure," *American Behavioral Scientist* 43, no. 3 (1999): 377–391; Susan L. Star and Karen Ruhleder, "Steps Towards an Ecology of Infrastructure: Design and Access for Large Information Spaces," *Information Systems Research* 7, no. 1 (1999): 111–134; Susan L. Star and James R. Griesemer, "Institutional Ecology, Translations and Boundary Objects: Amateurs and Professionals in Berkeley's Museum of Vertebrate Zoology, 1907–39," *Social Studies of Science* 19, no. 3 (1989): 387–420.

16. While some scholars in the social studies of science and technologies, like Chandra Mukerji, "Toward a Sociology of Material Culture: Science Studies, Cultural Studies and the Meanings of Things," in *The Sociology of Culture: Emerging Theoretical Perspectives,* ed. Diane Crane (Oxford: Blackwell, 1994), use the term *infrastructure* to refer to material structures and devices, such as dams, roads, etc., we conceive of infrastructures as assemblages that include the people and policies necessary to produce, operate, manage, and use these structures as well. Here we draw on studies of the construction of scientific and organizational knowledge rooted in actor-network theory (ANT). These studies explore the sociotechnical processes through which knowledge gets constructed as finished objects or

"facts," such as standardized test scores, teacher value-added estimates, etc. These socio-technical processes include both those through which information gets inscribed into various representations (e.g., school report cards, data files, test scores) and through which the networks of people, texts and devices that produce those representations gets assembled. Because we are studying information and the production of performance data, ANT studies of knowledge production are particularly relevant. See Bruno Latour and Steve Woolgar, *Laboratory Life: The Social Construction of Scientific Facts* (Beverly Hills, CA: Sage, 1979); John Law, "After ANT: Complexity, Naming and Topology," in *Actor Network Theory and After*, ed., John Law and John Hassard (Oxford: Blackwell, 1999), 1–14; John Law, "On the Methods of Long-Distance Control: Vessels, Navigation, and the Portuguese Route to India," in *Power, Action and Belief: A New Sociology of Knowledge?* ed. John Law (London: Routledge & Kegan Paul, 1986), 234–263; John Law, "Notes on the Theory of the Actor-Network: Ordering, Strategy and Heterogeneity, *Systems Practice 5*, no. 4 (1992): 379–393; Bruno Latour, *Reassembling the Social: An Introduction to Actor-Network Theory* (New York: Oxford University Press, 2005); Michael Callon, "Some Elements of a Sociology of Translation: Domestication of the Scallops and the Fishermen of St. Brieuc Bay," in *Power, Action and Belief: A New Sociology of Knowledge?* ed. John Law (London: Routledge & Kegan Paul, 1986), 196–233.

17. Earl Swift, *The Big Roads: The Untold Story of the Engineers, Visionaries, and Trailblazers Who Created the American Superhighways* (Boston: Houghton Mifflin Harcourt, 2011); Tom Lewis, *Divided Highways: Building the Interstate Highways, Transforming American Life* (New York: Penguin, 1999)

18. Susan L. Star, "The Ethnography of Infrastructure," *American Behavioral Scientist,* 43, no. 3(1999): 377–391

19. Mukerji, "Toward a Sociology of Material Culture," 143–162.

20. Swift, *The Big Roads*; Lewis, *Divided Highways*; Dianne Perrier, *Onramps and Overpasses: A Cultural History of Interstate Travel* (Gainesville: University Press of Florida, 2009).

21. Swift, *The Big Roads*; Lewis, *Divided Highways*

22. Chandra Mukerji, "The Territorial State as a Figured World of Power: Strategies, Logistics, and Impersonal Rule," *Sociological Theory* 28, no. 4 (2010): 402–424.

23. Bruno Latour, *Science in Action: How to Follow Scientists and Engineers Through Society* (Cambridge, MA: Harvard University Press, 1987).

24. Center for Education Policy, "Ten Big Effects of the No Child Left Behind Act on Public Schools," http://www.cep-dc.org/displayDocument.cfm?DocumentID=263; David N. Figlio and Lawrence S. Getzler, "Accountability, Ability and Disability: Gaming the System?" in *Improving School Accountability: Advances in Applied Microeconomics*, vol. 14, eds. Timothy J. Gronberg and Dennis W. Jansen (Bingley, UK: Emerald, 2006), 35–49; Julie Berry Cullen and Randal Reback, "Tinkering Toward Accolades: School Gaming Under a Performance Accountability System," in Gronberg and Jansen, *Improving School Accountability*, 1–34; Heinrich Mintrop, *Schools on Probation: How Accountability Works (And Doesn't Work)* (New York: Teachers College Press, 2004). See also Mintrop and Sunderman, chap. 1 this volume.

25. Groups, such as FairTest, and individuals, including standardized test designers, have long advocated against the high-stakes uses of standardized tests. In the spring of 2011, a group of educational, civil rights, and social service organizations issued "The National Testing Resolution," which called on governors, state legislatures, and state boards of education to reduce the reliance on standardized tests. The national resolution was based on anti-

testing resolutions signed by more than 360 schools in Texas, a state that has long been at the vanguard of the test-based accountability movement. See "The National Resolution on High Stakes Testing," http://timeoutfromtesting.org/nationalresolution/.

26. Coburn, Toure, and Yamashita, "Evidence, Interpretation, and Persuasion"; Coburn and Turner, "Research on Data Use."

27. Rothstein, Jacobsen, and Wilder, *Grading Education.*

28. David Tyack and William Tobin, "The Grammar of Schooling: Why Has It Been so Hard to Change?" *American Educational Research Journal* 31, no. 3 (1994): 453–479.

29. David F. Labaree, "The Lure of Statistics for Educational Researchers," in *Educational Research: Ethics and Esthetics of Statistics*, ed. Paul Smeyers and Marc Depaepe (Dordrecht, Germany: Springer, 2011), 12–25.

30. Mary H. Metz, "Real School: A Universal Drama amid Disparate Experience," in *Educational Politics for the New Century: The Twentieth Anniversary Yearbook of the Politics of Education Association*, ed. Douglas E. Mitchell and Margaret E. Goertz (Philadelphia: Falmer Press, 1990), 75–91.

31. Susan L. Star, "Power, Technologies and the Phenomenology of Standards: On Being Allergic to Onions," in *A Sociology of Monsters? Power, Technology and the Modern Word; Sociological Review Monograph 38*, ed. John Law (London: Routledge, 1991), 26–56; Martha Lampland and Susan L. Star, eds., *Standards and Their Stories: How Quantifying, Classifying, and Formalizing Practices Shape Everyday Life* (Ithaca, NY: Cornell University Press, 2009); Geoffrey C. Bowker and Susan L. Star, *Sorting Things Out: Classification and Its Consequences* (Cambridge, MA: MIT Press, 1999).

32. Heinrich Mintrop and Gail L. Sunderman, "The Predictable Failure of Federal Sanctions-Driven Accountability for School Improvement—And Why We May Retain It Anyway," *Educational Researcher* 38, no. 5 (2009): 353–364; Wayne Au, "High-Stakes Testing and Curricular Control: A Qualitative Metasynthesis," *Educational Researcher* 36, no. 5 (2007): 258–267; Center for Education Policy, "Ten Big Effects of the No Child Left Behind Act on Public Schools"; Julian Heilig and Linda Darling-Hammond, "Accountability Texas-Style: The Progress and Learning of Urban Minority Students in a High-Stakes Testing Context," *Educational Evaluation and Policy Analysis* 30, no. 2 (2008): 75–110.

33. Bowker and Star, *Sorting Things Out.*

34. Dorothea Anagnostopoulos and Stacey A. Rutledge, "Making Sense of School Sanctioning Policies in Urban High Schools," *Teachers College Record* 109, no. 5 (2007): 1261–1302; Kenneth Wong and Dorothea Anagnostopoulos, "Can Integrated Governance Reconstruct Teaching? Lessons Learned from Two Low-Performing Chicago High Schools," *Educational Policy* 12, no. 1 (1998): 31–47.

35. For example, Linda Skrla and James J Scheurich, "Displacing Deficit Thinking in School District Leadership," *Education and Urban Society* 33, no. 3 (2001): 235–259.

36. Christopher Ferguson, "The Progress of Education in Texas, Austin" (Austin, TX: Southwest Educational Development Laboratory, 2006); see also Mintrop and Sunderman, chap. 1, and Jennings and Sohn, chap. 10, this volume.

37. Labaree, "The Lure of Statistics," 19.

38. Mintrop and Sunderman, "The Predictable Failure."

39. Labaree, "The Lure of Statistics," 21.

40. Ibid.

41. Bowker and Star, *Sorting Things Out*, 34–46.

Chapter 1

1. Richard Sennett, *The Culture of the New Capitalism* (New Haven, CT: Yale University Press, 2006).

2. David Osborne and Ted Gaebler, *Reinventing Government: How the Entrepreneurial Spirit is Transforming America* (Reading, PA: Addison-Wesley, 1992); Christopher Hood, "A Public Management for All Seasons?" *Public Administration* 69, no. 1 (1991): 3–19; George H. Frederickson, "Comparing the Reinventing Government Movement with the New Public Administration," *Public Administration Review* 56, no. 3 (1996): 263–270; Hood, "A Public Management for All Seasons?"; Frederickson, "Comparing the Reinventing Government Movement."

3. Christopher Hood and Guy Peters, "The Middle Aging of New Public Management: Into the Age of Paradox?" *Journal of Public Administration Research and Theory* 14, no. 3 (2004): 267–282.

4. Heinrich Mintrop and Tina Trujillo, "Corrective Action in Low Performing Schools: Lessons for NCLB Implementation from First-Generation Accountability Systems," *Education Policy Analysis Archives* 13, no. 48 (2005), http://epaa.asu.edu/epaa/v13n48/; Heinrich Mintrop, *Schools on Probation: How Accountability Works (And Doesn't Work)* (New York: Teachers College, 2004).

5. Charles Thompson and John Zeuli, "The Frame and the Tapestry: Standards-Based Reform and Professional Development," in *Teaching as the Learning Profession: Handbook of Policy and Practice*, ed. Linda Darling-Hammond and Gary Sykes (San Francisco: Jossey-Bass, 1999).

6. Susan H. Fuhrman, *The New Accountability*, CPRE Policy Brief RB-27 (Philadelphia: Consortium for Policy Research in Education, University of Pennsylvania, 1999).

7. Heinrich Mintrop, "Low-Performing Schools' Programs and State Capacity Requirments: Meeting the NCLB Educational Goals," in *Holding NCLB Accountable: Achieving Accountability, Equity, and School Reform*, ed. Gail L. Sunderman (Thousand Oaks, CA: Corwin Press, 2008), 137–151; Dorothea Anagnostopoulos and Stacy Rutledge, "Making Sense of School Sanctioning Policies in Urban High Schools: Charting the Depth and Drift of School and Classroom Change," *Teachers College Record* 109, no. 5 (2007): 1261–1302; Mintrop, *Schools on Probation*; Kenneth Wong and Dorothea Anagnostopoulos, "Can Integrated Governance Reconstruct Teaching? Lessons Learned from Two Low-Performing Chicago High Schools," *Educational Policy* 12, no. 1 (1998): 31–47.

8. Caroline Kelley and Jean Protsik, "Risk and Reward: Perspectives on the Implementation of Kentucky's School-Based Performance Award Program," *Educational Administration Quarterly* 33, no. 4 (1997): 474–505; Linda Skrla and Joseph J. Scheurich, "Displacing Deficit Thinking in School District Leadership," in *Educational Equity and Accountability*, ed. Linda Skrla and Joseph J. Scheurich (New York: Routledge Farmer, 2004), 109–132; Eric A. Hanushek and Margaret E. Raymond, "Does School Accountability Lead to Improved Performance?" *Journal of Policy Analysis and Management* 24, no. 2 (2004): 297–327.

9. Kenneth Leithwood, Roseanne Steinbach, and Doris Jantzi, "School Leadership and Teachers' Motivation to Implement Accountability Policies," *Educational Administration Quarterly* 38, no. 1 (2002): 94–119; Richard F. Elmore, *School Reform from the Inside Out: Policy, Practice and Performance* (Cambridge, MA: Harvard Education Press, 2004); Kara Finnigan and Betheny Gross, "Do Accountability Policy Sanctions Influence Teacher Motivation? Lessons from Chicago's Low-Performing Schools," *American Educational Research Journal* 44, no. 3 (2007): 594–629.

10. Mintrop, *Schools on Probation;* Jennifer O'Day and Catherine Bitter, *Evaluation Study of the Immediate Intervention/Underperforming Schools Program and the High Achieving/Improving Schools Program of the Public Schools Accountability Act of 1999* (Sacramento, CA: American Institutes of Research, 2003); Jennifer A. O'Day, "Complexity, Accountability and School Improvement. *Harvard Educational Review* 72, no. 3 (2002): 293–329.

11. Joseph Pedulla, Lisa M. Abrams, George F. Madaus, Michael K. Russell, Miguel A. Ramos, and Jing Miao, *Perceived Effects of State-Mandated Testing Programs on Teaching and Learning: Findings from a National Survey of Teachers* (Boston: National Board on Educational Testing and Public Policy, 2003); George Madaus and Marguerite Clarke, "The Adverse Impact of High-Stakes Testing on Minority Students: Evidence from One Hundred Years of Test Data," in *Raising Standards or Raising Barriers? Inequality and High-Stakes Testing in Public Education*, ed. Gary Orfield and Mindy L. Kornhaber (New York: The Century Foundation Press, 2001), 85–106; David T. Conley and Paul Goldman, *Half Full, Half Empty? Educator Responses Over Time to State-Level Systematic Reforms; International Review of Industrial and Organizational Psychology* (Chichester, UK: Wiley, 2000).

12. Mintrop and Trujillo, "Corrective Action in Low Performing Schools."

13. Jennifer A. O'Day and Catherine Bitter, *Evaluation Study*; Jennifer A. O'Day, Catherine Bitter, M. Kirst, Martin Carnoy, Elisabeth Woody, Melissa Buttles, B. Fuller, and David Ruenzel, *Assessing California's Accountability System: Successes, Challenges, and Opportunities for Improvement* (Berkeley: Policy Analysis for California Education, 2004; Martha L. Thurlow, "Biting the Bullet: Including Special Needs Students in Accountability Systems," in *Redesigning Accountability Systems for Education,* ed. Susan Fuhrman and Richard Elmore (New York: Teachers College Press, 2004), 115–137.

14. Sharon L. Nichols, Gene V. Glass, and David C. Berliner, "High-Stakes Testing and Student Achievement: Does Accountability Pressure Increase Student Learning?" *Education Policy Analysis Archives* 14, no. 1 (2006), http://epaa.asu.edu/epaa/v14n1/.

15. Christopher Ferguson, "The Progress of Education in Texas, Austin" (Austin, TX: Southwest Educational Development Laboratory, 2006); Mintrop and Trujillo, "Corrective Action in Low Performing Schools."

16. "State Test Score Trends through 2008–09, Part 4: Is Achievement Improving and are Gaps Narrowing for Title I Students?" (Washington, DC: Center for Educational Policy, 2011); Lee Jaekyung, *Tracking Achievement Gaps and Assessing the Impact of NCLB on the Gaps: An In-depth Look into National and State Reading and Math Outcome Trends* (Cambridge, MA: The Civil Rights Project at Harvard University, 2006).

17. Jaekyung, *Tracking Achievement Gaps*; National Research Council, *Incentives and Test-Based Accountability in Education* (Washington, DC: National Academies Press, 2011); Jaekyung Lee, *The Testing Gap: Scientific Trials of Test-Driven School Accountability Systems for Excellence and Equity* (Charlotte, NC: Information Age, 2007); Erick Hanushek and Margaret E. Raymond, "Does School Sccountability Lead to Improved Performance?" *Journal of Policy Analysis and Management* 24, no. 2 (2004): 297–327; Jaekyung Lee and Todd Reeves, "Revisiting the Impact of NCLB High-Stakes School Accountability, Capacity and Resources: State NAEP 1990-2009 Reading and Math Achievement Gaps and Trends," *Educational Evaluation and Policy Analysis* 34, no. 2 (2012): 209–231.

18. Daniel M. Koretz, "The Validity of Score Gains on High-Stakes Tests," in *International Encyclopedia of Education,* 3rd ed., ed. Penelope L. Peterson and Eva Baker (Oxford: Elsevier, 2010); Daniel M. Koretz, "The Pending Reauthorization of NCLB: An Oppor-

tunity to Rethink the Basic Strategy," in Sunderman, *Holding NCLB Accountable*, 9–26. See also Jennings and Sohn, chap. 10 this volume.

19. Paul E. Peterson and Frederick M. Hess, "Few States Set World-Class Standards: In Fact, Most Render the Notion of Proficiency Meaningless," *Education Next* 8, no. 3 (2008): 70–73.

20. Gail L. Sunderman and Gary Orfield, "Domesticating a Revolution: No Child Left Behind and State Administrative Response," *Harvard Educational Review* 76, no. 4 (2006): 526–556.

21. Wayne Au, "High-Stakes Testing and Curricular Control: A Qualitative Metasynthesis," *Educational Researcher* 36, no. 5 (2007): 258–267; Gail L. Sunderman, Christopher A. Tracey, Jimmy S. Kim, and Gary Orfield, *Listening to Teachers: Classroom Realities and No Child Left Behind* (Cambridge, MA: The Civil Rights Project at Harvard University, 2004); Elmore, *School Reform from the Inside Out*.

22. Skrla and Scheurich, "Displacing Deficit Thinking in School District Leadership"; Douglas L. Lauen and Michael Gaddis, "Shining a Light or Fumbling in the Dark? The Effects of NCLB's Subgroup-Specific Accountability on Student Achievement," *Educational Evaluation and Policy Analysis* 34, no. 2 (2012): 185–208.

23. Derek Neal and Diane Whitmore Schanzenbach, *Left Behind by Design: Proficiency Counts and Test-Based Accountability* (Chicago: University of Chicago Press, 2008); Jennifer Booher-Jennings, "Below the Bubble: 'Educational Triage' and the Texas Accountability System," *American Educational Research Journal* 42 no. 2 (2005): 231–268; Walter M. Haney, "Evidence on Education Under NCLB (and How Florida Boosted NAEP Scores and Reduced the Race Gap)," in Sunderman, *Holding NCLB Accountable: Achieving Accountability, Equity and School Reform*, 91–101; Robert Balfanz and Nettie E. Legters, "NCLB and Reforming the Nation's Lowest-Performing High Schools," in ibid., 191–207; Jimmy S. Kim and Gail L. Sunderman, "Measuring Academic Proficiency Under the No Child Left Behind Act: Implications for Educational Equity," *Educational Researcher* 34, no. 8 (2005): 3–13; John Novak and Bruce Fuller, *Penalizing Diverse Schools? Similar Test Scores but Different Students Bring Federal Sanctions* (Berkeley: Policy Analysis for California Education, 2003); Robert L. Linn, "Conflicting Demands of No Child Left Behind and State Systems: Mixed Messages about School Performance," *Education Policy Analysis Archives* 13, no. 33 (2005), http://epaa.asu.edu/epaa/v13n33/; Heinrich Mintrop and Gail L. Sunderman, "Predictable Failure of Federal Sanctions-Driven Accountability for School Improvement—And Why We May Retain It Anyway," *Educational Researcher* 38, no. 1 (2009): 353–364.

24. Bronwyn Coltrane, "English Language Learners and High-Stakes Tests: An Overview of the Issues," *ERIC Digest* (2002), http://www.cal.org/ericcll/DIGEST; Laura Batt, Jimmy S. Kim, and Gail L. Sunderman, *Limited English Proficiency Students: Increased Accountability Under NCLB* (Cambridge, MA: The Civil Rights Project at Harvard University, 2005); Michael J. Kieffer, Nonie K. Lesaux, and Catherine E. Snow, "Promises and Pitfalls: Implications of NCLB for Identifying, Assessing, and Educating English Language Learners," in Sunderman, *Holding NCLB Accountable*, 57–74; Jay Heubert, "Disability, Race and High-Stakes Testing of Students," in *Racial Inequality in SpecialEeducation*, ed. Daniel J. Losen and Gary Orfield (New York: The Century Fund, 2002); Jamal Abedi, "The No Child Left Behind Act and English Language Learners: Assessment and Accountability Issues," *Educational Researcher* 33, no. 1 (2004): 4–14.

25. Nanette Asimov, "State Falling Way Behind No Child Left Behind," *San Francisco Chronicle*, September 5, 2008.

26. Richard Hackman and Greg Oldman, "Motivation Through the Design of Work: Test of a Theory," *Organizational Behavior and Human Performance* 16, no. 2 (1976): 250–279; Betty Achinstein and Rodney T. Ogawa, "(In)Fidelity: What the Resistance of New Teachers Reveals about Professional Principles and Prescriptive Educational Policies," *Harvard Educational Review* 76, no. 1 (2006): 30–63; Sheila W. Valencia et al., "Curriculum Materials for Elementary Reading: Shackles and Scaffolds for Four Beginning teachers," *Elementary School Journal* 107, no. 1 (2006): 93–120.

27. Achinstein and Ogawa, "(In)Fidelity"; Alan J. Daly, "Rigid Response in an Age of Accountability," *Educational Administration Quarterly* 45, no. 2 (2009): 168–216; Jim Cummins, "Pedagogies for the Poor? Realigning Reading Instruction for Low-Income Students with Scientifically Based Reading Research," *Educational Researcher* 36, no. 9 (2007): 564–572.

28. Lee and Reeves, "Revisiting the Impact of NCLB High-Stakes School Accountability, Capacity, and Resources."

29. Richard Rothstein, *Class and Schools: Using Social, Economic, and Educational Reform to Close the Black-White Achievement Gap* (New York: Teachers College Press, 2004); Sean F. Reardon, "The Widening Academic Achievement Gap Between the Rich and the Poor: New Evidence and Possible Explanations," in *Whither Opportunity? Rising Inequality, Schools, and Children's Life Chances*, ed. Greg, J. Duncan and Richard J. Murnane (New York: Russell Sage Foundation, 2011); Greg J. Duncan and Richard J. Murnane, ed. *Whither Opportunity? Rising Inequality, Schools, and Children's Life Chances* (New York: Russell Sage Foundation, 2011); Heather Schwartz, *Housing Policy Is School Policy: Economically Integrative Housing Promotes Academic Success in Montgomery County, Maryland* (Washington, DC: The Century Foundation, 2010).

30. Hood, "A Public Management for All Seasons?"

31. Christopher Pollitt and Geert Bouckaert, *Public Management Reform: A Comparative Analysis—New Public Management, Governance, and the Neo-Weberian State* (New York: Oxford University Press, 2011); Patrick Dunleavy, Helen Margetts, Simon Bastow, and Jane Tinkler, "New Public Management Is Dead—Long Live Digital-Era Governance," *Journal of Public Administration Research and Theory* 16, no. 3 (2006): 467–494; Robert Gregory, "New Public Management and the Ghost of Max Weber: Exorcized or Still Haunting," in *Transcending New Public Management: The Transformation of Public Sector Reforms*, ed. Tom Christensen and Per Laegreid (Farnham, UK: Ashgate, 2006); Christopher Pollitt, "Is the Emperor in His Underwear?" *Public Management* 2, no. 2 (2006): 181–200.

32. Hood and Peters, "The Middle Aging of New Public Management"; Sandra Van Thiel and Frans Leeuw, "The Performance Paradox in the Public," *Public Performance and Management Review* 25, no. 13 (2002): 267–281.

33. Pollitt and Bouckaert, *Public Management Reform.*

34. James Spillane, "Local Theories of Teacher Change: The Pedagogy of District Policies and Programs," *Teachers College Record*, 104, no. 3 (2002): 377–420.

35. Gail L. Sunderman, *The Unraveling of No Child Left Behind: How Negotiated Changes Transform the Law* (Cambridge, MA: The Civil Rights Project at Harvard University 2006); Sunderman, Tracey, Kim, and Orfield, *Listening to Teachers.*

36. Rod Paige, "Letter to Chief State School Officers Regarding Implementation of the No Child Left Behind Act 2002," *New York Times*, October 22, 2002; Nina Rees, "Public School Choice," letter to the editor, *New York Times*, October 8, 2003.

37. David Collingridge, *The Management of Scale: Big Organizations, Big Decisions, Big Mistakes* (London: Routledge, 1992); Hood and Peters, "The Middle Aging of New Public

Management"; Cynthia Coburn and Erica O. Turner, "Research on Data Use: A Framework and Analysis," *Measurement: Interdisciplinary Research and Perspective* 9, no. 4 (2011): 173–206.

38. Jenny Harrow, "Capacity Building as a Public Management Goal; Myth, Magic, or the Main Change?" *Public Management Review* 3, no. 2 (2010): 209–230.

39. Jennifer A. O'Day, "Complexity, Accountability, and School Improvement," *Harvard Educational Review* 72, no. 3 (2002): 293–329; Anthony S. Bryk, Penny Sebring, Ellen Allensworth, Stuart Luppescu, and John Q. Easton, *Organizing Schools for Improvement: Lessons from Chicago* (Chicago: University of Chicago Press, 2010); Eva L. Baker and Robert L. Linn, "Validity Issues for Accountability Systems," in *Redesigning Accountability Systems*, ed. Susan H. Fuhrman and Richard F. Elmore (New York: Teachers College Press, 2004), 47–72.

40. Jennifer A. O'Day and Catherine Bitter, *Evaluation Study of the Immediate Intervention/ Underperforming Schools Program and the High Achieving/Improving Schools Program of the Public Schools Accountability Act of 1999* (Sacramento, CA: American Institutes of Research, 2003); Ron Zimmer, Brian Gill, Kevin Booker, Stephane Lavertu, Tim R. Sass, and John F. Witte, *Charter Schools in Eight States: Effects on Achievement, Attainment, Integration and Competition* (Santa Monica, CA: RAND, 2009); Center for Research on Education Outcomes (CREDO), *Multiple Choice: Charter School Performance in 16 States* (Palo Alto, CA: Stanford University, 2009).

41. Jenny Harrow, "Capacity Building as a Public Management Goal: Myth, Magic, or the Main Change?" *Public Management Review* 3, no. 2 (2010): 209–230.

42. John R. Schwille, Andrew Porter, Linda Alford, Robert Floden, Donald Freeman, Susan Irwin, and William Schmidt, "State Policy and the Control of Curriculum Decisions," *Educational Policy* 2, no. 1 (1988): 29–50; Laura M. Desimone, Thomas M. Smith, Susan A. Hayes, and David Frisvold, "Beyond Accountability and Average Mathematics Scores: Relating State Education Policy Attributes to Cognitive Achievement Domains," *Educational Measurement: Issues and Practice* 24, no. 4 (2005): 5–18; Jason L. Pressman and Aaron Wildavsky, *Implementation: How Great Expectations in Washington Are Dashed in Oakland* (Berkeley: University of California Press, 1973).

43. Donald T. Campbell, "Assessing the Impact of Planned Social Change," *Evaluation and Program Planning* 2, no. 1 (1976): 67–90.

44. Bengt Holmstrom and Paul Milgrom, "Multitask Principal-Agent Analyses: Incentive Contracts, Asset Ownership, and Job Design," *Journal of Law, Economics, and Organization* 7 (Spring 1991): 24–52.

45. Sandra Van Thiel and Frans Leeuw, "The Performance Paradox in the Public," *Public Performance and Management Review* 25, no. 13 (2002): 267–281; Pollitt and Bouckaert, *Public Management Reform.*

46. Christensen and Laegreid, *Transcending New Public Management.*

47. Stephen Ball, "The Teacher's Soul and the Terrors of Performativity," *Journal of Education Policy* 18, no. 2 (2010): 215–228.

48. Jean-Francois Lyotard, *The Postmodern Condition: A Report on Knowledge* (Minneapolis: University of Minnesota Press, 2004).

49. Ball, "The Teacher's Soul and the Terrors of Performativity," 216.

50. Ibid.

51. See http://www.ed.gov/esea/flexibility; http://www2.ed.gov/programs/racetothetop/; http://www.corestandards.org/; http://www2.ed.gov/policy/elsec/leg/blueprint/; http://www.district administration.com/news/harkins.

52. Douglas Harris, "Would Accountability Based on Teacher Value Added Be Smart Policy? An Examination of the Statistical Properties and Policy Alternatives," *Education Finance and Policy* 4, no. 4 (2009): 319–350; Eva L. Baker and Robert L. Linn, "Validity Issues for Accountability Systems," in *Redesigning Accountability Systems*, ed. Susan H. Fuhrman and Richard F. Elmore (New York: Teachers College Press, 2004); Xiaxia A. Newton, Linda Darling-Hammond, Edward H. Haertel, and Ewart Thomas, "Value-Added Modeling of Teacher Effectiveness: An Exploration of Stability Across Models and Contexts," *Education Policy Analysis Archives* 18, no. 23 (2010), http://epaa.asu.edu/ojs/article/view/810.

53. Charlotte Danielson and Thomas McGreal, *Teacher Evaluation to Enhance Professional Practice* (Alexandria, VA: ASCD, 2000).

54. Jennifer A. O'Day, "Complexity, Accountability and School Improvement," *Harvard Educational Review* 72, no. 3 (2002): 293–329; Hans N. Weiler, "Comparative Perspectives on Educational Decentralization: An Exercise in Contradiction?" *Educational Evaluation and Policy Analysis* 12, no. 4 (1990): 433–448.

55. David Osborne and Ted Gaebler, *Reinventing Government: How the Entrepreneurial Spirit Is Transforming America* (Reading, PA: Addison-Wesley, 1992).

Chapter 2

1. Heinrich Mintrop, *Schools on Probation: How Accountability Works (and Doesn't Work)* (New York: Teachers College Press, 2004); Mintrop and Sunderman, chap. 1 this volume; Rutledge and Neal, chap. 6 this volume.

2. Data Quality Campaign, *Creating a Longitudinal Data System: Using Data to Improve Student Achievement*, http://www.dataqualitycampaign.org/tools/index.cfm#DQCResources.

3. Megan Tschannen-Moran and Wayne K. Hoy, "A Multidisciplinary Analysis of the Nature, Meaning, and Measurement of Trust," *Review of Educational Research* 70, no. 4 (2000): 556.

4. Anthony S. Bryk and Barbara Schneider, *Trust in Schools* (New York: Russell Sage Foundation, 2002); Mark A. Smylie, David Mayrowetz, Josephy Murphy, and Karen Seashore Louis, "Trust and the Development of Distributed Leadership," *Journal of School Leadership* 17 (2007): 469–503.

5. Roderick M. Kramer and Karen S. Cook, eds., *Trust and Distrust in Organizations: Dilemmas and Approaches* (New York: Russell Sage Foundation, 2004), 2.

6. Roderick M. Kramer, "Trust and Distrust in Organizations: Emerging Perspectives, Enduring Questions," *Annual Review of Psychology* 50 (1999): 590–592.

7. Wiebe E. Bijker and John Law, eds., *Shaping Technology/Building Society* (Cambridge, MA: MIT Press, 1992); John Law, *Aircraft Stories: Decentering the Object in Technoscience* (Durham, NC: Duke University Press, 2001); Bruno Latour, *Science in Action: How to Follow Scientists and Engineers Through Society* (Cambridge, MA: Harvard University Press, 1987); Michael Callon, "Some Elements of a Sociology of Translation: Domestication of the Scallops and the Fishermen of St. Brieuc Bay," in *Power, Action and Belief: A New Sociology of Knowledge?* ed. John Law (London: Routledge & Kegan Paul, 1989), 196–233.

8. Susan L. Star, "The Ethnography of Infrastructure," *American Behavioral Scientist* 43, no. 3 (1999): 377–391; Susan L. Star and Karen Ruhleder, "Steps Towards an Ecology of Infrastructure: Design and Access for Large Information Spaces," *Information Systems Research* 7, no.1 (1996): 111–134.

9. Dorothea Anagnostopoulos and Valentina Bali, *Implementing Statewide Student Longitudinal Data Systems: Lessons Learned from the States* (unpublished final report to the IBM Center for the Business of Government, 2008).

10. Tschannen-Moran and Hoy, "Nature, Meaning, and Measurement of Trust," 579.

11. Ibid., 578.

12. Ibid., 576–577.

13. Jeffrey Wayman, "Involving Teachers in Data-Driven Decision Making: Using Computer Data Systems to Support Teacher Inquiry and Reflection," *Journal of Education for Students Placed at Risk* 10, no. 3 (2005): 295–308; Richard Halverson, Jeffrey Grigg, Reid Prichett, and Chris Thomas, "The New Instructional Leadership: Creating Data-Driven Instructional Systems in Schools," *Journal of School Leadership* 17, no. 2 (2007): 159–194; Halverson and Shapiro, chap. 9 this volume.

14. Kramer, "Trust and Distrust in Organizations," 590–592.

Chapter 3

1. Douglas N. Harris, Stacey A. Rutledge, William K. Ingle, and Cynthia C. Thompson, "Mix and Match: What Principals Really Look for when Hiring Teachers," *Education Finance and Policy* 5, no. 2 (2010): 228–246.

2. Douglas N. Harris and Tim R. Sass, "Value-Added Models and the Measurement of Teacher Quality" (unpublished manuscript, Florida State University, Tallahassee, 2006); Douglas N. Harris, "Would Accountability Based on Teacher Value Added Be Smart Policy? An Examination of the Statistical Properties and Policy Alternatives," *Education Finance and Policy* 4, no. 4 (2009): 319–350; Douglas N. Harris, "Value-Added Measures and the Future of Educational Accountability," *Science* 333, no. 6044 (2011): 826–827; Steven Glazerman, Susanna Loeb, Dan Goldhaber, Douglas Staiger, Stephen Raudenbush, and Grover Whitehurst, *Evaluating Teachers: The Important Role of Value-Added* (Washington, DC: Brookings Institution, 2011).

3. See Thomas Kane and Douglas Staiger, *Gathering Feedback for Teaching: Combining High-Quality Observations with Student Surveys and Achievement Gains* (Seattle: Bill & Melinda Gates Foundation, 2012); Douglas N. Harris, *Value-Added Measures of Education Performance: Clearing Away the Smoke and Mirrors* (Palo Alto, CA: Policy Analysis for California Education, Stanford University, 2010).

4. See Jeffery Watson, Peter Witham, and Timothy St. Louis, *Evaluating Student-Teacher Linkage Data in Teacher Incentive Fund (TIF) Sites: Acquisition, Verification, and System Development* (Washington, DC: U.S. Department of Education, Office of Elementary and Secondary Education, 2010); *The Importance of Accurately Linking Instruction to Students to Determine Teacher Effectiveness* (Columbus, OH: Battelle for Kids, 2011).

5. See http://www.bushfoundation.org/education/network-excellence-teaching-next.

6. Caryn Mohr, Katie Broton, and Dan Muelle, *Bush Foundation Teacher Effectiveness Initiative: Phase II Feedback* (St. Paul, MN: The Archibald Bush Foundation, 2010).

7. Harris et al., "Mix and Match."

8. See http://theacademicvillage.blogspot.com/2011/04/bush-foundation-to-provide.html.

9. See Douglas N. Harris, *Value-Added Measures in Education* (Cambridge, MA: Harvard Education Press, 2011).

10. See http://www.bushfoundation.org/blog/investing-research-reduce-achievement-gap.

11. See http://blog.lib.umn.edu/cehd/teri/docs/Common%20Metrics.pdf.

12. See http://www.bushfoundation.org/blog/investing-research-reduce-achievement-gap

13. See http://www.maricopa.gov/schools/service-home.aspx?sid=1&cid=1; U.S. Department of Education, "Office of Elementary and Secondary Education: Overview Information; Teacher Incentive Fund; Notice Inviting Applications for New Awards for Fiscal Year (FY) 2006," *Federal Register* 71, no. 219 (2006): 66317–66321.

14. U.S. Department of Education, "Office of Elementary and Secondary Education: Overview Information; Teacher Incentive Fund; Notice Inviting Applications for New Awards for Fiscal Year (FY) 2010," *Federal Register* 75, no. 98 (2010): 28740–28749.

15. See http://www2.ed.gov/news/pressreleases/2010/05/05202010.html.

16. See http://www.maricopa.gov/schools/webcontent/docs/REIL_Learning_Obs_Instr_7-11-11_lr_51.pdf.

17. See the rollout plan at http://www.maricopa.gov/schools/webcontent/docs/REIL_Webcast LearningObservationInstrument_51.pdf.

18. See http://communication.sdhc.k12.fl.us/eethome/.

19. See http://www.sdhc.k12.fl.us/eet/v6/.

20. See http://www.convergenceconsultinggroup.com/convergence-consulting-group-recognized-as-premier-small-business/.

21. See http://communication.sdhc.k12.fl.us/empoweringteachers/.

22. See http://communication.sdhc.k12.fl.us/empoweringteachers/?page_id=706; and http://communication.sdhc.k12.fl.us/empoweringteachers/?page_id=313.

23. Jonathan Eckert, ed., *Local Labor Management Relationships as a Vehicle to Advance Reform: Findings from the U.S. Department of Education's Labor Management Conference* (Washington, DC: U.S. Department of Education, 2011).

24. Commission on Effective Teachers and Teaching, *Transforming Teaching: Connecting Professional Responsibility with Student Learning* (Washington, DC: National Education Association, 2011); American Federation of Teachers, "Weingarten Proposes Aligning Evaluation and due Process," http://www.aft.org/newspubs/news/2011/022411weingarten.cfm.

Chapter 4

1. Ellen C. Lagemann, *The Politics of Knowledge: The Carnegie Corporation, Philanthropy, and Public Policy* (Chicago: University of Chicago Press, 1992), 364; James D. Anderson, *The Education of Blacks in the South, 1860–1935* (Chapel Hill: University of North Carolina Press, 1988), 366; Nicholas Lemann, "Citizen 501(c)(3)," *Atlantic Monthly,* Februrary 6, 1997, 18–20; Dennis McIlnay, "Philanthropy at 50: Four moments in time," *Foundation News and Commentary,* 39, no. 5 (1998), http://www.foundationnews.org/CME/article.cfm?ID=1053.

2. David Tyack and Larry Cuban, *Tinkering Toward Utopia: A Century of Public School Reform* (Cambridge, MA: Harvard University Press, 1995), 178.

3. Venture philanthropies are foundations that assume a more active role than more traditional foundations in seeking out potential grantees or "investments," typically closely aligned with the policy preferences of the foundation or philanthropy. For more description of venture philanthropies, see Janelle Scott, "The Politics of Venture Philanthropy in Charter School Policy and Advocacy," *Educational Policy* 23, no. 1 (2009): 106–136; Sarah Reckhow, "Disseminating and Legitimating a New Approach: The Role of Foundations," in *Between Public and Private: Politics, Governance, and the New Portfolio Models for Urban School Reform*, ed. Katrina Bulkley, Jeffery R. Henig, and Henry M. Levin (Cambridge, MA: Harvard Education Press, 2010), 277–304.

4. See "J. P. Morgan Donates $1 Million to Train New York City Teachers," 2011, http://www.jpmorgan.com/cm/cs?pagename=JPM_redesign/JPM_Content_C/ Generic_Detail_Page_Template&cid=1299711962598&c=JPM_Content_C).

5. Janelle Scott and Catherine C. DiMartino, "Hybridized, Franchised, Duplicated, and Replicated: Charter Schools and Management Organizations," in *The Charter School Experiment: Expectations, Evidence, and Limitations,* ed. Christopher Lubienski and Peter Weitzel (Cambridge, MA: Harvard Education Press, 2010), 171–196.

6. Thomas Toch, "Educational Entrepreneurs on the Potomac," *Phi Delta Kappan* 92, no. 7 (2011): 68–69.

7. Christopher Lubienski, Janelle Scott, and Elizabeth DeBray, "The Rise of Intermediary Organizations in Knowledge Production, Advocacy, and Educational Policy," *Teachers College Record* (2011), ID No. 16487, http://www.tcr.org.

8. We thank the William T. Grant Foundation for its support of this research. Co–principal investigators are Professors Christopher Lubienski, Elizabeth DeBray, and Janelle Scott; research assistants are Huriya Jabbar, Matthew Linick, Priya Goel, and David Goldie.

9. Lagemann, *The Politics of Knowledge,* 364.

10. Scott, "The Politics of Venture Philanthropy."

11. John Kingdon, Agendas, Alternatives, and Public Policies (New York: Longman, 2003).

12. Lagemann, *The Politics of Knowledge,* 364.

13. Dennis McIlnay, "Philanthropy at 50: Four Moments in Time," *Foundation News and Commentary,* 1998, http://www.foundationnews.org/CME/article.cfm?ID=1053; Joan Roelofs, *Foundations and Public Policy: The Mask of Pluralism* (Albany: State University of New York Press, 2003).

14. John H. Stanfield, *Philanthropy and Jim Crow in American Social Science* (Westport, CT: Greenwood Press, 1985).

15. Francis Patrick Walsh and Basil M. Manly, *Final Report of the Commission on Industrial Relations: Including the Report of Basil M. Manly, Director of Research and Investigation, and the Individual Reports and Statements of the Several Commissioners* (Washington, DC: Government Printing Office, 1916).

16. Steve Barr, Frederick Hess, Vanessa Kirsch, Joel Klein, Tom Vander Ark, and Paul Tough, "How Many Billionaires Does It Take to Fix a School System?" *New York Times,* February 27, 2011.

17. David Tyack, *The One Best System: A History of American Urban Education* (Cambridge, MA: Harvard University Press, 1974).

18. Graham Bowley and Matthew Saltmarsh, "Goldman Earns $3.19 Billion, Beating Estimates," *New York Times,* October 16, 2009, http://www.nytimes.com/2009/10/16/business/16goldman.html?_r=1&hp.

19. Sam Dillon, "Gateses Give $290 Million for Education," New York Times, November 19, 2009; Malcolm Gladwell, "Most Likely to Succeed," New Yorker, December 15, 2008, http://www.new.yorker.com/reporting/2008/12/15/081215fa_fact_gladwell; Douglas McGray, "The Instigator," ibid., May 11, 2009, 66–74.

20. Fredrick M. Hess, *With the Best of Intentions: How Philanthropy Is Reshaping K–12 Education* (Cambridge, MA: Harvard Educational Publishing Group, 2005).

21. Cynthia Coburn, "The Role of Nonsystem Actors in the Relationship Between Policy and Practice: The Case of Reading Instruction in California," *Educational Evaluation and Policy Analysis* 27, no. 1 (2005): 23–52.

22. We requested a further breakdown of grants made by the Walton Foundation but were not able to obtain that information from the foundation, so we have not included them here.

Given that Walton is one of the largest donors to K–12 education, we would have liked to include its data. The Robertson and Fisher foundations also did not report this information on their Form 990s, so we were unable to include them as well.

23. These are the case study sites for our William T. Grant Foundation study on research use and incentivist reforms. We chose these cities because they all have active reform agendas that include one or more incentives-based reform. Washington, DC, allows us to consider the local-national networks around these reforms.

24. Janelle Scott and Catherine C. DiMartino, "Hybridized, Franchised, Duplicated, and Replicated: Charter Schools and Management Organizations," in Lubienski and Peter Weitzel, *The Charter School Experiment,* 171–196; Janelle Scott and Catherine C. DiMartino, "Public Education Under New Management: A Typology of Educational Privatization Applied to New York City's Restructuring," *Peabody Journal of Education* 83, no. 3 (2009): 432–452.

Chapter 5

1. Christopher Berry and William Howell, "Accountability and Local Elections: Rethinking Retrospective Voting," *Journal of Politics,* 69, no. 3 (2007): 844–858.

2. Ibid., 844.

3. Kenneth K. Wong, Francis X. Shen, Dorothea Anagnostopoulos, and Stacey Rutledge , *The Education Mayor: Improving America's Schools* (Washington, DC: Georgetown University Press, 2007).

4. Linda Jacobsen, "Project Aims to Tackle Dropout Problem, California-Style," *Education Week,* April 30, 2008, 8.

5. Achon Fung, *Empowered Participation: Reinventing Urban Democracy* (Princeton, NJ: Princeton University Press, 2004).

6. Sarah Reckhow, "Disseminating and Legitimating a New Approach," in *Between Public and Private,* ed. Katrina E. Bulkley, Jeffrey R. Henig, and Henry M. Levin (Cambridge, MA: Harvard Education Press, 2010), 277–304.

7. Jeffrey Henig, Richard C. Hula, Marion Orr, and Desiree S. Pedescleaux, *The Color of School Reform: Race, Politics, and the Challenge of Urban Education* (Princeton, NJ: Princeton University Press, 2001).

8. William Boyd, Jolley Bruce Christman, and Elizabeth Useem, "Radical Privatization in Philadelphia: School Leaders as Policy Entrepreneurs," in *The Transformation of Great American School Districts: How Big Cities Are Reshaping Public Education,* ed. William Boyd, Charles Kerchner, and Mark Blyth. (Cambridge, MA: Harvard Education Press, 2008), 33–60.

9. ARC, *Report to the School Reform Commission: The Status of 2009–2010 Academic Performance in the School District of Philadelphia* (Philadelphia: School District of Philadelphia, 2011).

10. Ibid., 33.

11. Ibid., 40–45.

12. Bruce Jolley, Eva Gold Christman, and Benjamin B. Herold, *Privatization "Philly Style": What Can Be Learned from Philadelphia's Diverse Provider Model of School Management?* updated ed. (Philadelphia: Research for Action, 2006).

13. Brian Gill, Laura S. Hamilton, J. R. Lockwood, Julie A. Marsh, Ron W. Zimmer, Deanna Hill, and Shana Pribesh, *Inspiration, Perspiration and Time: Operations and Achievement in Edison Schools* (Santa Monica, CA: RAND, 2005).

14. Brian Gill et al., *State Takeover, School Restructuring, Private Management, and Student Achievement in Philadelphia* (Santa Monica, CA: RAND, 2007).

15. Paul E. Peterson and Matthew M. Chingos, *Impact of For-Profit and Non-Profit Management on Student Achievement: The Philadelphia Story* (Cambridge, MA: Program on Education Policy and Governance, Kennedy School of Government, Harvard University, 2007).

16. ARC, *Report to the School Reform Commission.*

Chapter 6

1. Raj Chetty, John N. Friedman, and Jonah E. Rockoff, "The Long-Term Impacts of Teachers: Teacher Value-added and Student Outcomes in Adulthood" (working paper 17699, National Bureau of Economic Research, Cambridge, MA, 2011); Eric A. Hanushek, "The Economic Value of Higher Teacher Quality," *Economics of Education Review* 30, no. 2 (2011): 466–479.

2. Dorothea Anagnostopoulos, "The New Accountability, Student Failure, and Teachers' Work in Urban High Schools," *Educational Policy* 17, no. 3 (2003): 291–316; Wayne Au, "High-Stakes Testing and Curricular Control: A Qualitative Metasynthesis," *Educational Researcher* 36, no. 5 (2007): 258–267; Lora Cohen-Vogel, "Staffing to the Test": Are Today's School Personnel Practices Evidence Based?" *Educational Evaluation and Policy Analysis* 33, no. 4 (2011): 483–505; William A. Firestone, Lora Monfils, and Roberta Y. Schorr, "Test Preparation in New Jersey: Inquiry-Oriented and Didactic Responses," *Assessment in Education Principles Policy and Practice* 11, no. 1 (2004): 67–88; Helen F. Ladd and Arnaldo Zelli, "School-Based Accountability in North Carolina: The Responses of School Principals," *Educational Administration Quarterly* 38, no. 4 (2002): 494–529; Stacey A. Rutledge, "Contest for Jurisdiction: An Occupational Analysis of Principals' Responses to Test-Based Accountability," *Leadership and Policy in Schools* 9, no. 1 (2010): 78–107; Stacey A. Rutledge, Douglas N. Harris, and William K. Ingle, "How Principals 'Bridge and Buffer' the New Demands of Teacher Quality and Accountability: A Mixed-Methods Analysis of Teacher Hiring," *American Journal of Education* 116, no. 2 (2010): 211–242; Heinrich Mintrop, *Schools on Probation: How Accountability Works (and Doesn't Work)* (New York: Teachers College Press, 2003); James P. Spillane, John B. Diamond, Patricia Burch, Tim Hallett, Loyiso Jita, and Jennifer Zoltners, "Managing in the Middle: School Leaders and the Enactment of Accountability Policy," *Educational Policy* 16, no. 5 (2002): 731–762.

3. Jaekyung Lee, *Tracking Achievement Gaps and Assessing the Impact of NCLB on the Gaps: An in-Depth Look into National and State Reading and Math Outcome Trends* (Cambridge, MA: Harvard Education Publishing Group, 2006).

4. Cornelia Brunner, Chad Fasca, Juliette Heinze, Margaret Honey, Daniel Light, Ellen Mardinach, and Dara Wexler, "Linking Data and Learning: The Grow Network Study," *Journal of Education for Students Placed at Risk (JESPAR)* 10, no. 3 (2005): 241–267; Richard J. Murnane, Nancy S. Sharkey, and Kathryn P. Boudett, "Using Student Assessment Results to Improve Instruction: Lessons from a Workshop," *JESPAR* 10, no. 3 (2005): 265–280; Stephanie Sutherland, "Creating a Culture of Data Use for Continuous Improvement: Case Study of an Edison Project School," *American Journal of Evaluation* 25, no. 3 (2004): 277–293; Jeffrey C. Wayman and Sam Stringfield, "Technology-Supported Involvement of Entire Faculties in Examination of Student Data for Instructional Improvement," *American Journal of Education* 112, no. 4 (2006): 549–571; Jef-

frey C. Wayman, Sam Stringfield, and Mary Yakimowski, "Software Enabling School Improvement Through the Analysis of Student Data" (Report No. 67, Center for Research on the Education of Students Placed at Risk, Johns Hopkins University, Baltimore, 2004).

5. Wayman, Stringfield, and Yakimowski, "Software Enabling School Improvement," 1–67.

6. Alex J. Bowers, "Reconsidering Grades as Data for Decision Making: More Than Just Academic Knowledge," *Journal of Educational Administration* 47, no. 5 (2009): 609–629; Susan L. Star, "The Ethnography of Infrastructure," *American Behavioral Scientist* 43, no. 3 (1999): 377–391.

7. Richard Halverson, Jeffrey Grigg, Reid Prichett, and Chris Thomas, "The New Instructional Leadership: Creating Data-Driven Instructional Systems in Schools," *Journal of School Leadership* 17, no. 2 (2007): 159–194.

8. Star, "The Ethnography of Infrastructure."

9. Ibid.

10. Chandra Mukerji, "Toward a Sociology of Material Culture: Science Studies, Cultural Studies and the Meaning of Things," in *The Sociology of Culture: Emerging Theoretical Perspectives,* ed. D. Crane. (Oxford: Blackwell, 1994), 143–162.

11. Susan L. Star and Karen Ruhleder, "Steps Toward an Ecology of Infrastructure: Design and Access for Large Information Spaces," *Information Systems Research* 7 (1996): 111–134.

12. Steven Epstein, "Culture and Science/Technology: Rethinking Knowledge, Power, Materiality and Nature," *Annals of the American Academy of Political and Social Science* 619, no. 2 (2008): 165–182.

13. Under DA, schools that failed to meet AYP for two or more years faced different levels of sanction and district- and state-level intervention.

14. Fourteen participants were interviewed at each case study site. Interviews were conducted with administrators and teachers and were recorded and transcribed for accuracy and analytic purposes. The twenty-eight interviews were coded using NVivo software. Themes and patterns in the data were identified using thematic and pattern coding. Matthew B. Miles and A. Michael Huberman, *Qualitative Data Analysis* (Thousand Oaks, CA: Sage, 1994).

15. Mukerji, "Toward a Sociology of Material Culture."

16. David F. Labaree, "The Lure of Statistics for Educational Researchers," *Educational Theory* 61 (2011): 621–632.

17. Ibid., 628.

18. FCAT scores are reported between 1 and 5, with 1 being the lowest level of proficiency and 5 the highest.

19. Star and Ruhleder, "Steps Toward an Ecology of Infrastructure."

20. Robert Dreeben and Rebecca Barr, *Work in Schools* (Chicago: University of Chicago Press, 1983); Halverson et al., "The New Instructional Leadership"; Jeannie Oakes, *Keeping Track: How Schools Structure Inequality* (New Haven, CT: Yale University Press, 1986).

21. For a discussion on the range of information technologies schools have at their disposal to improve teaching and learning, see Halverson and Shapiro, chap. 9 this volume.

Chapter 7

1. Jeffrey Henig and Clarence Stone, "Rethinking School Reform: The Distractions of Dogma and the Potential for a New Politics of Progressive Pragmatism," *American Journal of Education* 114, no. 3 (2008): 191–218.

2. Ibid., 207.

3. Robert Crowson and Ellen Goldring, "The New Localism: Re-Examining Issues of Neighborhood and Community in Public Education," *Yearbook of the National Society for the Study of Education* 108, no. 1 (2009): 1–24.

4. Mintrop and Sunderman, chap. 1 this volume

5. Henig and Stone, "Rethinking School Reform."

6. James Spillane, Louis Gomez, and Leigh Mesler, "Notes on Reframing the Role of Organizations in Policy Implementation: Resources *for* Practice, *in* Practice," in *Handbook of Education Policy Research*, ed. Gary Sykes, Barbara Schneider, and David N. Plank (New York: Routledge, 2009), 409.

7. Wayne Au, "High-Stakes Testing and Curricular Control: A Qualitative Metasynthesis," *Educational Researcher* 36, no. 5 (2007): 258–267; Center for Education Policy, "Ten Big Effects of the No Child Left Behind Act on Public Schools," http://www.cep-dc.org/displayDocument.cfm?DocumentID=263; Lora Cohen-Vogel, "Staffing to the Test: Are Today's School Personnel Practices Evidence Based?" *Educational Evaluation and Policy Analysis* 33, no. 4 (2011): 483–505; Lora Cohen-Vogel and La'Tara Osborne-Lampkin, "Allocating Quality: Collective Bargaining Agreements and Administrative Discretion over Teacher Assignment," *Educational Administration Quarterly* 43, no. 4 (2007): 433–461; James E. Lyons and Bob Algozzine, "Perceptions of the Impact of Accountability on the Role of Principals," *Education Policy Analysis Archives* 14, no. 16. (2006), http://epaa.asu.edu/epaa/v14n16/.

8. Rodney Ogawa, "Improvement or Reinvention: Two Policy Approaches to School Reform," in *Handbook of Education Policy Research*, ed. Gary Sykes, Barbara Schneider, and David N. Plank (New York: Routledge, 2009), 535.

9. Lora Cohen-Vogel and Stacey A. Rutledge, "The Pushes and Pulls of New Localism: School-Level Instructional Arrangements, Instructional Resources, and Family-Community Partnerships," in *The New Localism in American Education: The Yearbook of the National Society for the Study of Education,* vol. 108, eds. Robert Crowson and Ellen Goldring (Chicago: University of Chicago Press, 2009).

10. Other responses to accountability and the threat of sanctions are possible as well. One such response involves manipulating the testing pool. Specifically, schools may attempt to increase aggregate test scores by (re)classifying students into test-excluded categories (Julie Cullen and Randall Reback, "Tinkering Toward Accolade: School Gaming under a Performance Accountability System" (working paper, National Bureau of Economic Research, Inc., Washington, DC, 2006). For example, schools or school systems may attempt to identify potentially failing students as disabled, and thus excluded from taking the test (David N. Figlio and Lawrence S. Getzer, *Accountability, Ability, and Disability: Gaming the System* [Cambridge, MA: National Bureau of Economic Research, 2002]). In a second example, schools may keep their lower-performing students out of tested grades or push them out of school altogether (Julian Heilig and Linda Darling-Hammond, "Accountability Texas-Style: The Progress and Learning of Urban Minority Students in a High-Stakes Testing Context," *Educational Evaluation and Policy Analysis* 30, no. 2 [2008]: 75–110). More egregious perhaps than manipulating the testing pool is manipulating test responses. Educators may cheat in order to make their students' test scores look better than they actually are; evidence suggests that teachers in the lowest-scoring classrooms are most likely to do so (Brian Jacob and Steven Levitt, "Rotten Apples: An Investigation of the Prevalence and Predictors of Teacher Cheating," *Quarterly Journal of Economics* 118, no. 3 [2003]: 843–877).

11. Lora Cohen-Vogel, Ellen Goldring, and Claire Smrekar, "The Influence of Local Conditions on Social Service Partnerships, Parent Involvement and Community Engagement in Neighborhood Schools," *American Journal of Education* 117, no. 1 (2009): 51–78.

12. Carl F. Kaestle, *Pillars of the Republic: Common Schools and American Society, 1780–1860* (New York: Hill & Wang, 1983); John Demos, *A Little Commonwealth: Family Life in Plymouth Colony,* 2nd ed. (New York: Oxford University Press, 1999).

13. Allen C. Ornstein, "Rural/Urban School Districts Trends in Consolidation and Decentralization," *The Clearing House,* 65, no. 5 (1992): 322–326.

14. It is generally agreed that school desegregation efforts were largely unsuccessful due to the persistence of entrenched, segregated housing patterns. Steven Rivkin, "Residential Segregation and School Integration," *Sociology of Education* 67, no. 4 (1994): 279–292.

15. James D. Anderson, *The Education of Blacks in the South, 1860–1935* (Chapel Hill: University of North Carolina Press, 1988); Vanessa S. Walker, *Their Highest Potential: An African American School Community in the Segregated South* (Chapel Hill: University of North Carolina Press, 1996); David S. Cecelski, *Along Freedom Road: Hyde County, North Carolina and the Fate of Black Schools in the South* (Chapel Hill: University of North Carolina Press, 1994).

16. Ronald P. Formasiano, *Boston Against Busing: Race, Class and Ethnicity in the 1960's and 1970's* (Chapel Hill: University of North Carolina Press, 1991).

17. See, for example, Eric Houck and Sheneka Williams, "To Turn Back Would Be a Huge Mistake": Race, Class, and Student Assignment in Wake County Public Schools" (paper presented at the annual meeting of the American Education Research Association, Denver, April 2010).

18. Civil Rights Project, "PICS One Year Later: Reflections on the Anniversary of the Supreme Court's Voluntary Integration Decision," http://civilrightsproject.ucla.edu/legal-developments/court-decisions/resources-on-u.s.-supreme-court-voluntary-school-desegregation-rulings/.

19. William. H. Clune, "The Shift from Equity to Adequacy in School Finance," *Educational Policy* 8, no. 4 (1994): 376–394.

20. Jennifer Hochschild, *The New American Dilemma: Liberal Democracy and School Desegregation* (New Haven, CT: Yale University Press, 1984).

21. Gary Orfield and Susan Eaton, *Dismantling Desegregation: The Quiet Reversal of Brown v. Board of Education* (New York: New Press, 1996).

22. *Public Agenda Online* (1999), http://www.publicagenda.com.

23. Ellen Goldring, Lora Cohen-Vogel, and Claire Smrekar, "Schooling Closer to Home: Desegregation Policy and Neighborhood Contexts," *American Journal of Education* 112, no. 3 (2006): 335–362.

24. Katherine Kersten, *Good Intentions Are Not Enough: The Peril Posed by Minnesota's New Desegregation Plan* (Minneapolis: Center for American Experiment, 2005), http://www.amexp.org/publications.

25. Cohen-Vogel, Goldring, and Smrekar, "The Influence of Local Conditions."

26. Harvard Civil Rights Project, "Selected Unitary Status Rulings Between 1990–2002," http://www.civilrightsproject.harvard.edu/research/reseg03/appendices.pdf.

27. Cohen-Vogel, Goldring, and Smrekar, "The Influence of Local Conditions."

28. A careful reading of the decision, however, reveals that districts not subject to an existing desegregation order are permitted to consider race when siting new schools, drawing or adjusting attendance lines, and tracking and disaggregating enrollment and student performance. Further, they are legally permitted to consider individual students' race as one

of several factors in school assignment plans after documenting that race-neutral alternatives, like socioeconomic or English language learner status, would not produce satisfactory integration levels. Civil Rights Project, "PICS One Year Later."

29. Orfield and Eaton, *Dismantling Desegregation;* Gary Orfield and John T. Yun, *Resegregation in American Schools* (Cambridge, MA: Civil Rights Project, Harvard University, 1996), http://www.eric.ed.gov/ERICWebPortal/detail?accno=ED445171; Eric Houck, "Teacher Quality and School Resegregation: A Resource Allocation Case Study," *Leadership and Policy in Schools* 9, no. 1 (2010): 49–77.

30. James Guthrie, Mathew G. Springer, Anthony R. Rolle, and Eric A. Houck, *Modern Education, Finance and Policy* (New York: Pearson, 2007).

31. See Erica Frankenberg and Elizabeth Debray-Pelot, *Integrating Schools in a Changing Society: New Policies and Legal Options for a Multiracial Generation* (Chapel Hill: University of North Carolina Press, 2011).

32. Eric Houck and Sheneka Williams, "To Turn Back Would Be a Huge Mistake": Race, Class, and Student Assignment in Wake County Public Schools" (paper presented at the annual meeting of the American Education Research Association, Denver, April 2010).

33. David Levine, "Public School Assignment Methods after Grutter and Gratz: The View from San Francisco," *Hastings Constitutional Law Quarterly* 30, no. 4 (2002): 511–540; Andrea Koskey, "New Student Assignment for San Francisco Schools Is in Place, but Remains Controversial," *San Francisco Examiner*, March 6, 2011, http://www.sfexaminer.com/local/education/2011/03/new-selection-san-francisco-schools-place-still-controversial.

34. William W. Cutler, "The Cathedral of Culture: The Schoolhouse in American Educational Thought and Practice Since 1920," *History of Education Quarterly* 29, no. 1 (1989): 1–40.

35. Robert Burns and DeWayne A. Mason, "Class Formation and Composition in Elementary Schools," *American Educational Research Journal* 35, no. 4 (1998): 739–772.

36. David Monk, "Assigning Elementary Pupils to their Teachers," *Elementary School Journal* 88, no. 2 (1987): 167–187.

37. Robert Burns and DeWayne A. Mason, "Class Composition and Student Achievement in Elementary Schools," *American Educational Research Journal* 39, no. 1 (2002): 207–233.

38. Burns and Mason, "Class Formation and Composition in Elementary Schools"; Monk, "Assigning Elementary Pupils to their Teachers"; Ronald Heck, George Marcoulides, and Naftaly Glasman, "The Application of Causal Modeling Techniques to Administrative Decision Making: The Case of Teacher Allocation," *Educational Administration Quarterly* 25, no. 3 (1989): 253–267.

39. They did not explore the relative weight of these concerns on principals' assignment decisions.

40. See Anne Elizabeth Harrison and Robert L. Sinclair, "Insights about the Perpetuation of Ability Grouping: Practices and Perceptions of Elementary School Teachers" (paper presented at the annual meeting of the American Educational Research Association, New Orleans, 1988).

41. Ability grouping takes a different form in elementary schools. See James H. Borland, Dawn Horton, Rena F. Subotnik, Shiang-Jiun Chen, Miran Chun, Cathy Freeman, Sabrina Goldberg, and Julie Yu Kim, "Ability-Grouping and Acceleration of Gifted Students," *Roeper Review* 24, no. 3 (2002): 100–102; and Robert E. Slavin, "Ability Grouping and Student Achievement in Elementary Schools: A Best-Evidence Synthesis," *Review of Educational Research* 57, no. 3 (1987): 293–336. Often called "within-class grouping," this practice divides a class of students into discrete instructional units for particu-

lar subjects (generally reading and math). The teacher then divides her time among these groups, adapting her teaching strategies to meet the needs and abilities of each. James A. Kulik, *An Analysis of the Research on Ability Grouping: Historical and Contemporary Perspectives (RBDM 9204)* (Storrs: National Research Center on the Gifted and Talented, University of Connecticut, 1992).

42. Dylan Conger, "Within-School Segregation in an Urban School District," *Educational Evaluation and Policy Analysis* 27, no. 3 (2005): 225–244; Daniel J. Losen, "Silent Segregation in Our Nation's Schools," *Harvard Civil Rights–Civil Liberties Law Review* 34 (1999): 1–27.

43. Jeannie Oakes, *Keeping Track: How Schools Structure Inequality* (New Haven, CT: Yale University Press, 1986).

44. Maureen Hallinan, "Tracking: From Theory to Practice." *Sociology of Education* 67, no. 2 (1994): 79–84.

45. Samuel Lucas, *Tracking Inequality* (New York: Teachers College Press, 1999).

46. Cohen-Vogel and Rutledge, "The Pushes and Pulls of New Localism," 52.

47. John Jenkins, "Looking Backward: Educational Reform in the Twentieth Century," *International Journal of Educational Reform* 9, no. 1 (2000): 110–113; Rebecca Barr and Robert Dreeben, *How Schools Work* (Chicago: University of Chicago Press, 1983).

48. Susan M. Johnson and Sarah E. Birkeland, "Pursuing a 'Sense of Success': New Teachers Explain Their Career Decisions," *American Educational Research Journal* 40, no. 3 (2003): 581–617.

49. Cohen-Vogel and Osborne-Lampkin, "Allocating Quality."

50. Jennifer Booher-Jennings, "Below the Bubble: Educational Triage and the Texas Accountability System," *American Educational Research Journal* 42, no. 2 (2005): 231–268; David Gillborn and Deborah Youdell, *Rationing Education: Policy, Practice, Reform and Equity* (Buckingham, UK: Open University Press, 2000).

51. La'Tara Osborne-Lampkin and Lora Cohen-Vogel, "Spreading the Wealth: How Principals Populate Elementary Schools" (paper presented at The Infrastructure of Accountability: Mapping Data Use and Its Consequences Across the American Education System conference, Florida State University, Tallahassee, February 2012).

52. Over time, the formula that calculates a school's grade has changed somewhat to include student test scores in more subject areas, graduation rates, enrollment in advanced courses, learning gains, and the progress of the lowest-performing 25 percent of its students.

53. Lora Cohen-Vogel, "Staffing to the Test: Are Today's School Personnel Practices Evidence Based?" *Educational Evaluation and Policy Analysis* 33, no. 4 (2011): 483–505.

54. Osborne-Lampkin and Cohen-Vogel, "Spreading the Wealth."

Chapter 8

1. To protect the site's anonymity, LICS and all other person and place names within this chapter are pseudonyms. For the same reason, percentages of the student body are rounded.

2. Diane J. Tedick, Donna Christian, and Tara Williams Fortune, ed., *Immersion Education: Practices, Policies, Possibilties* (Bristol, UK: Multilingual Matters, 2011).

3. Cynthia Coburn, "The Practice of Data Use: An Introduction," *American Journal of Education* 118, no. 2 (2012): 99–111; Jennifer L. Jennings, "School Choice or Schools' Choice? Managing in an Era of Accountability," *Sociology of Education* 83, no. 3 (2010): 227–247; Richard Elmore, "A Plea for Strong Practice," *Educational Leadership* 61, no. 3 (2003): 6–10; John B. Diamond, "Where the Rubber Meets the Road: Rethinking the

Connection Between High-Stakes Testing Policy and Classroom Instruction," *Sociology of Education* 80, no. 1 (2007): 285–313.

4. Patricia Burch, "Educational Policy and Practice from the Perspective of Institutional Theory: Crafting a Wider Lens," *Educational Researcher* 36, no. 2 (2007): 84–95.

5. Jeannette A. Colyvas, "Performance Metrics as Formal Structures and through the Lens of Social Mechanisms: When Do They Work and How Do They Influence?" *American Journal of Education* 118, no. 2 (2012): 167–197.

6. Walter W. Powell and Jeannette A. Colyvas, "Microfoundations of Institutional Theory," in *Handbook of Organizational Institutionalism*, ed. Royston Greenwood, Christine Oliver, Roy Suddaby, and Kerstin Sahlin-Andersson (Thousand Oaks, CA: Sage, 2008), 276–298.

7. Lisa M. Dorner, James P. Spillane, and James Pustejovsky, "Organizing for Instruction: A Comparative Study of Public, Charter, and Catholic Schools," *Journal of Educational Change* 12, no. 1 (2011): 71–98.

8. Dorothea Anagnostopoulos and Stacey A. Rutledge, "Making Sense of School Sanctioning Policies in Urban High Schools," *Teachers College Record* 109, no. 5 (2007): 1261–1302.

9. Cynthia E. Coburn, "Framing the Problem of Reading Instruction: Using Frame Analysis to Uncover the Microprocesses of Policy Implementation," *American Educational Research Journal* 43, no. 3 (2006): 343–379.

10. Rebecca Jacobsen, "The Voice of the People in Educational Policy," in *Handbook of Education Policy Research*, ed. D. Plank, G. Sykes, and B. Schneider (New York: Routledge, 2009), 307–318.

11. Lorraine M. McDonnell, *Politics, Persuasion, and Educational Testing* (Cambridge, MA: Harvard University Press, 2004), 248.

12. Damian W. Betebenner, Kenneth R. Howe, and Samara S. Foster, "On School Choice and Test-Based Accountability," *Education Policy Analysis Archives* 13, no. 41 (2005): 22.

13. Jean Johnson, "What Does the Public Say About Accountability?" *Educational Leadership* 61, no. 3 (2003): 36–40.

14. Justine S. Hastings and Jeffrey M. Weinstein, "Information, School Choice, and Academic Achievement: Evidence from Two Experiments," *Quarterly Journal of Economics* 123, no. 4 (2008): 1373–1414.

15. Kara S. Finnigan, "Charter School Autonomy: The Mismatch Between Theory and Practice," *Educational Policy* 21, no. 3 (2007): 503–526.

16. John Maddaus, "Parental Choice of School: What Parents Think and Do," *Review of Research in Education* 16, no. 1 (1990): 267–295.

17. Jennifer Jellison Holme, "Buying Homes, Buying Schools: School Choice and the Social Construction of School Quality," *Harvard Educational Review* 72, no. 2 (2002): 177–205.

18. Courtney A. Bell, "Space and Place: Urban Parents' Geographical Preferences for Schools," *The Urban Review* 39, no. 4 (2007): 375–403.

19. Katrina E. Bulkley and Priscilla Wohlstetter, ed., *Taking Account of Charter Schools: What's Happened and What's Next* (New York: Teachers College Press, 2004).

20. Critical Discourse Analysis (CDA) is especially concerned with the relationship between knowledge, discourse, and power within and across social contexts. See James Gee, *Social Linguistics and Literacies: Ideology in Discourses* (London: Taylor & Francis, 1990); Rebecca Rogers, *A Critical Discourse Analysis of Family Literacy Practices: Power In and Out of Print* (Matawah, NJ: Lawrence Erlbaum, 2003); Kathy Charmaz, "Grounded Theory: Objectivist and Constructivist Methods," in *Qualitative Educational Research: Readings in Reflexive Methodology and Transformative Practice*, ed. Wendy Luttrell (New York: Routledge, 2010), 183–207; N. L. Fairclough and R. Wodak, "Critical Dis-

course Analysis," in *Discourse Studies: A Multidisciplinary Introduction*, ed. T. A. van Dijk (London: Sage, 1997), 258–284. Our analysis began with a CDA of the charter. First we located all terms related to the scripts discussed above: (1) accountability and data (evaluate/evaluation, assess/assessment, measure/measurement); and (2) the innovation of language immersion (multilingual/ism, bilingual/ism) and a constructivist model of education (inquiry, authorship). See Table 8.1. In the next phase of analysis, we identified the agents/actors/actions related to each term and asked these guiding questions: (1) What are the *tools* set forth? For example, regarding accountability and data, what are the systems, tests, or standards proposed to assess each stakeholder at LICS (i.e., students' academic progress, teachers' effectiveness, and administrators' leadership)? (2) What *actions or practices* are ascribed to various agents? For example, who or what is evaluated, who conducts an evaluation, and to whom are agents accountable? In the final step of data analysis, we examined the field notes and interview transcripts. We coded for any mention of the three themes found in the charter: accountability/data, bi/multilingualism, and constructivism. Then, we considered how each of these themes related to particular scripts about schooling: good schools (1) have students that *perform* well on tests (shown through accountability systems/data); (2) are diverse and *multicultural* (multilingual); and (3) are *progressive* (following a constructivist model of schooling). Through axial coding and analytical memos, we examined the relative importance placed on each script by different stakeholders. The resulting analysis demonstrates how accountability systems have been produced and shape schooling—and become an important part of the competing notions that stakeholders have about good schooling—at new charter schools. We documented the schools' development through participant observation, creating more than 150 sets of field notes from planning meetings, board meetings, town hall forums, and parent organization meetings; collecting hundreds of artifacts, including the charter; and transcribing formal interviews with sixteen parents/caregivers, ten educators (staff, teachers, administrators, and founding board members), and one focus group with teachers.

21. Lisa M. Dorner, "English and Spanish 'Para Un Futuro'—Or Just English? Immigrant Family Perspectives on Two-Way Immersion," *International Journal of Bilingual Education and Bilingualism* 13, no. 3 (2010): 303–323.

22. Lesley Barlett and Ofelia García, *Additive Schooling in Subtractive Times: Bilingual Education and Dominican Immigrant Youth in the Heights* (Nashville, TN: Vanderbilt University Press, 2011).

23. Wayne P. Thomas and Virginia P. Collier, *A National Study of School Effectiveness for Language Minority Students' Long-Term Academic Achievement* (Washington, DC: Center for Research on Education, Diversity and Excellence, 2002).

24. Lisa Dorner, Emily Hager, and Angela Layton, "From Recruitment to Engagement: The Process of Developing Partnerships at New Charter Schools" (paper presented at the biennial meeting of the International Roundtable on School, Family, and Community Partnerships, Denver, April 30, 2010).

25. See also Rutledge and Neal, chap. 6 this volume.

Chapter 9

1. Susan Fuhrman and Richard Elmore, *Redesigning School Accountability Systems for Education* (New York: Teachers College Press, 2004).

2. Laura Hamilton, Richard Halverson, Sharnell Jackson, Ellen Mandinach, Jonathan Supovitz, and Jeffrey Wayman, *Using Student Achievement Data to Support Instructional Deci-*

sion-Making (Washington, DC: National Center for Education Evaluation and Regional Assistance, 2009).

3. Margaret Honig, Michael Copland, Lydia Rainey, Juli Anna Lorton, and Morena Newton, *School District Central Office Transformation for Teaching and Learning Improvement* (Seattle: Center for the Study of Teaching and Policy, 2010).

4. Patricia Burch, *Hidden Markets: The New Education Privatization* (London: Routledge, Taylor & Francis, 2009).

5. Jeffrey C. Wayman, "Involving Teachers in Data-Driven Decision Making: Using Computer Data Systems to Support Teacher Inquiry and Reflection," *Journal of Education for Students Placed at Risk* 10, no. 3 (2005): 295–308.

6. Barbara Means, Christine Padilla, and Larry Gallagher, *The Use of Education Data at the Local Level: From Accountability to Instructional Improvement,* U.S. Department of Education Office of Planning, Evaluation and Policy Development, 2010, http://www.ed.gov/about/offices/ list/opepd/ppss/reports.html#edtech. For a description of the SIS at the state level, see Anagnostopoulos and Bautista-Guerra, chap. 1 this volume.

7. Chris Thorn, "Knowledge Management for Educational Information Systems: What Is the State of the Field?" *Education Policy Analysis Archives* 9, no. 47 (2001), http://epaa.asu.edu/epaa/v9n47/.

8. Means et al., *The Use of Education Data at the Local Level.*

9. Jere Confrey and Katie Makar, "Critiquing and Improving Data Use from High Stakes Tests: Understanding Variation and Distribution in Relation to Equity Using Dynamic Statistics Software," in *Scaling Up Success: Lessons Learned from Technology-Based Educational Improvement,* ed. Chris Dede, James P. Homan, Laurence Peters and Ellen Condliffe Lagemann (San Francisco: Jossey-Bass, 2005), 198–226.

10. Thomas Toch, *Margins of Error: The Education Testing Industry in the No Child Left Behind Era* (Washington, DC: Education Sector, 2006).

11. See http://www.corestandards.org.

12. Margaret Heritage, "Learning Progressions: Supporting Instruction and Formative Assessment" (paper presented at the Council of Chief State School Officers, Washington DC, February 7, 2008), http://beta.ccsso.org/Resources/Publications /Learning_Progressions_Supporting_Instruction_and_Formative_Assessment.htm.

13. Shawn Stevens, Namsoo Shin, Carlos Delgado, Joseph Krajcik, and James Pellegrino, "Using Learning Progressions to Inform Curriculum, Instruction and Assessment Design" (paper presented at the National Association of Research in Science Teaching Conference, New Orleans, March 2002), http://hice.org/presentations/ documents /Shawn_etal_NARST_07.pdf.

14. Donald Norman, "Some Observations on Mental Models," in *Mental Models,* ed. D. Gentner and A. L. Stevens (Hillsdale, NJ: Lawrence Erlbaum, 1983), 1–9.

15. Alicia C. Alonzo and Maryl Gearhart, "Considering Learning Progressions from a Classroom Assessment Perspective," *Measurement: Interdisciplinary Research and Perspectives* 4, nos. 1 & 2 (2004): 99–108; Suzanne Blanc, Jolley Bruce Christman, Roseann Liu, Cecily Mitchell, Eva Travers, and Katrina E. Bulkley, "Learning to Learn from Data: Benchmarks and Instructional Communities," *Peabody Journal of Education* 85 no. 2 (2010): 205–225.

16. Lorie Shepard, "What the Marketplace Has Brought Us: Item-by-Item Teaching with Little Instructional Insight," *Peabody Journal of Education* 85, no. 2 (2010): 246–257.

17. Means et al., *The Use of Education Data at the Local Level.*

18. William Penuel and Louise Yarnall, "Designing Handheld Software to Support Classroom Assessment: An Analysis of Conditions for Teacher Adoption," *Journal of Technology, Learning, and Assessment* 3, no. 5 (2005): 4–45.

19. Valerie Crawford, Mark Schlager, William Penuel, and Yukie Toyama, "Supporting the Art of Teaching in a Data-Rich, High Performance Learning Environment," in *Linking Data and Learning*, ed. Ellen Mandinach and Margaret Honey (New York: Teachers College Press, 2008).

20. Ryann Ellis, *Field Guide to Learning Management Systems* (Alexandria, VA: ASTD Learning Circuits, 2009).

21. Jon Mott and David Wiley, "Open for Learning: The CMS and the Open Learning Network," *In Education* 16, no. 1 (2010): 3, http://ineducation.ca/article/open-learning-cms-and-open-learning-network.

22. danah boyd, "Why Youth (Heart) Social Network Sites: The Role of Networked Publics in Teenage Social Life," in *MacArthur Foundation Series on Digital Learning and Identity*, ed. David Buckingham (Cambridge, MA: MIT Press, 2008), 119–142.

23. Of course, we recognize the public debate that surrounds the potential of new media companies like Google, Facebook, and Apple to collect user information to advance the goals of the technological system. Like technologies for educators, new media tools generate considerable information about users as well as for users. Our point is that the widespread proliferation of new media tools depends on the value that the information tools provide to system users. Technologies for learners flourish in open systems that depend on the perception of value that users attribute to the system. This attention to the user experience creates the conditions for new media technologies to focus on issues such as user interface design and the accessibility of valued features in typical user experience.

24. See, for example, Sherry Turkle, *Alone Together* (New York: Basic Books, 2011).

25. Nicholas Carr, "Is Google Making Us Stupid?" *The Atlantic,* July 2008, 56–63; Alexander Jordan, Benoit Monin, Carol Dweck, Benjamin Lovett, Oliver John, and James Gross, "Misery Has More Company Than People Think: Underestimating the Prevalence of Others' Negative Emotions," *Personality and Social Psychology Bulletin* 37, no. 1 (2011): 120–135; Emma-Jane Cross, Richard Piggin, Thaddeus Douglas, and Jackson Von Kaenel-Flatt, *Virtual Violence II: Progress and Challenges in the Fight Against Cyberbullying* (London: BeatBullying, 2012); "Plagiarism and the Web," iParadigms White Paper, 2012, http://pages.turnitin.com/rs/iparadigms/images/Turnitin_WhitePaper_SourcesSECvsHE. pdf; Craig Anderson, Akiko Shibuya, Nobuko Ihori, Edward Swing, Brad Bushman, Akira Sakamoto, Hannah Rothstein, and Muniba Saleem, "Violent Video Game Effects on Aggression, Empathy, and Pro-Social Behavior in Eastern and Western Countries: A Meta-Analytic Review," *Psychological Bulletin* 136, no. 2 (2010): 151–173; Robert Weis and Brittany Cerankosky, "Effects of Video-Game Ownership on Young Boys' Academic and Behavioral Functioning: A Randomized, Controlled Study," *Psychological Science* 21, no. 4 (2010): 463–470.

26. Henry Jenkins, Ravi Purushotma, Katie Clinton, Margaret Weigel, and Alice Robison, *Confronting the Challenges of Participatory Culture: Media Education for the 21st Century,* MacArthur Foundation Digital Media and Learning White Paper Series, 2007, http://newmedialiteracies.org/files/ working/ NMLWhitePaper.pdf.

27. James Gee, *Situated Language and Learning: A Critique of Traditional Schooling* (New York: Routledge, 2004).

28. Colin Lankshear and Michelle Knobel, *New Literacies: Everyday Practices and Classroom Learning* (New York: Open University Press, 2006).

29. See http://newsroom.fb.com/imagelibrary/downloadmedia.ashx?Media DetailsID=4227& SizeId=-1.

30. See http://press.linkedin.com/about.

31. See, for example, John Bransford, Ann Brown, and Rodney Cocking, *How People Learn: Brain, Mind, Experience, and School* (Washington, DC: National Academies Press, 2000).

32. Jean Lave and Etienne Wenger, *Situated Learning: Legitimate Peripheral Participation* (New York: Cambridge University Press, 1991).

33. Ben Shapiro, Tene Gray, Akili Lee, and Nichole Pinkard, "Building a Community of Practice with SPACE and Remixworld" (paper presented at the annual conference of Games, Learning and Society, Madison, WI, July 2010).

34. See http://en.wikipedia.org/wiki/Special:Statistics.

35. James Giles, "Internet Encyclopedias Go Head to Head," *Nature* 438 (December 15, 2005): 900–901.

36. Paul Black and Dylan William, "Assessment and Classroom Learning," *Assessment in Education 5*, no. 1 (1998): 7–74.

37. See http://www.cinemablend.com/games/Video-Games-Market-Grow-From-52-Billion-2009-86-Billion-By-2014-30363.html.

38. Victoria Rideout, Ulla Foehr, and Donald Roberts, *Generation M2: Media in the Lives of 8- to 18-Year-Olds,* Kaiser Family Foundation, 2010, http://kff.org/entmedia/upload/8010.pdf.

39. Jane McGonigal, *Reality Is Broken: Why Games Make Us Better and How They Can Change the World* (New York: Penguin, 2011).

40. James Gee, *What Video Games Have to Teach Us About Learning and Literacy* (New York: Palgrave Macmillan, 2003).

41. Kurt Squire, "From Content to Context: Videogames as Designed Experience," *Educational Researcher 35*, no. 8 (2006): 19–29.

42. James Gee, *Good Video Games and Good Learning* (New York: Peter Lang, 2005).

43. William James, *Psychology* (New York, Henry Holt, 1890): 293–295.

44. Erica Halverson, "Participatory Media Spaces: A Design Perspective on Learning with Media and Technology in the 21st Century," in *Games, Learning and Society,* ed. Constance Steinkuehler, Kurt Squire, and Sasha Barab (London: Cambridge University Press, 2012).

45. Joseph Kahne, Jacqueline Ullman, and Ellen Middaugh, "Digital Opportunities for Civic Education" (paper presented at the American Enterprise Institute Conference Civics 2.0: Citizenship Education for a New Generation, October 20, 2011, Washington, DC), http://www.civicsurvey.org/Digital%20opportunities%20for %20civic%20education.pdf

46. See http://www.macfound.org/site/c.lkLXJ8MQKrH/b.5852881/k.CD8/ReImagining_Learning__Assessing_Learning.htm.

47. Jane McGonigal, *Reality Is Broken: Why Gaming Makes Us Better and How They Can Change the World* (New York: Penguin, 2011).

48. See http://iremix.org/.

Chapter 10

1. *Has Student Achievement Increased Since 2002? State Test Score Trends Through 2006–07* (Washington, DC: Center on Education Policy, 2008); and *Is the Emphasis on Proficiency Shortchanging Higher and Lower Achieving Students?* (Washington, DC: Center on Education Policy, 2009).

2. Stephen P. Klein, Laura S. Hamilton, Daniel F. McCaffrey, and Brian M. Stecher, *What Do Test Scores in Texas Tell Us?* (Santa Monica, CA: RAND, 2000); Daniel Koretz, Robert L. Linn, Stephen B. Dunbar, and Lorrie A. Shepard, "The Effects of High-Stakes Testing: Preliminary Evidence about Generalization Across Tests" (paper presented at the annual meetings of the American Educational Research Association and the National Council on Measurement in Education, Chicago, April 1991); Daniel M. Koretz and Sheila I. Barron, *The Validity of Gains on the Kentucky Instructional Results Information System (KIRIS)* (Santa Monica, CA: RAND, 1998).

3. Karl E. Weick, "Administering Education in Loosely Coupled Schools," *Phi Delta Kappan* 63, no. 10 (1982): 673–676.

4. Jennifer L. Jennings, Jonathan Bearak, and Daniel Koretz, "Accountability and Racial Inequality in American Education" (paper presented at the Annual Meetings of the American Sociological Association, Las Vegas, August 2011).

5. Jennifer Booher-Jennings, "Below the Bubble: 'Educational Triage' and the Texas Accountability System," *American Educational Research Journal* 42, no. 2 (2005): 231–268.

6. Derek Neal and Diane Whitmore Schanzenbach, "Left Behind by Design: Proficiency Counts and Test-Based Accountability" (working paper, Derek Neal Department of Economics, Harris School, University of Chicago, 2007); Randall Reback, "Teaching to the Rating: School Accountability and the Distribution of Student Achievement," *Journal of Public Economics* 92, nos. 5–6 (2008): 1394–1415.

7. Brian A. Jacob, "Accountability, Incentives, and Behavior: Evidence from School Reform in Chicago," *Journal of Public Economics* 89 (2005): 761–796; Matthew Springer, "The Influence of an NCLB Accountability Plan on the Distribution of Student Test Score Gains," *Economics of Education Review* 27, no. 5 (2007): 556–563; Jeff Krieg, "Are Students Left Behind? The Distributional Effects of No Child Left Behind. *Education Finance and Policy* 3, no. 2 (2008): 250–281; Helen F. Ladd and Douglas Lee Lauen, "Status Versus Growth: The Distributional Effects of Accountability Policies," *Journal of Policy Analysis and Management* 29, no. 3 (2010): 426–450; Thomas Dee and Brian Jacob, "The Impact of No Child Left Behind on Student Achievement," National Bureau of Economic Research Working Paper 15531, 2009, http://www.nber.org/papers/w15531; Reback, "Teaching to the Rating."

8. Our methods are described in more detail in Jennifer Jennings and Heeju Sohn, "Measure for Measure: Measuring Inequality in an Era of Accountability" (paper presented at the annual meeting of the American Sociological Association, Denver, August 2012).

9. For the complex ways in which accountability data affect public perception, see Jacobsen and Saultz, chap. 11 this volume.

10. David Labaree, *How to Succeed in School Without Really Learning* (New Haven, CT: Yale University Press, 1999).

11. Barbara Heyns, *Summer Learning and the Effects of Schooling* (New York: Academic Press, 1978); Karl L. Alexander, Doris R. Entwisle, and Linda S. Olsen, "Schools, Achievement, and Inequality: A Seasonal Perspective," *Educational Evaluation and Policy Analysis* 23, no. 2 (2001): 171–191; Douglas B. Downey, Paul T. von Hippel, and Beckett Broh, "Are Schools the Great Equalizer? Cognitive Inequality During the Summer Months and the School Year," *American Sociological Review* 69, no. 5 (2004): 613–635.

12. This is discussed in more depth in Jennifer Jennings and Aaron Pallas, "The Racial Achievement Gap in New York City," in *New York City Schools Under Bloomberg and Klein*, ed. Leonie Haimson and Ann Kjellberg (New York: Class Size Matters, 2009).

Chapter 11

1. Lorraine M. McDonnell, "Defining Democratic Purposes," in *Rediscovering the Democratic Purposes of Education,* ed. Lorraine M. McDonnell, Michael P. Timpane, and Roger Benjamin (Lawrence: University of Kansas Press, 2000), 1–20; William T. Gormley Jr. and David L. Weimer, *Organizational Report Cards* (Cambridge, MA: Harvard University Press, 1999); Michael Mintrom, "Educational Governance and Democratic Practice," *Educational Policy* 15, no. 5 (2001): 615–642; William E. Lyons and David Lowery, "The Organization and Political Space and Citizen Responses to Dissatisfaction in Urban Communities: An Integrative Model," *Journal of Politics* 48, no. 2 (1986): 321–346: Mark A. Glaser and Bartley W. Hildreth, "Service Delivery Satisfaction and Willingness to Pay Taxes: Citizen Recognition of Local Government Performance," *Public Productivity and Management Review* 23, no. 1 (1999): 48–67; Bill Simonsen and Mark D. Robbins, "Reasonableness, Satisfaction and Willingness to Pay Property Taxes," *Urban Affairs Review* 38, no. 6 (2003): 831–854.

2. Arne Duncan, "Secretary Arne Duncan's Remarks at the Statehouse Convention Center in Little Rock, Arkansas," August 25, 2010, http://www.ed.gov/news/speeches/secretary-arne-duncans-remarks-statehouse-convention-center-little-rock-arkansas.

3. David N. Figlio and Maurice E. Lucas, "What's in a Grade? School Report Cards and the Housing Market," *American Economic Review* 94, no. 3 (2004): 591–604: Justin S. Hastings, Richard Van Weelden, and Jeffery Weinstein, "Preferences, Information, and Parental Choice Behavior in Public School Choice" (National Bureau of Economic Research Working Paper No. 12995, Cambridge, MA, 2007); Sandra E. Black and Stephen Machin, "Housing Valuations of School Performance," in *Handbook of Economic of Education,* ed. Erick Hanushek, Stephen Machin, and Ludger Woessmann (San Diego, CA: North-Holland, 2011), 485–516.

4. Lorraine McDonnell, *Politics Persuasion and Education Testing* (Cambridge, MA: Harvard University Press, 2004), 34.

5. Daniel P. Moynihan, *The Dynamics of Performance Management: Constructing Information and Reform* (Washington, DC: Georgetown University Press, 2008), 5.

6. Because the average school satisfaction may be highly unrepresentative in schools with low response rates, we excluded schools with a response rate lower than 30 percent.

7. Our main independent variable, the overall Progress Report letter grade, is coded on a four-point scale with a letter grade of F receiving a zero and a school with an A receiving a 4. Our dependent variable, parent satisfaction with school quality, is collected on the annual parent satisfaction survey. Specifically, we use the question, "How satisfied were you with the education your child has received this year?" We use a linear regression model for each school year examined in our study to predict whether the publicly available accountability data influenced perceptions of school quality.

8. *Digest of Education Statistics, 2010* (Washington, DC: Department of Education, National Center for Education Statistics, 2011), table 188, http://nces.ed.gov/fastfacts/display.asp?id=66.

9. Lorraine M. McDonnell, "The Politics of Educational Accountability: Can the Clock Be Turned Back?" in *The Future of Test-Based Educational Accountability,* ed. Katherine Ryan and Lorrie Shepard (New York: Routledge, 2008), 47–67; Lorraine M. McDonnell, "Assessment and Accountability from the Policymaker's Perspective," *Yearbook of the National Society for the Study of Education* 104, no. 2 (2005): 35–54.

10. Michael X. Delli Carpini and Scott Keeter, *What Americans Know About Politics and Why It Matters* (New Haven, CT: Yale University Press, 1989).

11. Associated Press/Stanford University Poll, September 2010, iPOLL Databank, Roper Center for Public Opinion Research, University of Connecticut, http://www.ropercenter. uconn.edu.proxy2.cl.msu.edu/data_access/ipoll/ipoll.html.

12. McDonnell, *Politics, Persuasion, and Education Testing*; Paul E. Peterson and Martin R. West, *No Child Left Behind? The Politics and Practice of School Accountability* (Washington, DC: Brookings Institution Press, 2003).

13. Paul E. Peterson, *The Price of Federalism* (Washington, DC: Brookings Institute, 1995); William J. Reese, *America's Public Schools: From the Common School to "No Child Left Behind"* (Baltimore: Johns Hopkins University Press, 2005).

14. Michael Feuer, "Future Directions for Educational Accountability: Notes for a Political Economy of Measurement," in *The Future of Test-Based Educational Accountability*, ed. Katherine Ryan and Lorrie Shepard (New York: Routledge, 2008), 293–307; Lorraine M. McDonnell, "The Politics of Educational Accountability: Can the Clock Be Turned Back?" in *The Future of Test-Based Educational Accountability*, ed. Katherine Ryan and Lorrie Shepard (New York: Routledge, 2008), 47–67.

15. Archon Fung, Mary Graham, and David Weil, *Full Disclosure: The Perils and Promise of Transparency* (Cambridge: Cambridge University Press, 2007).

16. William T. Gormley Jr. and David L. Weimer, *Organizational Report Cards* (Cambridge, MA: Harvard University Press, 1999), 3.

17. Ibid.

18. Bill Gates, "Shame Is Not the Solution" *New York Times*, February 22, 2012, http://www. nytimes.com/2012/02/23/opinion/for-teachers-shame-is-no-solution.html.

19. Harry P. Hartey, *Performance Measurement: Getting Results*, 2nd ed. (Washington, DC: Urban Institute Press, 2006).

20. Tom Loveless, "The Structure of Public Confidence in Education," *American Journal of Education* 105, no. 2 (1997): 127–159; Rebecca Jacobsen, "The Voice of the People in Education Policy," in *Handbook of Education Policy Research*, ed. Gary Sykes, Barbara Schneider, and David Planks (New York: Routledge Press, 2009), 307–317.

21. Daniel P. Moynihan, *The Dynamics of Performance Management: Constructing Information and Reform* (Washington, DC: Georgetown University Press, 2008), 5.

22. Fung et al., *Full Disclosure*; McDonnell, *Politics, Persuasion, and Education Testing*; Moynihan, *The Dynamics of Performance Management*.

23. Richard Pride, "How Critical Events Rather Than Performance Trends Shape Public Evaluations of the Schools," *Urban Review* 34, no. 2 (2002): 159–177.

24. Charles Hausman and Ellen Goldring, "Parent Involvement, Influence, and Satisfaction in Magnet Schools: Do Reasons for Choice Matter?" *Urban Review* 32, no. 2 (2000): 105–121; Jennifer Jellison Holme, "Buying Homes, Buying Schools: School Choice and the Social Construction of School Quality," *Harvard Educational Review* 72, no. 2 (2002): 177–205; Hastings et al., "Preferences, Information, and Parental Choice Behavior."

25. Etienne Charbonneau and Gregg Van Ryzin, "Performance Measures and Parental Satisfaction with New York City Schools," *American Review of Public Administration* 42, no. 1 (2012): 54–65.

26. Jason Felch, Jason Song, and Doug Smith, "Who's Teaching L.A.'s Kids?" *Los Angeles Times*, August 14, 2010, http://latimes.com/news/local/la-me-teachers-value-20100815,0,2695044 .story.

27. "Los Angeles Teacher Ratings," *Los Angeles Times*, April 11, 2011, http://projects. latimes.com/value-added/.

28. Shantor Iyengar, Mark Peters, and Donald Kinder, "Experimental Demonstrations of the 'Not-So-Minimal' Consequences of Television News Programs," in *Media Power in Politics,* ed. Doris Graber (Washington, DC: CQ Press, 1984), 54–60; Shantor Iyengar and Donald Kinder, *News That Matters: Television and American Opinion* (Chicago: University of Chicago Press, 1987).

29. Dietram Scheufele and David Tewksbury, "Framing, Agenda Setting, and Priming: The Evolution of Three Media Effects Models," *Journal of Communication* 57, no. 1 (2007): 9–20.

30. Robert Erickson and Kent L. Tedin, *American Public Opinion: It's Origins, Content and Impact* (New York: Pearson Education, 2005); Dietram Scheufele and David Tewskbury, "Framing, Agenda Setting, and Priming: The Evolution of Three Media Effects Models," *Journal of Communication* 57, no. 1 (2007): 9–20.

31. Dietram Scheufele and David Tewksbury, "Framing, Agenda Setting, and Priming: The Evolution of Three Media Effects Models," *Journal of Communication* 57, no. 1 (2007): 12.

32. Kenneth Wong and Pushpam Jain, "Newspapers as Policy Actors in Urban School Systems: The Chicago Story," *Urban Affairs Review* 35, no. 2 (1999): 210–246; Christopher Berry and William Howell, "Accountability and Local Elections: Rethinking Retrospective Voting," *Journal of Politics* 69, no. 3 (2007): 844–858.

33. McDonnell, *Politics, Persuasion, and Education Testing.*

34. For a discussion of how test scores shape the public's ideas about achievement and inequality, see Jennings and Sohn, chap. 10 this volume.

35. Julie Bosman, "Schools Wait, Teeth Gritted: Their Grades Are Coming," *New York Times,* September 1, 2007, B1; Jennifer Medina and Robert Gebeloff, "In Rating Schools, New York Hands Out Mostly A's and B's," *New York Times,* September 3, 2009, A23.

36. Jennifer Medina and Elissa Gootman, "Schools Brace to Be Scored on a Scale of A to F," *New York Times,* November 4, 2007.

37. Jennifer Medina and Robert Gebeloff, "Schools Get More A's and Fewer F's," *New York Times,* September 17, 2008, B1.

38. Ibid.

39. Robin Finn, "Shaping the System That Grades City Schools," *New York Times,* November 16, 2007.

40. New York City School Survey, http://schools.nyc.gov/Accountability/tools/survey/default.htm.

41. Op-ed, "Stupid Card Trick: Grade Inflation Sabotaged this Year's School Progress Reports," *Daily News,* September 5, 2009.

42. McDonnell, *Politics, Persuasion, and Education Testing.*

43. Deborah Stone, *Policy Paradox: The Art of Political Decision Making* (New York: Norton, 2001).

Conclusion

1. See http://www.whitehouse.gov/news/releases/2007/08/20070829-5.html.

2. Heinrich Mintrop and Gail L. Sunderman, "Predictable Failure of Federal Sanctions-Driven Accountability for School Improvement—And Why We May Retain It Anyway," *Educational Researcher* 38, no. 5 (2009): 353–364.

3. Organization for Economic Cooperation and Development, "An Overview of Growing Income Inequality in OECD Countries: Main Findings," http://www.oecd.org/general/

searchresults/?q=Income%20inequality%20United%20States&cx=01243260174851139
1518:xzeadub0b0a&cof=FORID:11&ie=UTF-8.

4. Jeffrey C. Wayman, "Involving Teachers in Data-Based Decision-Making: Using Computer Data Systems to Support Teacher Inquiry and Reflection," *Journal of Education for Students Placed at Risk* 10, no. 1 (2005): 295–308; Richard Halverson, Jeffrey Grigg, Reid Prichett, and Chris Thomas, "The New Instructional Leadership: Creating Data-Driven Instructional Systems in Schools," *Journal of School Leadership* 17, no. 2 (2007):159–194; Amanda Datnow, Vicki Park, and Priscilla Wohlstetter, *Achieving with Data: How High-Performing School Systems Use Data to Improve Instruction for Elementary Students* (Los Angeles: University of Southern California, Rossier School of Education, Center on Educational Governance, 2007); Cynthia E. Coburn, Judith Toure, and Mika Yamashita, "Evidence, Interpretation, and Persuasion: Instructional Decision Making in the District Central Office," *Teachers College Record* 111, no. 4 (2009): 1115–1161.

5. Roderick M. Kramer and Karen S. Cook, eds., *Trust and Distrust in Organizations: Dilemmas and Approaches* (New York: Russell Sage Foundation, 2004); Roderick M. Kramer, "Trust and Distrust in Organizations: Emerging Perspectives, Enduring Questions," *Annual Review of Psychology* 50 (1999): 590–592.

6. Wayman, "Involving Teachers in Data-Driven Decision Making"; Halverson et al., "The New Instructional Leadership"; Regional Educational Laboratory, *"Getting the Evidence for Evidence-Based Initiatives: How the Midwest States Use Data Systems to Improve Education Processes and Outcomes,"* http://ies.ed.gov/ncee/edlabs/projects/project.asp?id=29.

Acknowledgments

We thank the many individuals who have supported the work that has gone into this volume. Dean Marcy Driscoll and the Florida State University (FSU) College of Education enthusiastically provided funding and organizational support for The Infrastructure of Accountability conference held at FSU in February 2012. The conference provided invaluable opportunities for the authors to share preliminary versions of their chapters and further develop the ideas in this volume. We also thank Patrice Iatarola, who as department chair for the Department of Educational Leadership and Policy at FSU provided logistical and moral support. And we thank Gale Neal for her tireless coordination and attention to detail in making the conference a success.

We also thank Suzanne Wilson, who, as chair of the Teacher Education department at Michigan State University, provided us support to complete this manuscript and who has generously offered her time and considerable insight to help us pursue the ideas in this book. Gary Sykes has also been of immeasurable assistance in pushing our ideas forward. His unwavering enthusiasm for this work has been a source of key support for us. We also thank David Labaree for his encouragement. His ideas about the processes and consequences of quantification inform this volume in important ways. We appreciate the work that Betty Okwako did on the final preparation of this manuscript. We also thank Bob Floden and the Education Policy Center at Michigan State University for supporting Juanita Bautista-Guerra's work on this volume.

Finally, we thank Caroline Chauncey, editor-in-chief and assistant director of Harvard Education Press. Her feedback at every stage of the production of this volume has been tremendously helpful. She has responded to our ongoing questions and anxieties with grace and insight.

About the Editors

Dorothea Anagnostopoulos is an associate professor in the Department of Teacher Education at Michigan State University. She earned her PhD in education from the University of Chicago, where she also earned an MAT/English. Her research crosses several domains, including educational policy, urban education, teacher education, and classroom discourse, and has been widely published in journals such as *Research in the Teaching of English, Discourse and Society, Education Evaluation and Policy Analysis,* and the *American Educational Research Journal.* Her policy research uses a cultural sociological perspective to examine how teachers and students make sense of educational accountability policies and how such policies shape the distribution of resources, opportunities, and social identities in urban high schools. She is coauthor with Kenneth K. Wong, Francis Shen, and Stacey Rutledge of *The Education Mayor* (Georgetown University Press, 2007). Anagnostopoulos taught high school English in rural, suburban, and urban schools prior to receiving her doctorate.

Rebecca Jacobsen is an assistant professor in the Department of Teacher Education at Michigan State University. Rebecca received a PhD in the politics of education from Teachers College, Columbia University. Her dissertation, entitled "Priorities in Public Education: An Analysis of Elite and Popular Opinion on the Goals of Public Education," received a 2007 dissertation fellowship award from the Spencer Foundation. Her work focuses on the ways in which public opinion is shaped by school accountability data. She has published articles in *Public Opinion Quarterly, American Education Research Journal,* and *Education Finance and Policy.* She is coauthor with Richard Rothstein and Tamara Wilder of *Grading Education: Getting Accountability Right* (Teachers College Press, 2008) and with Martin Carnoy, Larry Mischel, and Richard Rothstein of *The Charter School Dust Up* (Economic Policy Institute and Teachers College Press, 2005). Jacobsen taught in the New York City Public School system prior to earning her doctorate.

Stacey A. Rutledge is an associate professor of educational leadership and policy at Florida State University. She received a master's in teaching social studies from Brown University and a doctor of philosophy in education from the University of Chicago. Her research explores how policies at multiple levels of the school system aimed at improving teaching and learning, such as test-based accountability and teacher quality, shape the work of district and school administrators and teachers, and, ultimately, students' learning opportunities. Rutledge is currently serving as a lead investigator for the National Center for Research and Development on Scaling Up Effective Schools, which is aimed at identifying the policies and practices of effective high schools. Her research has been published in *American Journal of Education, Teachers College Record,* and *Leadership and Policy in Schools.* She also taught high school social studies in Chile and Massachusetts before beginning her doctoral degree.

About the Contributors

Juanita Bautista-Guerra is a doctoral candidate in the educational policy PhD program in Michigan State University's College of Education. Her research interests are in the areas of educational policy, rural schooling, and rural-urban migration. Her dissertation uses actor network theory to explore how educational policy intersects with rural youths' decisions to migrate to the city in her home country of Colombia.

Lora Cohen-Vogel is the Robena and Walter E. Hussman Jr. Distinguished Associate Professor of Policy and Education Reform at University of North Carolina at Chapel Hill. As a co–principal investigator and associate director of the National Center for Research and Development on Scaling Up Effective Schools, Cohen-Vogel is interested in identifying the programs, policies, and practices of schools that are successfully raising schooling outcomes for traditionally underperforming student populations. Among other foci, this work looks at how schools use data to help raise learning outcomes for low-income, minority, and ELL students. In related work, Cohen-Vogel considers what she calls "evidence-based assignment," the ways student performance data is used by principals to hire, assign, and dismiss their teachers. Articles by Cohen-Vogel have been published in the *American Educational Research Journal, Educational Evaluation and Policy Analysis, American Journal of Education,* and *Educational Administration Quarterly,* among others.

Lisa M. Dorner, an assistant professor at the University of Missouri–St. Louis, received her PhD in human development and social policy from Northwestern University. Her main research interests include immigrant childhoods, language politics, and the implementation of educational policies. One of her most recent projects has documented the development of a new network of language immersion schools. Within this case study, she examined parents' and children's roles in the creation of schoolwide policies and practices. She is especially interested in how local policies intersect—and conflict—with state and federal mandates. She has published articles recently in the *American Educational Research Journal, Educational Policy,* and *Journal of Educational Change.* Dorner also works with area school districts, nonprofit organizations, and educators to develop curricula and materials relating to the immigrant experience (see www.lacesproject.org).

Richard Halverson is a professor in the School of Education at the University of Wisconsin at Madison. His research explores the use of data-driven instructional systems in schools and the development of game and simulation-based tools for professional learning. He currently codirects the Comprehensive Assessment of Leadership for Learning (CALL) study to develop an online, 360-degree formative evaluation system for school leadership. Halverson cofounded the Games Learning and Society research group at UW-Madison. He is a fellow at the Wisconsin Institutes for Discovery, an affiliate member of the UW-Madison Curriculum and Instruction and Educational Psychology departments, and a founding member of the UW-Madison learning sciences program area.

Douglas N. Harris, an associate professor of economics and the University Endowed Chair in Public Education at Tulane University, has been at the forefront of research attempting to identify policies that improve teacher effectiveness. His book *Value-Added Measures in Education: What Every Educator Needs to Know* (Harvard Education Press, 2011) was nominated for the national Grawemeyer Award in Education. He is also branching out into two new areas. In his new position at Tulane, Harris is creating a new research consortium to study New Orleans school choice and "portfolio district" reforms. He has also created two of the first randomized trials of college financial aid, the Wisconsin Scholars Longitudinal Study (WSLS) and the Milwaukee College Access Project for Success (M-CAPS). He has been the principal investigator on more than $6 million in research grants, and the results of this work have been published in dozens of academic publications. His research is frequently cited in the national media, and he consults widely on policy matters with elected officials, state departments of education, and organizations such as the National Council of State Legislators, the National Governors Association, and the National Academy of Sciences. Until recently, Harris was an associate professor of educational policy and public affairs at UW-Madison, where he remains an affiliate of the Wisconsin Center for the Advancement of Postsecondary Education and Institute for Research on Poverty.

Jeffrey R. Henig is a professor of political science and education at Teachers College and a professor of political science at Columbia University. He is the author or coauthor of eight books, including *The Color of School Reform: Race, Politics and the Challenge of Urban Education* (Princeton University Press, 1999) and *Building Civic Capacity: The Politics of Reforming Urban Schools* (University Press of Kansas, 2001), both of which were named the best books written on urban politics by the Urban Politics Section of the American Political Science Association. *Spin Cycle: How Research Gets Used in Policy Debates: The Case of Charter Schools* (Sage, 2008) won the American Educational Research Association's (AERA) Outstanding Book Award of 2010. Most recently, he is co-editor with Katrina E. Bulkley & Henry M. Levin and contributor to *Between Public and Private: Politics, Governance, and the New Portfolio Models for Urban School Reform* (Harvard Education

Press, 2010), winner of the AERA Districts in Research and Reform Special Interest Group Outstanding Publications Award for 2012.

Eric A. Houck is an associate professor of educational leadership and policy at the University of North Carolina at Chapel Hill. A specialist in school finance and educational policy, Dr. Houck's work has appeared in numerous academic and legal publications, including the *Journal of Education Finance, Peabody Journal of Education, School Business Affairs,* and *The School Administrator.* His research interests include intradistrict school finance and student assignment policies.

Huriya Jabbar is a doctoral candidate at the University of California at Berkeley in the Graduate School of Education. She earned an MA in economics from the New School for Social Research and a BA in economics from the University of California at Santa Cruz. Before her doctoral work, Jabbar worked at a nonprofit organization in New York assisting low-income families with short-term financial emergencies. She studies school choice, privatization, and the use of research by policy makers.

Jennifer Jennings is an assistant professor of sociology at New York University. She earned her PhD in sociology from Columbia University and her master's in education from the University of Cambridge. Her research focuses on the effects of accountability systems in education and health care on racial and socioeconomic inequality in education and health outcomes. She is working on two projects about educational accountability systems. The first attempts to identify the sources of score inflation in multiple states and to establish whether poor and minority students are disproportionately affected. The second asks whether the high schools that are good at increasing students' test score value-added are similarly good at promoting other long-term outcomes of education, such as college attendance and completion.

Angela Layton is a doctoral student in the College of Education at the University of Missouri–St. Louis, Department of Educational Psychology, Research, and Evaluation. Her previous work includes teaching English as a second language in the United States and in Istanbul, Turkey. Her major research interests include language, literacy, and identity development in multilingual contexts, immigrant childhoods, and teaching English as a second language. Her dissertation work examines how multilingual children develop as writers in a Spanish immersion school.

Heinrich Mintrop, currently professor at the University of California, Berkeley, was a high school teacher in both the United States and Germany before he entered into his academic career. He received an MA in political science and German literature at the Freie Universität Berlin and a PhD in education from Stanford University. He is the director of the doctoral program in Leadership for Educational Equity (LEEP), which aims to prepare strong leaders for high-need urban schools. As a researcher, he explores the issues of school quality, accountability, incentives, and school improvement. His research on school accountability has resulted in, among other publications, the book *Schools on Probation: How Accountability Works (and Doesn't Work)* (Teachers College Press, 2004) and the 2009 *Educational Researcher* article, coauthored with Gail L. Sunderman, "Predictable Failure of Federal Sanctions-Driven Accountability for School Improvement—And Why We May Retain It Anyway."

Brenda Gale Neal is a PhD candidate in educational leadership and policy studies at Florida State University, where she also completed her education specialist degree in educational leadership in 2011. She taught in a variety of public and private elementary schools for eighteen years. Currently, Neal works as a graduate research assistant and is interested in researching alternative teacher compensation methods and teacher evaluation.

La'Tara Osborne-Lampkin is a postdoctoral research associate with the National Center on Scaling up Effective Schools at Florida State University. Prior to her postdoctoral research position, La'Tara served as an assistant professor of educational leadership and policy studies at the University of North Florida. Her research seeks to build an understanding about how politics play out in educational institutions, how stakeholders wield their political influence, and the implications of these political processes for educational access and equity, particularly for traditionally low-performing students. Over the past few years, her research has focused on the role of teacher unions and school and district administrators, looking in particular at the collective bargaining process and its impact on educational decision making. Her most recent work is published in the *Journal of School Leadership* and *Educational Administration Quarterly*.

Andrew Saultz is a student in the educational policy program at Michigan State University. Prior to his graduate work, he taught high school social studies in Michigan. He was also elected to the Okemos (MI) Public Schools school board, where he served as the vice president and on the negotiation team. His research interests include the politics of education, federalism, and educational policy.

R. Benjamin Shapiro is the McDonnell Family Assistant Professor of Engineering Education at Tufts University, where he is a member of the Departments of Computer Science and Education and of the Center for Engineering Education and Outreach. His work focuses on the design of interactive technologies for learning and the development of data analysis and support systems to support teaching with them. He earned a PhD in the learning sciences from Northwestern University and was a postdoctoral fellow in the Games+Learning+Society theme of the Wisconsin Institutes for Discovery at the University of Wisconsin at Madison.

Heeju Sohn is a PhD candidate in demography and sociology at the University of Pennsylvania. She earned her master's and bachelor's degrees at Cornell University. Before beginning her doctoral work, she was a research assistant at the Harvard

School of Public Health. She also has experience working in economic consulting with Charles River Associates. Her current research interests focus on population health and inequalities in access to health care. Her most recent project studies the relationship between health insurance and marital dissolution.

Gail L. Sunderman is a researcher who focuses on educational policy and politics, urban school reform, and the impact of policy on the educational opportunities of low-income and minority students. She directed the Mid-Atlantic Equity Center at the George Washington University Center for Equity and Excellence in Education, where she spearheaded the development of the Equity Planning Tool, a research-based instrument designed to assist districts to assess for equity. She is coauthor of the book, *NCLB Meets School Realities: Lessons from the Field* (with James S. Kim and Gary Orfield, Sage, 2005) and editor of *Holding NCLB Accountable: Achieving Accountability, Equity, and School Reform* (Sage, 2007). Sunderman's work has appeared in *Review of Research in Education, Harvard Educational Review, Teacher's College Record,* and *Educational Researcher,* among other journals, including practitioner publications. She is a former Fulbright scholar to Afghanistan, and she received her PhD in political science from the University of Chicago.

Chris Thorn is currently the director of the Assessing-Teaching Improving-Learning project at the Carnegie Foundation for the Advancement of Teaching. Previously he was an associate research scientist at the Wisconsin Center for Education Research, where he was the director for the Center for Data Quality and Systems Innovation, which was an outgrowth of the success of the Value-Added Research Center, and also the associate director of the Value-Added Research Center, which he assisted in its mission to promote the development, application, and dissemination of value-added research methods to evaluate the performance and effectiveness of schools, teachers, programs, and policies. His work focuses on identifying and addressing organizational and technical gaps between operational information systems, measures of student and teacher performance, and decision support systems at the state, district, and school levels. His PhD in sociology and postdoctoral work focused on private-private and public-private cooperation in research and development.

Index

ability grouping, 139–142
Accelerated Reader program, 122
accountability
  assessment, 177
  case studies, 62–69
  data-based, vii
  data systems, viii
  good schooling scripts, 148
  high-stakes tests, 31, 185
  Hillsborough County, Florida, 68–69
  information infrastructure, 13–17
  mandates and pressures, 118
  principals, 58
  school-level, 58
  standardized test scores, 13, 166
  teachers, 58–60, 63–65
  technologies, 175
  test-based, 1
  value-added-based, 59
accountability data, 199, 201–202
  assumptions, 202–205
  "if you build it, they will use it"
    assumption, 202–203
  influence of, 205–209
  interpretations of, 210
  New York City (NYC), 205
  political pressure, 202
  public use or influence by, 200
  "Truth in Numbers" assumption,
    203–205, 207–209
accountability infrastructure, ix, 129
accountability logic, 163–164
accountability movement
  good schools, 146
  institutional reach of, 160
accountability regimes, xi
Accountability Review Council (ARC)
    (Philadelphia), 223

accountability, 110
achievement gaps, 110
alternative high schools, 109–110
data and analysis from metrics, 102–103
data-based policy evaluation, 105–109
data collaboration, 110
data transparency, 110
districts, 102–103
diverse stakeholders, 103–104
dropout rates, 108
EMO management, 106
English language learners (ELLs), 109
institutional stability and independence,
  101
key policy stakeholders, 101
key reform initiatives, 102, 105–109
NCLB-like accountability, 102
parents, 107
policies, 101–102, 106
proficiency goals, 102
racial achievement gap, 103
racial equity, 110
Rand evaluation, 106
reading improvement, 103
research and evaluation activities, 102
Research for Action study, 107
student achievement data, 106
supporting student learning, 108
test cheating incidents, 104
accountability systems
  achievement gaps, 197
  assessments, 165
  common elements, 24
  costs, xi–xii
  democratic regimes, xii–xiii
  educational inequality, 195
  educator evaluations, 24
  first-generation, 25–27

accountability systems, *continued*
  high-stakes testing, 147
  incentivizing, 197
  legislation and bureaucratic practice, xi
  math tests, 191
  measuring, 197
  No Child Left Behind Act of 2001
    (NCLB), 24
  nonschool factors, xi–xii
  output and outcomes, 35
  politics, xii
  proficiency-based, 191, 195
  ramifications, ix
  second-generation, 27–30
  standardized achievement tests, 23–24
  state designs, 23–25, 189
  systematic qualitative assessments, ix
  teaching, xi
  third-generation, 36–39
achievement gaps, 110, 216–217
  closing, 195–196
  narrowing, 183
  schools accountable for, 197
  test scores, 190–195
Ackerman, Arlene, 107, 110
actors
  coordinating activities, 58–59
  external consultants, 55
Acuity, 166
Adequate Yearly Progress (AYP), 102,
  115, 186
administrators
  customizing activities and classifying
    students, 127
  influencing instruction, 38
  performance data, 215
  scientific management, viii
advocacy groups and incentivist reforms, 90
AEI. *See* The American Enterprise Institute
  (AEI)
African American parents and good
  schools, 149
African American students, 133, 196
age-based, grade level system, 138–139
AIR. *See* American Institutes for Research
  (AIR)

Alliance for Education, 87
alternative high schools, 108–110
The American Enterprise Institute (AEI), 91
American Federation of Teachers, 71–72
American Institutes for Research (AIR),
  60, 72
A Nation at Risk, x
A+ Plan (1999), 141
Appalshop, 177
ARC. *See* Accountability Review Council
  (ARC)
Arizona Education Association, 66–67
Aspen Institute, 87, 88
assessments, 166–168, 177
assessment technologies, 165–167
assigning students to classes, 138–140
assignment to teachers, 138–140
attribution problem, 61
AYP. *See* Adequate Yearly Progress (AYP)

badges, 178
Bali, Valentina, 42
Barnett, Ross, 133
Battelle for Kids, 61, 72, 81, 224
"beating the odds" narrative, 198
benchmark assessments, 166, 167
BFK-Link, 61
Bill & Melinda Gates Foundation, 7, 72,
  77, 99
  assessment, 85–86
  data analysis, 84–85
  educational documentaries, 86
  hard data, 81, 84–86
  Intensive Partnerships for Effective
    Teaching, 68
  policy and advocacy networks, 87–88
  print and broadcast journalism
    organizations, 86
  public information, 86–87
  school reform issues, 86
  soft data, 86–88
  teacher effectiveness, 81, 84
  teacher evaluation, 81, 84
Blackboard, 167
Bloomberg, Michael, 97, 205, 208
British Ministry for Education, 224

Brookings Institution, 84
bubble kids
    focusing on, 188
    strategic distribution, 136
    targeting resources on, 141
Bush, George W., 216
Bush Foundation, 63, 65
busing, 134

CAI systems. *See* computer-assisted
    instruction (CAI) systems
California Dropout Research Project
    (CDRP), 97–98
CAP. *See* Center for American Progress
    (CAP)
Cappacione v. Charlotte-Mecklenburg, 137
caricaturing game players, 174
Carnegie Corporation, 78
case studies
    system restructuring, 62–69
    teacher accountability, 62–69
    themes, 69–70
CCSR. *See* Chicago Consortium for School
    Research (CCSR)
CDA. *See* critical discourse analysis (CDA)
CDRP. *See* California Dropout Research
    Project (CDRP)
Celt Corporation, 84
Center for American Progress (CAP), 91
Center for Assessment, 60, 72
Center on Education Policy, 85
Chancellor Beacon Academies, 105
change and local practice, 130–132
Charles G. Koch Foundation, 78
Charlotte-Mecklenburg Schools, 84, 86
Charlotte (SC) Chamber of Commerce, 86
charter schools, 135, 148
    data for school improvement, 146
    educational innovation, 160–161
    educational management organizations
        (EMOs), 150
    legislation, 149
    new model of schooling, 149–150
    performance-based accountability, 146
Chicago Consortium for School Research
    (CCSR), 97–98

Chicago Public Schools, 97–98
Chicago School Reform Act (1988), 97
choice-based student assignment, 135
Civic Enterprises, 97–98
class-based student assignment, 136
classes
    student assignment to, 138–140
    test-based assignment to, 140–143
classifications, 13–17, 126, 215–216, 226
CODE, 61
collaborative problem solving, 170
College Ready Promise, 81
Commission on Hispanic Affairs, 87
Common Core State Standards, 66–67, 80,
    129, 166
    aspirational educational goals, 36
    tying to assessments and curriculum, 85
Common Education Data Standards
    initiative, 6–7
Common School, 4, 12
communication, 44
computer-adaptive assessments, 166
computer-assisted instruction (CAI)
    systems, 167–168
Consent Decree, 100, 110
Convergence Consulting Group, 68
costs, xi–xii, 70
Council of Chief State School Officers,
    84–85
critical discourse analysis (CDA), 150–160
cultural scripts, 147–148
    data, 150–160
    good schooling, 149
customization, 219–220
    activities and services, 123–124
    critical elements of time, 125–126
    instructional practices, 124–125
    student scores, 123–124
    technological infrastructure, 121–126
Cypress Elementary
    ability grouping, 125
    accountability, 120–121, 128
    assistant principal, 120–121
    benchmark assessments, 123
    classifying students, 126
    critical elements of time, 125–126

Cypress Elementary, *continued*
 data-driven conclusions, 121
 differentiation instruction, 124
 district and state intervention, 118
 expectations, 121
 Florida Comprehensive Assessment Test
  (FCAT), 116, 123, 125
 low socioeconomic student population,
  117
 standardization, 122–123
 student learning, 125
 teachers, 125
 work practices, 118

Daily News, 207, 208
DA initiative. *See* Differentiated
 Accountability (DA) initiative
Dallas Independent School District, 84
data
 accuracy, 61
 analyses, 224
 authority, 117–121
 change and, 200
 coalitions and relationships, 226
 constraining, 13, 96
 cultural authority, 117–121
 cultural scripts, 150–160
 district governance role, 95–100
 educational outcomes, 200
 electoral accountability, 95–97
 goal setting and performance monitoring,
  23
 good schooling, 160–161
 governing with, 95–111
 independent review panel, 98–100
 integration, 58
 outside organizations, 97–98
 overcoming limitations, 61–62
 policy decisions, 110
 politics and, xii
 production in education, 199
 public and, 96, 223–224
 quality, 50
 state tests, 189
 student achievement, 118, 128
 student assignment, 139–140

 student performance, 114–115
 tailoring instruction to students' needs,
  124
 test-based accountability, 2
 use of, 117–121
data analysis, 60–62, 84–85
data-based accountability, vii
data-based decision making, 152
data collection, 60–62
data-driven decision making, 164
data-driven school reform paradoxes,
 23–39
data-driven technologies, 163
data infrastructure, 115–116
 facilitating standardization, 123
 test-based accountability, 127
data management organizations, 59
Data Quality Campaign (DQC), 42
data systems, viii, 129
 accountability, viii
 audits of, 224
 feedback loops and indicators, x
 foundations, 76
 funding, 79
 Language Immersion Charter Schools
  (LICS), 146, 150
 local, 160
 power and influence, xii
 student assignment, 135–138
 teacher accountability, 59
data technologies
 assessment technologies, 165–167
 instructional technologies, 167–168
 student information systems (SIS),
  164–165
 technologies for learners, 168–175
data warehouses, 23, 62, 70
decentralized school governance, 45
decision-making process, 111
democracy
 availability of information, 4
 intersection with accountability, xii
 trust and distrust, 220
democratic considerations, 91–92
democratic equality, 192–193, 195
Denver Public Schools, 84

departmentalization and ability grouping, 142
desegregation, 132–135
Dewey, John, xii
DiBELS, 167
Differentiated Accountability (DA) initiative, 116
Digital Youth Network (DYN), 172, 178
districts, 30
  allocating resources, 56
  data analytic capacity, 99
  data collection, 215
  data reporting systems, 203
  data sharing agreements, 64
  English as a second language classes, 156
  first-generation systems, 32
  information systems, 5–6, 218
  just-in-time support, 49
  key accountability recipients, 27
  local assessments, 218
  low-cost simplistic strategies, 28
  lower-performing kids, 136
  micro-controls of teaching, 38
  monitoring progress, 102–103
  performance data, 214, 215
  program silos, 50
  public and, 111
  reshaping relationships, 55
  restructuring roles and relationships, 57–58
  role of data, 95–100
  SEA tensions, 45–46
  SSIS, 48–52
  standardized information, 219
  standardizing practices, 117
  streamlining operations, 33
  technological resources and capacities, 50
  value-added measures for accountability, 73
distrust
  democracy, 220
  educational system, 221
  technologies of surveillance, 43
  tensions, 220–221
diverse providers, 101
  key reform initiatives, 105–109
    low-achieving schools, 105–109
    Philadelphia style, 105
    Renaissance 2014, 107
DOE. *See* U.S. Department of Education (DOE)
DQC. *See* Data Quality Campaign (DQC)
Duncan, Arne, x, 98, 199
DYN. *See* Digital Youth Network (DYN)
dynamic social networks, 8–10

Edison Learning, Inc., 150
Edison Project, 101, 105
Edison schools performance, 106
Editorial Projects in Education, 86
education
  accountability, x, 23–24
  achievement gaps, xi
  goals, 31–32, 218
  measuring success, 57
  municipal government and, viii
  outputs, 134
  performance report cards, 202
  policy regimes, x–xi
  shaper of citizens, xii
  struggles for control, 78
  technologies for, 163–164
educational inequality, 184, 195
educational management organizations (EMOs), 150
educational performance data, 41
educational policy and foundations or philanthropies, 77–79
educational reforms, 29, 76
educational systems
  distrust, 221
  goals, 36
  political and bureaucratic structures, 31–32
  trust, 221
Educational Testing Service, 81
education journalism and media, 79
education management organizations (EMOs), 101, 105–106
"Education Nation" event, 85
education reform and foundations, 91
Education Writers Association, 86

educators
accountability, 57
evaluating, 24, 36
effectiveness, 216–218
electoral accountability, 95–97
Elementary and Secondary Education Act, 88, 147
elementary schools
age-based, grade level system, 138–139
heterogeneous classes, 143
Eli and Edythe Broad Foundation, 79
ELL. *See* English language learners (ELL)
EMOs. *See* education management organizations (EMOs)
Empowering Effective Teachers, 68, 71
end-of-grade tests, 60
English, focus on student test scores in, 156
English language learners (ELL), 139
enrollment, 43–44
equity, 216–218
ESE. *See* exceptional student education (ESE)
ESEA flexibility waiver programs, 36
Exceptional Student Education (ESE)
teachers, 124, 139
expressions, 170
external consultants, 49, 55

Facebook, 168, 171–173
fairness, 143
Faubus, Orval, 133
FCAT. *See* Florida Comprehensive Assessment Test (FCAT)
federal education agencies, 5, 11
federal government and state information systems, 6–7
Fenty, Adrian, 97
Field of Dreams, 203
first-generation accountability systems, 25–27, 32
Florida
accountability context, 116
A+ Plan (1999), 116, 141
elementary schools, 127
Florida Comprehensive Assessment Test (FCAT), 118

Florida Comprehensive Assessment Test (FCAT), 116, 118, 126, 141
Florida Department of Education, 128
formative feedback, 173–174
for-profit database management companies, 62
foundations, 75–78, 214
accountability systems, 86
data collection and evaluation, 90
democratic considerations, 91–92
educational policy, 77–79
education reform, 91
education reporting, 79
funding, 89, 91
infrastructure of accountability, 80, 91–92
knowledge production spending, 79–80
local contexts, 88–91
state information systems, 6
urban districts, 98
4th Circuit Court of Appeals, 137
The Fund for Public Schools, Inc., 84

Gates, Bill, x, 80, 202
Georgia Department of Education, 85
gifted and talented education (GTE), 139
goals
test-based accountability, 57–58
third-generation accountability systems, 38
good instruction, 38
good schools
accountability movement, 146
African American parents, 149
competing discourses about, 160–161
constructivist approach to, 158
data, 160–161
high test scores/data, 149
innovation, 148–149
multicultural and progressive scripts, 158
multilingualism, 158
Google Groups, 172
grants, conferences, and workshops, 80
Great Schools, 85, 86
Grockit.com, 172

GTE. *See* gifted and talented education (GTE)

Harris, Douglas, 59
Harvard Civil Rights Project, 135
Harvard University, 84
Heritage Foundation, 91
heterogeneous classes, 143
higher-achieving students, 188–190
high-performing teachers, 37–38
high-stakes accountability, 31–32
  motivating work behavior, 37
  what worked and did not work, 24–25
high-stakes incentives, 28
high-stakes tests, 147
  accountability, 185
  gains, 189–190, 198
  improving scores, 33
  Language Immersion Charter Schools (LICS), 157
  low-stakes tests, 34
  results, 28
Hillsborough County (Florida) Public Schools, 62, 68–69, 81
HISD. *See* Houston Independent School District (HISD)
Hispanic students, 196, 198
homework, 176–177
Houston Independent School District (HISD), 185–187

i3. *See* Investing in Innovation (i3)
"if you build it, they will use it" assumption, 202–203, 206–207
Imagine 2014, 108–109
IMPACT, 89
incentivist educational reforms, 76, 90
independent review panels, 214
  as critical friend, 98–100
  functions of, 100–109
  urban districts, 110–111
indicator corruption, 24
  new public management (NPM), 33–34, 35
inequalities
  obscuring, 220

proficiency rates measuring, 195–196
public schools, 191–195
reproducing and legitimating, 196–198
standardized test scores, 190–195, 217
informatic power, 10–13, 11–12, 215
information
  availability, 4
  collecting, 2, 7
  democratic control over schools, 12–13
  performance measures and ratings, 2
  serving interests of users, 168
information infrastructure
  accountability, 13–17
  classification, 13–17
  constitutive, 9
  district and school-level information systems, 6
  as dynamic sociotechnical networks, 8–10
  implications, 222–226
  informatic power, 10–13
  information systems, 5–6
  knowledge production role, 227
  multiplicity, 10
  new actors, 9–10
  performance measures, 11
  policy makers, 222–225
  quantification, 13–17
  redistributing power, 226
  resources required, 225
  schooling practices, 10, 226
  standardization, 13–17
  state education agencies, 8–9
  surveillance technology, 223
  test-based accountability, 3
  tools and technologies, 226
  trust, 117, 220
information systems
  affecting behavior, 222
  classification systems, 226
  collaboration among actors, 222–223
  districts, 5–6, 218
  early, 4–5
  information infrastructure of accountability, 5–7
  large-scale, 3–4, 160, 225

information systems, *continued*
  public-private partnerships, 10
  schools, 5–6, 218
  state education agencies, 5
  statewide consequences, 53–56
  test-based accountability, 4–7
information technologies, 169
infrastructure of accountability, 161
  actors relationships, 214
  administrators' and teachers' activities,
    128
  foundations, 91–92
  informatic power, 215
  making visible, 214–216
  mapping, 2
  New York City lessons, 209–211
  public role, 210–211
  researchers, 225–227
  schooling and learning opportunities,
    127
  state and local context, 115
  tensions, 216–221
  winners and losers, 227
infrastructure of data, 127–128
infrastructure perspective
  altering social and material worlds, 9
  cultural authority of numbers, 12
  information systems, 7
  local narratives of schooling, 12
  power, 10–13
  quantification, standardization, and
    classification, 14
  recovering practical politics, 15
  sociotechnical networks, 8–10
  test-based accountability, 7–17
In Progress, 177
instruction
  customization, 124
  elements, 131
  institutionalized relationships and links,
    38
  standardizing evaluation of, 37
instructional technologies, 167–168
intermediary organizations, 88–91
International Baccalaureate Fund USA, 85
Investing in Innovation (i3), 76

Jim Crow legislation, 133
JP Mogan Foundation, 76

key reform initiatives, 105, 108–109
KIPP charter school. *See* Knowledge Is
    Power Program (KIPP) charter school
knowledge, 16–17
  funding strategies, 78–80
  information infrastructures role, 227
knowledge communities, 171–172
Knowledge Is Power Program (KIPP)
    charter school, 76

labor unions, 71–72
Language Immersion Charter Schools
    (LICS)
  accountability, 155
  charter, 145, 151–155
  competing cultural scripts, 150–160
  constructivists, 145, 151–152
  data-based decision making, 146, 152
  data collection, 152
  data/performance script, 150
  data systems, 146, 150
  English language learners (ELLs), 157
  family satisfaction measurement, 158–
    160
  high-stakes state tests, 157
  immigrant families, 156
  language immersion, 151–152
  local control, 155
  merit-based raises, 153, 155
  multicultural and progressive scripts,
    150–155
  multilingualism, 146, 156
  ownership, 155
  parent meetings, 158–160
  Parent Satisfaction Survey, 159
  performance and assessment data, 161
  performance-based accountability, 150
  public language immersion schools, 150
  success measurement, 160
  teachers, 152–153, 155
  360° Performance Evaluation, 153, 155
large-scale information systems, 3–4, 160,
    214, 225

dynamic nature of, 55
standardization, 219
leadership, 69
learning
accountability-driven environments, 169
achieving specified goals, 168
formative feedback, 173–174
information technologies, 169
infrastructure of data, 127–128
knowledge communities participation, 169
real-world, 169
technologies for, 168–175
learning management systems (LMS), 167–168, 176
Learning Matters, Inc., 86
LICS. *See* Language Immersion Charter Schools (LICS)
Liebman, James, 206
Linden Elementary
accountability demands, 118–120
classifying students, 126
data use, 120
enrichment opportunities, 122
extensive pullout program, 124–125
extra activities for students, 123
Florida Comprehensive Assessment Test (FCAT), 116
modifying curriculum for students, 124
standardization, 118, 122–123
students needing individual attention, 120
work practices, 118
LinkedIn, 171–172
LMS. *See* learning management systems (LMS)
local control, 132
local data systems, 160
local practical knowledge, 16–17
local practice, 130–132
Local School Councils, 97–98
logistical power, 10–11
Los Angeles Times, 204
Los Angeles Unified School District, 204
lower-performing schools, 142
lower-performing students

accountability, 189
focusing on, 131, 136
further marginalizing, 141
high- and low-stakes tests, 190
score inflation, 198
test score inequalities, 188–190
Lowi, Theodore, viii
low-income students, 217
low-performing schools, 33, 101
low-stakes tests, 185
discrepancy with high-stakes tests, 34
gains, 190, 198
results, 28

MacArthur Foundation 21st Century Assessment project, 178
magnet schools, 148–149
mandatory desegregation order, 134–135
Mann, Horace, 4–5, 192
MAP. *See* Measures of Academic Progress (MAP)
marginalized students, 29, 189
Maricopa County Educational Services Agency (MCESA), 62, 66–67
Mathematica Policy Research, Inc., 108–109
MCESA. *See* Maricopa County Educational Services Agency (MCESA)
McFarland v. Jefferson County Public Schools, 135
McGraw Hill Acuity, 166
mClass products, 167
measurement, 152
Measures of Academic Progress (MAP), 65, 166
Measures of Effective Teaching study, 70–71
media, 96, 204
Memphis City Schools, 84
Memphis Schools Foundation, 87
Metametrics, 85
Michael & Susan Dell Foundation, 79
microprocesses, 147
Milliken v. Bradley, 134
minority students, 185–186
diminished learning opportunities, 217

minority students, *continued*
 performance accountability, 183
 score inflation, 185–186
"mission accomplished" narrative, 198
mobilization, 43–44
Moodle, 167
multicultural scripts, 151–156
multilingualism, 156

NAEP. *See* National Assessment of
 Educational Progress (NAEP)
National Alliance for Public Charter
 Schools (NAPCS), 87–88
National Assessment of Educational
 Progress (NAEP), 113, 183–184
 achievement gap, 28
 New York State, 187–188
National Board for Professional Teaching
 Standards, 84
National Center for Education Statistics,
 66–67
National Education Association, 71–72
National Institute for Excellence in
 Teaching, 61, 224
National Public Radio, 86
National School Boards Association, 85
A Nation at Risk, 134
NBC Universal, Inc., 86
NCLB. *See* No Child Left Behind (NCLB)
neighborhood schools, 134
neo-institutionalism, 147–148
Network of Effective Teaching (NExT),
 62–65, 72
New America Foundation, 86
Newark (NJ) Public Schools, 81
New Machines, viii
New Progressives, vii–viii
new public management (NPM), 24, 31–36
NewSchools Venture Fund, 81
newspapers and education topics, 204
The New Teacher Project, 84, 89
New York City (NYC)
 accountability data, 205
 Board of Education, 206
 Charter School Center, 86
 elementary schools, 200–201

infrastructure of accountability, 209–211
 newspapers, 207–210
 performance data, 205–206
 Progress Reports, 205–208, 210
New York Post, 207–208
New York State, 185, 187–188
New York Times, 202, 204, 207
NExT. *See* Network of Effective Teaching
 (NExT)
ning.com, 172
No Child Left Behind Act (NCLB), x, 145,
 147, 183, 216–218
 accountability, 32
 achievement gaps, 28, 217
 Adequate Yearly Progress (AYP), 116,
 186
 assessments, 165–166
 communication, 31–32
 educational reform, 29
 effects of, 183
 failing schools, 16
 federal funding, 148
 goals, 29–30
 high-stakes accountability, 27–28
 high-stakes state tests, 28
 implementation consequences, 190
 mandates, 47
 middle managers in districts, 32
 public dissemination of data, 201
 sanctions, 28–30, 188
 school accountability data, 199
 state governments, 28
 states opting out of requirements, 24
 state test scores, 183
 student achievement, 217
 test-based accountability, 57, 217
 theoretical explanations of failure, 30–36
nonschool factors, xi–xii
Northwest Education Association, 65, 72,
 166
Northwest Ordinances, 132
NPM. *See* new public management (NPM)
NYC. *See* New York City (NYC)

Obama administration incentivist
 educational reforms, 76

Office of Accountability, 110
Ohio Business Roundtable, 81
online participation, 177
organizational legitimacy, 194
organizations
  data, 23
  funding for sustaining, 89
  influence of elite or wealthy, 78
  pressure on school governance, 97–98
outcome-driven public management
    systems, 33
outputs of educational process, 134
output trumps outcome, 35

*Parents Involved in Community Schools v.
    Seattle School District No. 1 (PICS),*
    135
Participant Media, LLC, 86
participation assessment, 177
participatory cultures, 170–171, 173, 175,
    179
partnerships with external actors, 71–73
Pearson SuccessMaker program, 118
Pennsylvania Department of Education,
    103
Pennsylvania Human Relations
    Commission, 110
Pennsylvania System of School Assessment
    (PSSA), 102
performance-based accountability, 145
  charter schools, 146
  Language Immersion Charter Schools
    (LICS), 150
  multicultural and progressive scripts,
    151–155
  states, 148
performance-based compensation, 65–67
performance data, 2, 199
  administrators, 215
  districts, 214–215
  New York City (NYC), 205–206
  public and, 199–200, 202
  reforming schools, 213–214
  selecting schools, 203
  state education agencies (SEAs), 214
  teachers, 215

performance measures, 4, 11–13
  trust, 220–221
performance script competing with
    multilingualism, 156
performativity, 24, 34–35, 37
Phi Delta Kappan, 89
Philadelphia Department of Education, 104
Philadelphia district test-cheating problem,
    110
Philadelphia Diverse Provider Model, 106
philanthropies, 77–79
  incentive-based reforms, 90
  shaping public education, 75
PICS decision, 136
PLATO, 167
Plessy v. Ferguson, 133
Policy Innovators in Education Network,
    87
policy makers
  decision making, 224
  incentivist reforms, 90
  information infrastructures, 222–225
  information systems, 222
  numeric indicators of performance, 225
  school reform, 76
policy regimes, x–xi
politicized goal setting, 24, 31–32
politics relationship with data, xii
poor schools, 149
poor students, 183, 185–186
poverty rates, 184
premix, 178
principals and accountability, 58
problematization, 43–44, 47
problem solving, 170
ProComp, 88, 90
professional development, 63, 69–70
proficiency-based accountability systems,
    195
Progressive reformers, vii–viii
progressive scripts and performance-based
    accountability, 151–155
Progress Reports, 205–208
Promise Academies, 107–108
PSSA. *See* Pennsylvania System of School
    Assessment (PSSA)

public
accountability data, 200–202
debates on public education, 196–198
language immersion schools, 150
Public Agenda pools, 148
public and infrastructure of accountability, 210–211
public education
philanthropists and foundations influencing, 75
public debates, 196–198
public management, 24
public-private partnerships, 10
public relations, 86–87
public schools
accountability, 148
Adequate Yearly Progress (AYP), 102
assessing progress, 96
broad support for, 12
democratic equality, 192–193
funding, 201
goals and purposes, 218
governance, vii, 95
incentives and sanctions, 1
inequality, 191–195
integrating technologies for learners, 179
performance-based compensation, 65–67
social mobility, 193–194
student test scores, 127
test-based accountability, 113

quantification, 13–17, 215–216

race-based assignment, 133–135
race-neutral student assignment, 135
Race to the Top (RttT), x, 1, 36, 57, 72–73, 76, 129
racial achievement gap, 108–109
Rand study, 106
Read180, 168
real-world learning, 169, 172
ReelWorks, 177
reform
data-driven paradoxes, 23–39
superficial and symbolic, ix

REIL. *See* Rewarding Excellence in Instruction and Leadership (REIL)
relative equality, 193
Relay School of Education, 76
RemixWorld, 172
Renaissance 2014, 107
Renaissance schools, 107–108
research-based organizations, 97–98
researchers and infrastructure of accountability, 225–227
Research for Action, 85, 107
residential assignment, 132–133
resources, distributing between students, 195–196
response to intervention (RTI), 61
Rewarding Excellence in Instruction and Leadership (REIL), 66–67
Ridge, Tom, 105
RttT. *See* Race to the Top (RttT)

sanctions, 36, 188
San Francisco (CA), 132
San Francisco Unified School District, 136–138
SAS Inc., 60, 72
school boards
elections, 96
independent voices, 111
policy making, vii
school choice, 132, 148–149
School District of Philadelphia, 101–103, 105, 110, 223
school governance
decentralized, 45
independent review panel, 98–100
School Improvements Grants program, 36
school-level standardization, 122
school of education (SOE), 63–64
School Progress Reports in New York City, 200, 210
School Reform Commission (SRC), 100–101, 107
schools
accountability, 24, 183
achievement and computing technologies, 227

achievement gap, 197
affluent students, 128
allocating resources, 56
classification, 13–17
collecting information on, 4–7
corrective action and sanctions stages, 30
data collection, 215
data infrastructure, 115–116
decision making, 57
educational practices, 219–220
failure, 30, 221
goals, 192–194
high-stakes tests, 12, 33
inequality, 196–198
information systems, 5–6, 218
instructional arrangements, 130
just-in-time support, 49
leadership, 95
local assessments, 218
lower-performing students, 136, 217
low-performing schools, 33
management, 69
organizational legitimacy, 194
performance data, 14, 96, 214
performance indicators, 33
performance targets, 28
poor students, 128
quality, 207
quantification, 13–17
racial makeup, 134–135
reshaping relationships, 55
sanctions, 217
selecting teachers, 63
SSIS, 48–51
standardization, 13–17
state education associations (SEA),
     45–46
student assignment to, 132–135
technological resources and capacities, 50
test-based accountability, 130–131
test scores, 192
trust, 42–44
what makes good, 146–161
schools of education (SOE), 58–59
science, 3
score inflation, 185–187

SDP. *See* Strategic Data Project (SDP)
SEAs. *See* state education agencies (SEAs)
SEA staff, 51, 54
second-generation accountability systems,
     27–30, 32–33
SIG, 72
SIS. *See* student information systems (SIS)
social classifications, 13
social efficiency, 192
social inequality, 193
social mobility, 193–195
social networks, 159, 171–173, 176
social policy, 184
social studies of science and technology
     (SSST), 115
socioeconomic status, 137
SOE. *See* school of education (SOE)
Spanish Immersion Elementary School, 145,
     156
special-needs students, 183, 217
SRC. *See* School Reform Commission
     (SRC)
SSIS. *See* statewide student information
     systems (SSIS)
SSIS staff, 48–53
SSST. *See* social studies of science and
     technology (SSST)
stability and local practice, 130–132
stakeholders, 103–104
standardization, 44, 152, 215–216, 219–
     220
convergence and divergence, 14–15
core curricular guidelines and materials,
     122
data infrastructure facilitating, 123
FCAT scores, 122
information infrastructure, 13–17
intensification of, 16
large-scale information systems, 219
practical politics of, 15
school-level, 122
schools, 13–17
state- and federal-mandated activities,
     14, 122
technological infrastructure, 121–126
test preparation, 122

standardized performance data and trust, 220

standardized tests, x
  accountability, 166
  measuring learning, 218
  skills and knowledge, 13

standardized test scores, 12–14
  effectiveness and equity measures, 217–218
  inequity, 217
  narrowing curriculum, 219–218
  negative sanctions, 217
  practical, political, and moral consequences, 217–218
  quantitative indicators with focus, 194
  student achievement, 118

Stanford Achievement Test, 186

state and national learning standards, 14

state education agencies (SEAs)
  districts and schools tensions, 45–46
  external consultants, 49
  information infrastructure, 8–9
  information systems, 5
  IT departments, 55
  performance data, 214
  problem solving, 51
  reshaping relationships, 55
  statewide student information systems (SSIS), 41, 48–51
  trust, 54

state education agents, 11

state information systems, 6–7, 214–215

state legislature and SSIS, 52–53

states
  assessments, 28
  data reporting systems, 203
  departments of education, 84
  No Child Left Behind (NCLB), 28
  performance-based accountability, 148
  residential assignment, 132–133
  standardized information, 219
  standards, 148
  student demographics, 30
  teacher evaluation systems, 223

state tests, 183, 185–189

Statewide Longitudinal Data Systems Grant program, 6

statewide student information systems (SSIS)
  Accelerated State, 42, 46
  coercion limits, 47–48
  collecting and reporting data to, 41
  comprehensiveness, 44
  computerized data system, 47–48
  consequences of, 53–56
  Data Quality Campaign (DQC), 42
  development and operation, 44–47
  districts, 47–48
  Emergent State, 42, 45–46
  enrollment and trust, 48–51
  Established State, 42, 47
  fiscal resources, 45
  funding, 47
  legislation or statutes, 44
  mobilizing support for, 52
  overview of states, 44–47
  performance data, 42
  quality of information, 48
  reshaping work and relationships, 54
  schools, 47, 48
  spokespeople, 52
  state education agencies (SEAs), 41
  state legislative support, 45–47
  systems of surveillance, 56
  trust, 41, 43–44, 46

Strategic Data Project (SDP), 99, 109

strategic power, 10

Street Level, 177

structuration, 122

student assignment, 132–135
  ability grouping, 140
  balance, 141–142
  busing, 134, 137
  choice-based, 135
  class-based, 136
  classes, 138–140
  data, 139–140
  desegregation, 132, 133–135
  differentiated course levels, 140
  diversity, 143
  equity, 143

fairness, 142–143
gender and parental requests, 139
heterogeneity and balance, 140
multifactor plans, 136
performance data, 141
PICS decision, 136
race-based, 133–135, 141
race-neutral, 135–136
residential assignment, 132–134
school choice, 132
school preferences, 137
socioeconomic status, 137
special services, 141
student performance, 136–137
teachers, 138–140
test-based, 135–138, 140–143
tracking, 140
student information system (SIS), 61–62,
168, 176
student performance, 114–115, 137
students
achievement, 60, 223
assessment development, 85–86
assignment and test scores, 129–144
classifying, 127
distributing resources between, 195–196
human capital, 192
performance categories, 14
preparing for success in workplace,
192
progress, 60
pushed to sidelines, 29–30
socioeconomic status, 136
sorting, 126
test scores, 184
SuccessMaker lab, 123
surveillance, 56, 221
system leaders, 84–85
system restructuring case studies, 62–69

TAAS/TAKS. *See* Texas Assessment of
Academic Skills/Texas Assessment of
Knowledge and Skills (TAAS/TAKS)
TAP. *See* Teacher Advancement Program
(TAP)
Teacher Advancement Program (TAP), 61

Teacher Incentive Fund (TIF), 58, 65–67,
72
teachers, 90
accountability, 58–60, 63–65, 70–72,
155
accountability case studies, 62–69
administration, 38
attribution, 61
as authors and accountants, 155
certifications, 139
community relations, 38
decision support, 69
evaluating, 58–59
fairness to, 142–143
internal relationships with colleagues, 38
merit-based raises, 88–89, 153, 155
performance, 14, 36, 58–59, 215
preparation, 58–59, 63–65
professional development, 63, 69
sanctions, 37
school failure, 221
standardized district resources, 127
student assignment to, 138–140
teaching to the test, 185
test-based assignment, 140–143
value-added estimates, 59, 60–62
teacher unions, 69
Teach for America (TFA), 84, 87
teaching
complex standards embedded into
practice, 38–39
exciting and rewarding career, 63–65
infrastructure of data, 127–128
upgrading quality, 37–38
teaching to the test, 185
Teachscape Inc., 81
technological infrastructure, 121–126
technologies, 163–164
accountability, 175
accountability cultures, 164
agenda for integration, 178–179
data-driven, 163
data use and generation, 171
estimating learning progress, 168
feedback, 178
infrastructural perspective, 3

technologies, *continued*
  integration challenges, 175–178
  orchestrating convergence, 176
  participatory cultures, 175
technologies, continued
  participatory learning spaces, 176–177
  system progress, 175
technologies for learners, 168–175
  civic participation, 177
  data use and generation, 171
  detrimental effects, 169–170
  feedback, 178
  guiding progress, 175
  information relevant for learning, 178
  interests and goals of, 179
  participatory cultures, 170–171
  public schools, 179
  reinvigorating learning experience, 179
  reshaping technologies for education,
    178
  social networks, 171–173
  user interest and motivation, 169
  video games, 174–175
  Wikipedia, 173–174
technologies of surveillance, 43, 56
Temple University, 106
tensions
  customization, 219–220
  distrust, 220–221
  effectiveness, 216–218
  equity, 216–218
  infrastructure of accountability, 216–221
  outputs and outcomes, 218–219
  standardization, 219–220
  trust, 220–221
test-based accountability, xi, 1, 47, 129
  allocating instructional time, 218
  American education policy, 183
  computing and data network, 114
  consequences, 225–226
  data, 2
  data infrastructure, 127
  documenting impact, 114
  educational landscape, 130–144
  extending power, 12, 215
  goals, 57–58

high-stakes pressures, 122
information infrastructure, 1–3, 220
information systems, 4–7
infrastructural perspective, 7–17
local practice, 130–132
new technologies and types of work, 130
outputs and outcomes, 218–219
performance data, 2
performance measures, 11–12, 220–221
policies, 113, 130
public schools, 113, 227
research, 3
schools responding to, 130–131
standardized test scores, 12
state assessments, 131
state information systems (SIS), 214–215
student assignment, 131, 135–138, 143
technically and politically complex, 222
test scores, 6, 12, 184
theory of action, 15
test-based assignment, 140–143
test-based school accountability, 57
test cheating incidents, 104
test-cheating incidents, 110
tests, 60
test scores
  achievement and inequality, 190–195
  achievement gap, 195
  democratic equality goal, 193
  diminished learning opportunities, 217
  lower- and higher-achieving students,
    188–190
  public debates, 191, 196–198
  reducing validity of, 217
  schools' effectiveness measurement, 192
  student assignment, 129–144
Texas Assessment of Academic Skills/Texas
    Assessment of Knowledge and Skills
    (TAAS/TAKS), 186
TFA. *See* Teach for America (TFA)
themed schools, 133
think tanks, 88–91
third-generation accountability systems,
    36–39
Thomas B. Fordham Institute, 87
Thorn, Chris, 59

TIF. *See* Teacher Incentive Fund (TIF)
time-management studies, viii
tracking, 140
traditional
  badges, 178
  foundations, 75
  public schools, 65–67
trust
  collection and reporting data, 43
  cooperation, 43
  critical resource for schools, 42–44
  democracy, 220
  educational system, 221
  information infrastructure, 220
  problem solving, 43
  provisional, 43
  school reform efforts, 42
  SEAs, districts, and schools, 48–51
  sharing information, 43
  standardized performance data, 220
  statewide student information systems
    (SSIS), 41
  student achievement, 42
  tensions, 220–221
  test-based accountability, 220–221
"truth in numbers" assumptions, 203–205,
  207–209
Tulsa Public Schools, 84
20th Anniversary Summit, 87
Twitter, 171

underperforming schools, 107
unemployment rates, 184
unitary status grant, 134–135
United States
  collecting information on schools, 4–7
  policy and test-based accountability, 183
  school accountability, 23–24
  schools and social efficiency, 192
Universal Companies, 106
University of California Berkeley, 85

University of Chicago, 85
University of Florida, 78
University of Pennsylvania, 106
University of Wisconsin, 84
University of Wisconsin at Madison, 59
urban districts
  data, 95
  external experts, 99
  governance accountability, 95–100
  independent review panels, 110–111,
    214
  large-scale information systems, 214
  mayoral control, 96–97
  political climate, 98
  school boards, 96
U.S. Department of Education (DOE), x, 4,
  6, 49, 65–66
  2011 budget, 80
  signature policy initiatives, 76

Vallas, Paul, 98, 105
value-added-based accountability, 59
value-added measures, 61
value-added models, 60
Value-Added Research Center (VARC),
  59–60, 65, 69, 72
Victory Schools, 106
video games, 174–175, 177–178
voucher systems, 135

Waiting for Superman, 86
Wake County (NC), 132–133, 136
Wake County Public School System
  (WCPSS), 137
WestEd, 67
Wikipedia, 173–174
Wikis, 173
William and Flora Hewlett Foundation, 79
Wireless Generation mClass products, 167
W. K. Kellogg Foundation, 79
World of Warcraft (WoW), 174, 175

DATE DUE
